INDIA AND THE SOVIET UNION

INDIA AND THE SOVIET UNION

The Nehru Era

ARTHUR STEIN

UNIVERSITY OF CHICAGO PRESS

Chicago and London

Standard Book Number: 226-77172-5
Library of Congress Catalog Card Number: 73-91656

The University of Chicago Press, Chicago 60637
The University of Chicago Press, Ltd., London

To my parents
SAMUEL AND MARY STEIN

Contents

Preface

IN the prologue to his study, *Asian Drama*, Gunnar Myrdal observed: "So far as Western countries, scholars, and scholarly institutions are concerned, it is clear that [the international tensions, culminating in the cold war have] been foremost in arousing interest in the problems of the underdeveloped countries. In the underdeveloped countries themselves it is fairly well understood . . . that the readiness to give aid and, more fundamentally, the interest of both the West and the Soviet Union in their conditions and problems were largely due to the world tensions that give significance to their internal affairs abroad."[1]

1. Gunnar Myrdal, *Asian Drama*, (New York: Pantheon, 1968), 1: 8. Further on in his prologue, "The Beam in our Eyes," Professor Myrdal adds: "Consideration of Western political and military interests in saving the underdeveloped countries from Communism invites inhibitions, for instance, about observing and analyzing the shortcomings of political regimes in those countries—provided, let it be noted, that they are not friendly with the enemy in the cold war. . . . This opportunistic approach to a research task is not necessarily, or even ordinarily, egoistic and hard-hearted in its conclusions. A study may have as its purpose to discover better based and politically appealing reasons for giving more generous aid to the underdeveloped countries. The political influences on Western social research do not usually encourage unkind treatment of underdeveloped countries—as long as they are not hopelessly lost to the enemy bloc. On the contrary, what national communities more or less overtly demand from their social scientists are essays in practical diplomacy pleading certain directions

To this writer, there is a great deal of validity in Myrdal's assessment. For example, studies by Western scholars of relations between the nonaligned nations of Asia and the Communist nations have generally been most concerned with how these relations affect Western policies. As a consequence there have been relatively few attempts at analysis from the standpoint of the "third world" countries themselves.

Among the most extensive and complex of these relationships has been that between India and the Soviet Union. Of all the non-Communist nations in the post-Stalin years, India has had the widest range of associations with the USSR. The relations between these two nations, whose peoples together number more than a fifth of the world's population, have been of major significance in the international sphere.

This study, then, examines the interaction between India and the USSR primarily from the Indian viewpoint, focusing on the rationale underlying India's policy and the factors which led to the close involvement with the Soviet state. Among the basic questions asked are: What has New Delhi attempted to achieve and to what extent have these objectives been realized? Also, how did India's dealings with the USSR mesh or clash with her relations with China, Pakistan, the United States, Great Britain, and "Afro-Asia," and with other aspects of her diplomacy?

A secondary purpose is to view the Soviet Union's evolving policy toward South Asia in the context of overall Soviet policies. To do this systematically would require a second book written from a different perspective, but groundwork is provided here for an understanding of the Soviet position. The narrative focuses on

---

of external and internal policy and giving a more solid and scholarly foundation to such pleas." (p. 14)

Myrdal's observations are not confined to Western scholarship alone: "In the Communist countries, bias is massively and systematically incorporated in the approach to all social, economic, and political problems and has been hardened into a stale dogma. . . . It is no accident that we may search in vain for important and original contributions by social scientists in the Communist countries to the scientific discussion of development problems in the poor countries." (p. 11)

the multifaceted relations between New Delhi and Moscow as they developed over a fifteen year period, on how these relations have affected and/or been affected by domestic and international developments, and on how each government attempted to influence the other's policies.

In brief summary, from 1947 to 1952 Soviet hostility toward India made it very difficult for a measure of rapport to develop. The more flexible approach by Stalin's successors led to changes in Soviet policy toward India. Desiring to weaken and perhaps supplant Western influence in India, the USSR in the mid-1950s hailed Indian nonalignment as a "positive force" in world affairs, made India the leading recipient of its foreign aid program, and gave unreserved support to India's position on such sensitive issues as Kashmir and Goa. On its part, India welcomed the willingness of the USSR to coexist as equals. From 1959 onward China posed an increasing concern for both New Delhi and Moscow. By then the Indo-Soviet relationship had passed through a stage of cautious coexistence to a phase which might be termed "peaceful cooperation." The latter period has extended to the present— despite the presence of some tensions and disagreements. One such tension, which has developed since 1965, stems from the Soviet tendency toward neutralizing its pro-Indian stance on certain Indo-Pakistani disputes, most notably Kashmir. Also, despite the fact that the USSR in 1965 became the leading supplier of military weaponry to India, the Soviet decision in mid-1968 to give Pakistan a limited amount of military aid has been unfavorably received by India. But the differences which exist on some issues have not been permitted to interfere seriously with the broad accord that developed during the Nehru-Khrushchev era.

There are many problems involved in transforming today's fragile international system into a more harmonious world community. The ever-present danger of nuclear holocaust underscores the need for the most powerful nations to learn to use their power judiciously during a transitional period in which a more just and stable international system can evolve. One requisite first step is for nations with differing cultural heritages and sociopolitical systems to reach *modi vivendi*. Another is for the major world powers to reduce the spillover of their rivalries into their relations with developing nations. In the early 1960s a de facto detente began to develop between the United States and the USSR in South Asia, in the sense that both superpowers wished to see an end to Indo-Pakistani strife and to foster political stability and economic development programs of India and Pakistan. This accord, however limited, contrasts with the confrontations between the USSR and the United States elsewhere in Asia, particularly in Vietnam and the Middle East.

The limitations inherent in any inquiry into the relationship of two or more nations are present in this study. The closed nature of the Soviet system added somewhat to the problems ordinarily encountered. There are also the limitations involved when an American writer attempts to view the world from the perspectives of New Delhi and Moscow.

Essentially, this book tries to reconstruct the step-by-step developments and to identify the emerging patterns within the Indo-Soviet relationship. While we obviously cannot "know" what goes on in the minds of individual policy makers at any given moment, we can discern the consequences of their thoughts over a period of time. We cannot, for instance, presume to identify conclusively Nehru's order of priorities in making various decisions, but we can evaluate the results and to some degree the intent of these decisions. Pieced together, the integral parts of his policy emerge as a reasonably coherent whole.

In the introductory chapter an attempt has been made to provide a general historic background, focusing on Russia and British India, Soviet policy toward the British Raj and the Indian National Congress, and Nehru's views on the USSR and communism. Aspects emphasized in the main body of the book include (1) the interaction between India's domestic considerations and foreign policy and her conception of her international role; (2) the evolving Soviet policy toward South Asia and how it was interpreted by Nehru, other political leaders, the opposition parties,

and the Indian press; (3) Kashmir; (4) India as a factor in the
Sino-Soviet conflict; (5) the Sino-Indian border confrontation;
(6) the role of the Communist party of India in Indo-Soviet
relations; (7) the Soviet program of economic and technological
assistance to India, and the commerce and other transactions
between the two governments; (8) the nature of contacts between
the two peoples; (9) the extent to which the USSR has established
a "presence" in India; and (10) the interplay of Indian and
Soviet diplomacy during various international crises and other
prominent events of the past two decades. A final chapter reviews
the Nehru era and notes the more important developments which
have taken place since the leadership changes of 1964 through
mid-1968.

My interest in this subject began in 1961 after I had spent
several months as a visitor in India and the Soviet Union. In 1963
I returned to India for a year of field work, and in December
1968 I spent an additional month in New Delhi and Moscow.

Many individuals in India kindly gave of their time for extensive
discussions on various aspects of their nation's foreign affairs and
added greatly to the author's general understanding of the Indian
political system. Among these are several Indian diplomats who
have served in the Soviet Union, members of the External Affairs
Ministry and other government ministries, several former members
of Mr. Nehru's cabinet, active politicians (particularly members
of the Congress and Communist parties), journalists, and members
of the academic profession. While not acknowledging these per-
sons individually in deference to some who hold public positions
and might prefer to remain anonymous, I wish to express my
thanks for their assistance.

I am indebted to Professors Norman D. Palmer, Donald E.
Smith, Richard L. Park, Margaret W. Fisher, Lloyd I. Rudolph,
Dr. Leo E. Rose, Gary Thurston, and Mark Juergensmeier who
read all or parts of the manuscript and offered many valuable
criticisms and suggestions. Others who gave much help included
Professors Karl Deutsch, Alexander V. Riasanovsky, Alvin Z.

Rubinstein, and Messrs. Selig S. Harrison, C. N. Satyapalan,
James Greene, and Philip Lindsay. I am also appreciative of
interviews and other assistance provided by a number of Soviet,
Polish, and Yugoslav diplomats and scholars. I wish to acknowledge
the following institutions for their support: The Woodrow Wilson
Foundation for a fellowship which helped me complete my graduate studies, the University of Pennsylvania for a Penfield Travel-
ing Fellowship which enabled me to do a year's field work in India
in 1963–64, the University of Rhode Island for a grant supporting my work on the manuscript during the summer of 1966,
and the U.S. Department of Education which provided a post-
doctoral fellowship in 1967–68 for language study and research
at the University of California's Center for South Asian Studies in
Berkeley. My wife and I also recall the warm hospitality of Deen
and Eunice Gupta and Drs. C. J. and Dorothy Chacko in New
Delhi. To all of the above I offer my sincere thanks. Needless to
say, the views expressed in the study and the remaining errors
of omission and commission are my responsibility alone.

Much of the research on this project was done at the South Asian
section of the University of Pennsylvania library; the library of
the Indian School of International Studies and the I.C.W.A. in
Sapru House, New Delhi; and the library of the University of
California (Berkeley). I wish to thank those librarians, especially
Mrs. Ruth Madera of the University of Pennsylvania, who helped
me locate materials for the study.

Finally, I express gratitude to my wife Karen, without whose
patient editing, encouragement, and occasional hassling the book
would not have been completed. And also to our young daughter
Lisa Natanya for her forebearance in not shredding accessible
portions of the manuscript scattered around the house.

1 The Historic Backdrop

The Pre-Soviet Period

EXPANSES of arid land and the almost impenetrable mountain ranges of Central Asia impose a formidable physical barrier between European Russia and the Indian subcontinent. A few traders and travelers made their way between the two regions as early as the twelfth century, but contacts over the years were extremely limited.[1] By the seventeenth century an expanding Muscovite state had finally succeeded in breaking the bonds of Tartary. Motivated by the prospects of trade, Czar Alexis sought

1. One of the earliest and the best-documented visits by a Russian to India is the diary of a merchant from Tver, Afanasii Nikitin, who made journeys in the fifteenth century: *Khozhdenie za tri moria* [Journey beyond the three seas] (Moscow: Geografizdat, 1960). Also see P. M. Kemp, *Bharat-Rus: An Introduction to Indo-Russian Contacts and Travels from Medieval Times to the October Revolution* (New Delhi: The Indo-Soviet Cultural Society, 1958).

Trade between Moghul India and Russia was minimal. In the eighteenth century there were at any given time no more than a few dozen Indian merchants in Russia, most of whom were in Astrakhan. A few went beyond Astrakhan to Novgorod, Moscow and Saint Petersburg. See *Russko-Indiiskia Otnosheniia b XVIII Beke* [Russian-Indian relations in the eighteenth century], a collection of documents, (Moscow, 1965).

After Soviet-Indian political relations improved in the mid-1950s, Soviet academics greatly intensified their search to discover the historic contacts between Russia and pre-British India.

1

in 1675 to make contact with the wealthy Moghul Empire of Northern India, then at the zenith of its power. But the Emperor Aurengzeb was suspicious of the Christian infidels' motives and rejected the Czar's delegation. Over the following decades the Russian state continued to expand while the Moghul power declined. Still, India remained a repository of great wealth envied by the monarchs of Europe. Peter the Great often spoke of the riches of India, but Russian expansion during his rule was directed toward obtaining outlets on the Baltic and Black Seas. The main interests of Peter's successors also lay in Europe.

By the beginning of the nineteenth century the British had supplanted the Moghuls as the leading force in India, while the Russian Empire began its expansion into the vast reaches of Central Asia. The imperial aspirations of the two European powers then began to come into conflict.[2] In a physical sense, however, Russia did not constitute a threat to British India until late in the reign of Alexander II (1855–81) when Russian control was extended over the weakened Khanates in Central Asia up to the Oxus region in the land of Afghans.

The British feared that Russia coveted the richest jewel in the Empire, a vast land of several hundred million people, tenuously controlled by a few thousand soldiers and administrators. Over the years some Russian rulers[3] and generals would have liked to take advantage of the vulnerable British position in India, but the opportunity was never present for them to do so. Russian interests lay primarily in Europe, and the major Russian effort at expansion was in the direction of Constantinople. Generally speaking, Russian diplomacy was fairly conservative, attempting to

---

2. See C. S. Samra, *Indian and Anglo-Soviet Relations*, pp. 1–19, and A. Lobanov-Rostovsky, *Russia and Asia* (Ann Arbor: George Wahl 1953).

3. For example, in 1801 during the time of the Napoleonic wars, the Russian emperor Paul called for the creation of an invasion force to cross the deserts and mountains to the Indus valley while England's attentions were engaged elsewhere. The ill-conceived notion came to naught when Paul was assassinated six weeks later.

prevent coalitions of other European powers from forming against her. The events leading to the Crimean War constituted a break-down in this strategy of Russian diplomacy; thereafter Russian expansionist efforts were directed primarily to the Far East where British interests were not immediately involved. Nonetheless, Russia's position in Central Asia and the spectre of the Russian threat to India provided a useful diplomatic foil in countering British moves elsewhere, particularly in Europe.

To deal with the ostensible Russian threat, the British in India developed a strategy that came to be known as the "forward" move-ment. The plan called for buffer states in which British-Indian in-flunces would predominate. Afghanistan, with its Khyber Pass—the traditional invasion route to the Indian subcontinent—was the focal point of contention.[4] For several decades beginning in 1838 the British sought to extend their control over the region with no lasting success.

From 1880 to 1884 the Russian Empire for the first time had extended its area of effective control as far as the Merv oasis on the northern frontier of Afghanistan. Since neither the British nor the Russians wanted a conflict to develop, they agreed to set up a border commission to demarcate the Russo-Afghan border. A settlement was finally reached in 1887, and the boundary was formally agreed upon. The British agreed in 1895 to delimit the southern borders of Afghanistan, and the Durand Line was drawn to demarcate the Indo-Afghan border. A strip of land was ceded to Afghanistan in the Pamir Mountains region in order that the British and Russian controlled territories would not come into contact with each other. (This boundary was retained after 1947; thus Soviet Russia and independent India do not share a common frontier. Actually, the section of the former Indian princely state of Kashmir bordering on Afghanistan today is part of Pakistan's Azad Kashmir.)

4. Cf. W. K. Fraser-Tytler, *Afghanistan: A Study of Political Developments* (London: Oxford University Press, 1953), and Owen Lattimore, *Pivot of Asia* (Boston: Little Brown, 1950).

A final resurgence of the British forward policy came during the viceroyalty of Lord Curzon (1898–1905).[5] Counterintrigues again flourished over Afghanistan for a few years, but the major British concern was with growing Russian influence in Tibet. In 1903 a ravaging army entered Lhasa, only to find that the fears of a Russian presence there were largely without foundation. The Tibetan campaign, however, was in most ways a departure from the general trend of British-Russian relations. The close of the nineteenth century had found both London and St. Petersburg searching for allies as the result of both having been rejected by Kaiser Wilhelm's Germany. Their decision to forge a Russo-British alliance necessitated the delimiting of their respective spheres of influence. The remaining British-Russian conflicts of interest in Asia were largely settled as part of the general entente of 1907. Among other terms, each agreed to delimit spheres of influence in Persia and to respect the territorial integrity of Tibet.[6] The exigencies of pre–World War diplomacy had for the time sublimated the rivalry between the two European powers.

It is often asked: to what extent has there been change and to what extent has there been continuity in the foreign policy objectives of Czarist Russia and the Soviet Union? The complex question is not easily resolved, but in the case of policy toward the Indian subcontinent there is at least one very basic similarity. Neither before nor after the revolution has Russia ever been in a

5. Lord George E. Curzon gave the following dedication to his book *Russia in Central Asia in 1889 and the Anglo-Russo Question* (London: Longmans, Green, 1889): "To the great army of Russophobes who mislead others, and Russophiles whom others mislead I dedicate this book which will be found equally disrespectful to the ignoble terrors of the one and the perverse complacency of the others." For an evaluation of the Curzon era see Michael Edwardes, *High Noon of Empire: India Under Curzon* (London, 1965). (When Curzon himself later became viceroy of India, his policy gradually came to resemble that of the Russophobes whom he had deplored.)

6. For accounts of great power diplomacy in Tibet see Alastair Lamb, *Britain and Chinese Central Asia* (London: Routledge and Kegan Paul, 1960), and H. E. Richardson, *Tibet and Its History* (London: Oxford University Press, 1961).

position to extend its control over the subcontinent by force of
arms. Of equal importance, there has never been a threat to the
Russian state from South Asia. The mountains and deserts of Central Asia provided a natural defensive barrier. Also, the vital
centers of the Russian state are not within striking distance of a
potential enemy in South Asia (except of course through the use
of air power). From the seventeenth century until the present
the Russians have been primarily concerned with the problems
of their western boundaries and their relations with the European
states. The eastern frontiers—first with Japan and then (in recent
years) with the People's Republic of China—have been the area
of secondary concern over the past eighty years. In contrast, by far
the least volatile of Russia's borders in the twentieth century has
been the "southern tier" in Central Asia. The leaders of the Indian
Independence movement, prior to 1947 and after, were aware of
these geopolitical conditions and consequently did not share the
apprehensions of other peoples on or near the periphery of the
Russian state.

Soviet Policy toward India, 1917–52

Like Karl Marx,[7] Lenin emphasized the imperial powers'
exploitation of the resources and markets of colonial and semi-
colonial regions. He did not concern himself much in his pre-
Revolutionary writings with the potential role of the colonial
peoples in bringing about revolutionary change. But by 1916 he
suggested the possible efficacy of "an epoch of civil war against

7. Marx's writings dealing specifically with India consisted largely of a series
of articles for the *New York Herald Tribune* in 1853. He described the British
rule of India as pernicious and exploitative, but on another level noted that the
British unconsciously performed the progressive step in the dialectical process of
bringing India from the feudal stage of "Oriental despotism" to the capitalistic
stage of historical development. See Karl Marx, *Articles on India*, 2nd ed. (Bombay: Peoples Publishing House, 1951).

For discussion of Karl Marx's views on British rule and the Indian caste
system see the section "Marx, Modernity and Mobilization," in Rudolph and
Rudolph, *The Modernity of Tradition*, 17–24.

the bourgeoisie in the advanced countries combined with a whole series of democratic and revolutionary movements . . . in the underdeveloped, backward and oppressed nations."[8]

The immediate focus of the new Soviet state was westward. Yet the East was not neglected in the midst of the turmoil of the civil war and the call for revolution elsewhere in Europe. Some attention was given first to the Moslem world and then to India.

An old dictum that the road to Paris lay through Calcutta and Peking reflected the belief that the most vulnerable points of the imperialist powers lay in their colonial holdings and spheres of influence in Asia. The potential of a revolutionary India for furthering the cause of world revolution and—perhaps of more immediate importance—for deterring British intervention in Russia itself, was emphasized in the Soviet *Blue Book* on India published in 1918. This document reveals how important the Soviets considered the British possession of India to be to the cause of world imperialism. It read in part, "there cannot be a social catastrophe in the West while the West can still live and exploit itself upon the East, while there is still a submissive object of exploitation." Moreover, a revolt in India could touch off a series of upheavals in other Asian lands.[9]

But revolution in India could not be fomented by documents alone. The young Bengali revolutionary, M. N. Roy, and other Indian emigrés were encouraged to form an Indian communist movement, and in the winter of 1920–21 Roy set up a training program for several dozen Indian revolutionaries in Tashkent.[10] The prospects for a meaningful Communist movement in India

8. Lenin, "Concerning a Caricature of Marxian and Imperialist Economics" (October 1916), *Sochineniia*, 4th ed., xxiii, p. 48. Cited in Charles McLane, *Soviet Strategies in Southeast Asia* (Princeton: Princeton University Press, 1966), p. 6.

9. *Siniaia Kniga* [Blue book], *India for the Indians* (Moscow, 1918). Reprinted in *Records of the Department of State Related to International Affairs of India, 1910–29*, p. 7. (National Archives of USA, 1934, microfilm).

10. Cf. X. J. Eudin and Robert C. North, *Soviet Russia and the East, 1920–27* (Stanford University Press, 1957), pp. 86–88.

were crushed, however, by the mass arrests and extended trials of the so-called Cawnpore Conspiracy. After the setback in India, the Comintern's main interest turned to China.

Although Lenin supported the Indian Communists in the early 1920s, he recognized that the hoped-for Communist revolutions in the industrially advanced countries of Europe were not going to take place. His attention turned to relieving the external pressures on the Soviet state and rebuilding the shattered economy. Accordingly, the USSR concluded a trade agreement with Britain in 1921 and obtained diplomatic recognition by Britain three years later. Sending substantial numbers of agitators to India would have been incompatible with the more basic objective of lessening Anglo-Soviet tensions.

One of the great theoretical and, at the same time, practical problems confronting the Soviets was the proper attitude to adopt toward the "national bourgeoisie of the colonial areas." At the Second Party Comintern Congress in 1920, Lenin pragmatically called upon the young Communist movements to collaborate with the much stronger bourgeoisie in the struggle for national independence. His argument stressed that independence should first be won from the imperial rulers; then Communists, utilizing the class struggle, could win power from the bourgeoisie.[11] Lenin asked M. N. Roy to provide some supplementary theses for the Comintern Congress to consider. While not contradicting Lenin, Roy pointed to the necessity for the Communist parties to attempt to lead the national revolutionary movements from their inception. The bourgeoisie could not be trusted and had to be confronted immediately. Roy emphasized the importance of the Asian up-

11. A documented analysis of the Comintern proceedings is included by Edward H. Carr in *The Bolshevik Revolution, 1917–23* (New York: Macmillan, 1953), 3: 251–59. M. N. Roy's later reflections on the subject are included in several installments of his uncompleted memoirs in the *Radical Humanist:* "International Concourse at Moscow," *Radical Humanist,* January 3, 1954, and "Disagreement with Lenin over Colonial Countries," *Radical Humanist,* January 24, 1954.

risings to conditions in Europe. The Comintern accepted Lenin's theses, but the question of alliances with the "national bourgeoisie," has never been fully resolved. Through the years the emphasis has fluctuated between collaboration with the bourgeoisie and opposition to it. Communists remain divided on this issue today as in the past.

For a short while the Indian Communists cooperated with the Indian National Congress, but turned away after Gandhi called off his massive noncooperation campaign in February 1922. Gandhi's commitment to nonviolence was anathema to Roy, who denounced the suspension of civil disobedience against the British as a "veritable betrayal of the revolutionary rank and file by the nonrevolutionary and reactionary leadership."

From 1923 to 1926 the Communist line toward the Indian National Congress vacillated.[12] But after the 1927 Chinese debacle in which the Kuomintang liquidated the Communist faction within its ranks, the Sixth Comintern Congress hardened its general policy toward the "bourgeois democrats." Stalin, who had recently consolidated his controlling position within the CPSU by expelling Trotsky, adopted a position on colonial questions and the national bourgeoisie similar to that advocated earlier by M. N. Roy. The new "leftist strategy," as applied to India, denounced Gandhism as "idealizing the most backward and economically reactionary forms of social life" and termed Nehru a "tepid reformist" with "Kerenskyite tendencies." In 1929, Roy, who had argued for years against cooperating with the Indian National Congress, was expelled from the Comintern.

The Communist party of India (CPI)[13] continued its strong

12. Several well-documented studies have been made of the interaction of the Soviet and Indian Communist parties. The most extensive of these is by Gene Overstreet and Marshall Windmiller, *Communism in India*. The summary in the following paragraphs is derived in large part from that work and from John Kautsky, *Moscow and the Communist Party of India*.

13. The Communist party of India (CPI) formally came into existence in December 1929 when the leaders of the Workers' and Peasants' Party reconstituted themselves as the CPI.

opposition to the Indian National Congress until 1934–35 when the USSR called upon overseas Communist parties to cooperate with non-Communists in combating the rising menace of fascism. After some problems of readjustment, the CPI followed the Comintern directive to work within the Natural Congress while maintaining its complete organizational independence. In its "united front from below" strategy, the CPI attempted to penetrate the Indian National Congress and transform its policies.

Then came a rapid shift in Soviet diplomacy which created considerable confusion for Communist parties throughout the world. After the Munich Treaty of 1938, the Russians sought to make their own settlement—at least temporarily—with the Nazis. For a year after the conclusion of the Soviet-German Nonaggression Pact of August 1939, there was little coordination between the Comintern and the CPI. The German invasion of the USSR in June 1941 clarified matters, and the CPI was called upon to back the British war effort in the People's War against fascism.[14] A ban on the legality of the CPI, which had been in effect for two years, was removed by the British in July 1942. The Communist support for the British from 1942 to 1945 hurt the CPI in one important respect, however, for it incurred the resentment of the leaders of the Indian National Congress, many of whom were imprisoned because of the "Quit India" campaign.

For some time after the close of the war, the USSR refrained from sharp criticism of its British ally. Not until early 1946 did the CPI members join the mass anti-British demonstrations that had broken out months earlier. As Anglo-Russian relations in Europe deteriorated seriously in 1947, the Soviets became overtly critical of the British plan to partition India. The Mountbatten Plan of June 1947 was described as a means for the British "to perpetuate imperialist control" by dividing the subcontinent. To hasten the British departure from India, the CPI, acting upon Soviet advice, adopted a "united front from above" policy of

14. Overstreet and Windmiller, *Communism in India*, pp. 192–222.

cooperation with the Indian National Congress. The CPI supported the Nehru government's efforts to quell the communal disorders in the critical months immediately before and after partition of the subcontinent in August 1947.

The contacts between the Indian Provisional Government and the USSR in 1946–47 were reasonably cordial. On April 14, 1947, the two governments announced their intention to exchange diplomats on the ambassadorial level. Earlier, representatives of several Soviet Central Asian Republics had participated in the Inter-Asian Conference held in Delhi from March 23 to April 12. These contacts, limited as they were, stood in contrast to earlier days when the British had kept India insulated from the Soviets. No authorized Soviet national came to India prior to the outbreak of World War II. All of the Soviet press information on India was second-hand until a TASS representative arrived in 1942 for the duration of the period of wartime cooperation.

But Soviet support for the independent government of India was short-lived.[15] The initial meeting of the Cominform in September 1947 put forth the thesis that the world was divided into "imperialist and anti-imperialist camps."[16] It became apparent in the following months that Moscow had little regard for the Nehru Government, which had allegedly permitted India to be drawn toward the Anglo-American sphere.

The British withdrawal from the Indian subcontinent was the initial and most decisive step in the process which dismembered

15. An early indication that the Soviets did not favor a policy of continued CPI support for the Congress party can be seen in the speeches delivered at a conference on Indian studies held by the USSR Academy of Science in June 1947. Several leading academicians emphasized the reactionary nature of both the Congress and the Muslim League and declared that the class struggle in the subcontinent would be abetted by the growing size of the working classes. See Kautsky, *Moscow and the Communist Party of India*, pp. 24–26.

16. A. Zhdanov, "The International Situation," *For A Lasting Peace, For A People's Democracy*, November 10, 1947, pp. 2–4. Zhdanov's only reference to India in his address was a rather ambiguous remark that the Soviet-led camp had the "sympathy of Syria, Egypt and India."

the European colonial empires in Asia. But the new rulers of independent India, Pakistan, Ceylon, Burma, and Indonesia were members of the "national bourgeoisie," and thus subject to distrust by Moscow. The old stereotypes about the national bourgeoisie still prevailed. This was not surprising, however, in the context of Stalin's distrust of even those Communist leaders who did not owe their postwar emergence to power directly to his patronage. This frame of mind was reinforced by his fallout with Tito's Yugoslavia. In Asia the only Communist-led struggle for national liberation from European colonial rule was in Vietnam, and there also the indigenous leadership was not beholden to the USSR. By their criticism (1947–50) of the leadership in the newly independent countries, the Soviets dissipated much of the latent good will which the elites in these countries had held for the USSR.

Within India the "leftist" faction of the CPI gained control of the party leadership by December 1947 and, using the "two camps" thesis for justification, resolved that conditions in India were ripe for militant action. A Communist-inspired peasant revolt broke out in the Telengana region of Hyderabad, and disruptive tactics were pursued in West Bengal and elsewhere. Almost simultaneous with the inception of the CPI militancy was an upsurge in revolutionary activity by the Communist parties in Burma, Malaya, and Indonesia.

Moscow was undoubtedly skeptical of the prospect for a successful revolution in India, but nonetheless adopted a wait-and-see attitude. Interestingly enough, no comment on the December 1947 CPI resolutions appeared in any of the major Soviet or international Communist publications in 1948–49. By the end of 1949 it became apparent to the Soviets that the "adventurous" policy of the CPI was alienating many supporters of the party. The insurgency in Hyderabad, although still smouldering, had been checked. CPI membership dropped from an estimated 89,200 in 1948 to 20,000 in 1950.[17] In January 1950 an editorial in the Cominform

17. Overstreet and Windmiller, *Communism in India*, p. 357.

journal, *For A Lasting Peace, For A People's Democracy*, disapproved of the "leftist" tactics pursued by the CPI. It declared
armed uprisings inappropriate to the Indian situation and
recommended that the CPI "unite all classes, parties, groups, and
organizations willing to defend the national independence and freedom of India."[18]

The problem of coordinating Soviet and CPI policies was a
difficult one. India's Communists naturally looked to the USSR
for political guidance and sometimes financial assistance. Still,
India's Communists were often divided among themselves; factionalism generally was more prevalent in the Indian party than in
most other Communist parties, due in large measure to a party
membership that came from diverse geographic areas and family
and occupational backgrounds. Because of this division, it often
took time to adjust to shifts in Soviet foreign policy.

The movement developed strength only in a few areas—mainly
in Bengal, Hyderabad, and the Malabar Coast, and its members
reflected most of the diversities and regional differences inherent
in contemporary India. Other problems also existed: for instance,
some party leaders of high caste backgrounds retained some of
their traditional attitudes toward lower caste workers and peasants
—a troublesome situation for a movement purportedly committed
to the creation of a casteless and classless society.

With Soviet encouragement a more moderate faction gained
control of the CPI leadership in the early months of 1951. In
India's first national elections held in 1951–52, the CPI made a
surprisingly good showing, winning 16 seats in the lower house
of Parliament, the Lok Sabha.[19] That the USSR advised the CPI
to work within the framework of the parliamentary system, however, did not signify approval of such Indian policies as member-

18. "Mighty Advance of the National Liberation Movement in the Colonial
and Dependent Countries," *For a Lasting Peace. . . . ,*" January 27, 1950, p. 1.

19. The CPI and its electoral allies contested 70 of the 489 seats in the Lok
Sabha Their candidates received only 5.4 percent of the popular vote; but by

ship in the Commonwealth, adherence to an essentially capitalistic economic system, and support of "anti-popular regimes" in Asia.

Prior to the Korean War the USSR had been sharply critical of India's declarations of impartiality in world affairs.[20] But India's support for the seating of the People's Republic of China in the United Nations, coupled with India's overall attitude on the Korean War, led to a partial reappraisal of Indian foreign policy.[21] While by no means wholly satisfied with Nehru's policies, the Soviet and British Communist parties wished to encourage any Indian tendency toward disengagement from the West. The CPI, however, maintained until early 1953 that the Congress Party was indebted to the imperialists and therefore could not pursue an independent and "progressive" foreign policy.

In his last year, Stalin began to recognize that Nehru was genuinely interested in pursuing a course independent from the Western Powers on Cold War issues in Asia. Therefore, the Soviets made a number of gestures (noted on page 30) toward India in 1952–53; yet their suspicion of Indian motives still prevailed.[22]

---

concentrating its efforts in such areas of party strength as Hyderabad, Travancore-Cochin, and West Bengal, the CPI and allied groups emerged with more (27) parliamentary seats than any other opposition party. See Norman D. Palmer, *The Indian Political System* (Boston, Houghton Mifflin, 1961), pp. 222–23.

20. Cf. V. Berezhkov, "Foreign Policy Maneuvers of Indian Reactionaries," *New Times*, no. 22 (May 31, 1950), p. 31. The Russian attitude toward India during this period is discussed by Asoka Mehta, "India's Foreign Policy: The Soviet View," *India Quarterly* (April–June, 1951).

21. India refused to join the Western powers in condemning the Chinese entrance into the Korean War in October 1950. The USSR thereafter was generally satisfied with India's stance on the Korean question and noted with approval the growing divergence between India and the USA on the Korean and Chinese questions. See Iu. M. Vinnik, "Imperialisticheskaia agressiia protiv K.N.D.R. i politika Indii (iun 1950–ianvar 1954)" [The imperialist aggression against the Korean Democratic Peoples' Republic and Indian policy]. *Nekotorye voprosy mezhdunarodnykh Otnoshenii* [Some questions of international relations] (Moscow: Higher Party School and Academy of Social Sciences, 1960), pp. 173–74.

22. On one such occasion in the United Nations the Soviet representatives, Andrei Vyshinsky, made some scathing remarks against an Indian draft resolu-

It should also be remembered that Stalin, concerned with more pressing developments in the Far East and Europe and preoccupied with his own physical and mental problems, had little time for such secondary matters as improving relations with India.

Nehru's Views on the USSR and Communism (1917–52)

The Bolshevik revolution of 1917 posed a new concern for the British. Expansion by Czarist Russia into India could have been achieved only by military means, as the autocratic, orthodox Russia of the Romanovs had no appeal whatsoever for the peoples of India. But the concepts of Marx and Lenin provided an ideological attraction for many who wished to alter the status quo in India and other colonial regions.

The British in India censored the news of the October revolution and subsequent developments in Russia. The great amount of confusion in India over what was happening is not at all surprising in view of the extremely fluid situation in Russia, the poor press coverage of events, and the constant effort of the British to quarantine their colonial subjects from Leninism. Most Indian nationalists felt that anything which the British Indian government sought so hard to discredit must have merit.[23]

World War I quickened the process of change within India and made the attainment of Swaraj (independence) a potentially realizable goal. The initial sympathy among Indian nationalists for the Bolsheviks stemmed partly from the Indians' realization that the principle of self-determination proclaimed by the Allies was not being applied to India and other colonial areas. By contrast, the Soviet government not only promised but also imple-

---

tion dealing with the repatriation of Korean War prisoners. Vyshinsky was provoked because he felt that the Indian delegate, V. K. Krishna Menon, presumed to speak on behalf of the Chinese People's Republic—a perogative the Soviets in those days reserved for themselves. See UN, *General Assembly Official Records*, First Committee, 529th mtg., Nov. 24, 1952, p. 137.

23. See Zafar Imam, "The Effects of the Russian Revolution on India, 1917–1920," in *South Asian Affairs*, no. 2, ed. S. N. Mukherjee, St. Antony Papers, no. 18 (Oxford, 1966), pp. 74–98.

mented (for several years) its pledge to grant self-determination to non-Russian peoples in the Czarist Empire.

The embattled Soviets won the sympathy of the great majority of Indian nationalists. In this vein the influential *Modern Review* of Calcutta published a series of articles beginning in January 1918. A representative excerpt reads:

It is refreshing to turn from the chorus of abuses and misrepresentation directed against the Russian Soviets by the capitalist press to the illuminating sketch of the framework of the Soviet state. . . . We are at last given an insight into the mighty efforts of the revolutionary Russia to organize herself and work out her communist ideals. . . . In fact [the Bolshevik] is striving to make Russia better and nobler than anything she has ever been.[24]

The October Revolution helped to stimulate the political consciousness of the Indian proletariat. Labor unions were formed after the war in some of the larger urban centers to help improve the very poor working and living conditions of the workers. As a result, in October 1920 the All-India Trade Union Council came into existence.

The emergent leader of the Indian National Congress, Mohandas K. Gandhi, derided the crude anti-Bolshevik propaganda disseminated by the British. But Gandhi stressed his dislike for the chaos and anarchy that he saw inherent in the violence of Bolshevism. Also, he did not think that any movement utilizing violence would stir the Indian masses to action.[25]

Gandhi had expected the British to deal generously with India after the war, but was disappointed by the tepid Chelmsford-

24. *Modern Review* (Calcutta), June 1919. Cited by Imam, "The Effects of the Russian Revolution," p. 77.

25. Gandhi wrote in his weekly, *Young India:* "India does not want Bolshevism. The people are too peaceful to stand anarchy. They will bow to the knees to anyone who restores order. Let us recognize the Indian psychology. The average Mussalman of India is quite different from the average Mussalman of the other part of the world. . . . The Hindus are proverbially almost contemptibly mild." M. K. Gandhi, *Young India, 1919–1922* (Madras, 1924), p 279.

Montagu reforms of 1918, which gave only partial self-govern-
ment to the provinces. The repressive use of the preventative detention powers of the Rowlatt Bills in 1919 led to the Amritsar
tragedy and a further loss of British moral authority in the eyes
of Indian nationalists.

It was at this juncture that the young Cambridge-trained Allahabad barrister, Jawaharlal Nehru, became seriously involved in
the Congress movement. He was impressed by Gandhi's high personal standards and capacity to stimulate the Indian masses. Under
Gandhi's leadership he participated in the nonviolent civil disobedience movement against the British in the early 1920s, sharing
with many of his contemporaries the initial hopes and frustrations
of the indecisive campaigns.

Nehru's pre-independence attitudes toward the USSR and communism tempered his later assessments of Soviet policy. Impressed
by Moscow's encouragement to Asian peoples seeking an end to
colonial rule, he wished to learn more about the Soviet experiment.
His first strong exposure to Marxist analysis of the world scene
came during an extended tour of Europe in 1927. In Brussels he
participated in the Congress of Oppressed Nationalities where he
met other nationalists from Asia and Africa and European intellectuals sympathetic to the plight of the colonial peoples.[26] Before
returning to India, he and his father accepted an invitation to
spend several days in Moscow. On the whole Jawaharlal was well
disposed toward what he saw there. Of particular interest to him
was the apparent trend toward social and economic leveling in
the new society. In one of his letters home he observed that "the
contrasts between extreme luxury and poverty are not visible, nor
does one notice the hierarchy of class or caste." He was also impressed by the Soviet penal system and by the manner in which
the Soviets seemingly dealt with minority and language problems
in their multinational state. Recognizing the possible relevance

26. Nehru's recollection of the Congress of Oppressed Nationalities is included in his *Toward Freedom*, pp. 123–27. Also see Dorothy Norman's useful
compilation of Nehru's writings: *Nehru: The First Sixty Years* 1: 121–28.

of the Soviet experiences to problems in India, he wrote that "India's path would be made easier" if the USSR were to find satisfactory solutions to the problems of poverty, illiteracy, and the need for industrialization.[27] While admiring the boldness of the Soviet experiment, however, Nehru did express some reservation about certain Soviet practices. "There is much," he wrote, "that I do not understand and much that I do not like." But the general tone of the letters reflects his interest in the Soviet attempt to reshape the political and social life of the world's largest country.

Nehru's favorable view of the USSR at this time also derived in large measure from the fact that the USSR was the only European nation calling for an end to British colonial rule in India. Speaking to a group of students in Calcutta in 1928, he emphasized the anti-imperialist record of the USSR: "And Russia, what of her? An outcast like us from nations and much slandered and often erring. But in spite of her many mistakes she stands today as the greatest opponent of imperialism and her record with the nations of the East has been just and generous."[28] Unlike Great Britain, the USSR did not hinder India's national aspirations. Nehru speculated that when India received its independence, "Russia and India should live as the best neighbors with [the] fewest points of friction. . . . Is there any reason why we in India should inherit the age-long rivalry of England against Russia?" He believed it was in India's own interest to understand the new order in Russia. Russia was India's neighbor, "a powerful neighbor, which may be friendly to us and cooperate with us, or may be a thorn in our side. In either event, we have to know her and understand her and shape our policy accordingly."[29]

27. Excerpts from Nehru, *Soviet Russia.* For a perceptive discussion of Nehru's early views on the USSR see Brecher, *Nehru,* pp. 116–20.

28. Jagat Bright, ed., *Before and After Independence: A Collection of the Important Speeches of Jawaharlal Nehru, 1922–50* (New Delhi: Indian Printing Works, 1950), p. 66.

29. J. Nehru, *Soviet Russia,* pp. 131 ff.

After 1927 Nehru was increasingly impatient with the gradualist approach to ending British rule. In forming the Independence for India League he joined with Subhas Chandra Bose, S. S. Iyengar, and others of differing political outlooks, all of whom shared one basic point—the desire to achieve immediate independence for India. Along with other Indian nationalists Nehru sympathized with the leaders of the CPI who were arrested in the drawn-out Meerut Conspiracy Case (1929–34). At this stage he and other "left" members of the Congress movement would have welcomed a cooperative relationship with the CPI. But ironically the Indian Communists, despite their harrassment by the British, were under Comintern instructions to denounce the Indian National Congress and the independence for India movements.

An incident in 1931 gave Nehru a firsthand insight into the workings of Soviet policy. Earlier, on behalf of the Indian National Congress, he had joined the newly-formed League Against Imperialism. But after the adoption of the hard line against "bourgeois nationalists" by the Sixth Comintern Congress in 1928, Nehru fell from grace. When Gandhi called off the 1931 civil disobedience campaign against the British, the Comintern declared that both he and Nehru had "practically gone over to the camp of the British rulers." The Indian National Congress was then dropped from the League Against Imperialism, and Nehru was removed from his office as one of the League's honorary presidents. He was not even given a chance to explain his and the Congress's position before the League.

Severely disillusioned, Nehru knew that Moscow was responsible for his expulsion from the League.[30] Nevertheless the bitter experience did not affect for long his view that the USSR represented a progressive force for altering the existing international order. The extent to which he was aware of the Stalinist abuses within the USSR in the 1930s is not known. In any event his writings

30. See Donald E. Smith, *Nehru and Democracy*.

never dwelt upon the liquidation of the kulaks, the mass purges, or other such occurrences.

Nehru's reservations about conditions within the USSR were soon subordinated to his abhorrence for the fascism and parochial nationalism rising in Europe and Japan. He hailed the USSR as the world's leading opponent of fascism and praised the "United Front" strategy adopted by the Comintern in 1934. These feelings were reinforced by Nehru's visit to Spain in the midst of the Civil War and by the tepid response of Britain and France to Axis conquests in Abyssinia and China. Like many European intellectuals of the political left, he in large part accepted Moscow's explanation that the 1938 Munich Agreement was simply an Anglo-French conspiracy to turn Germany eastward at the USSR's expense. Although puzzled and disappointed by the German-Soviet Non-aggression Pact the following year, he held that the USSR had no other alternative after their efforts to contain Germany through common action with the West had failed.[31]

When war broke out in Europe, Nehru, along with other Congress Party leaders, hoped that Indian support for the British war effort could be used as a leverage point in the struggle for national independence. However, without even consulting the Congress leaders, the British declared India to be at war with the Axis powers. Later the Cripps mission was willing to concede dominion status for India after the war ended. But this was unacceptable to Gandhi, who launched his "Quit India" campaign in 1942. Nehru had strong reservations about the campaign, for noncooperation with the British indirectly hindered the struggle against facism. Unlike some Indian nationalists, he did not welcome the British military setbacks in Asia. But loyalty to Gandhi prevailed, and Nehru followed the Mahatma's lead.

Jailed for much of the 1942–45 period, Nehru for the first time

31. See J. Nehru, *China, Spain, and the War* (Allahabad: Kitabistan, 1940) and *A Bunch of Old Letters* (New York: Asia Publishing House, 1960).

in years had ample time for reading and reflection. In his *Discovery of India*, written during the internment, Nehru sought to analyze the various influences on the totality of his thought. Marx and Lenin, he wrote, had given to the "long chain of history and of social development . . . some meaning, some sequence." There was much in Marxist philosophy that he "could accept without difficulty," but it did not satisfy him completely, "nor answer all the questions in [his] mind." He termed the achievements of the USSR "tremendously impressive," although some developments seemed to be "too closely concerned with the opportunities of the moment or the power politics of the day." Nehru felt that "the Soviet revolution had advanced human society by a great leap," but he expressed distaste for the overregimentation of the society. Nonetheless it was understandable, he wrote, that "in a complex social structure individual freedom had to be limited."[32]

At no time, even during his days of imprisonment, could Nehru be termed a doctrinaire Marxist. His readings on the subject were limited to a few standard works of Marx and Lenin and exegeses by British Marxists. Their theories were attractive to him in that they provided new perspectives with which to view political and social phenomena. His intellect was too independent however, to be subjected to the rigid discipline of any dogma. The insights of Marx and Lenin were added to those of reformist Indian, liberal, and Fabian thinkers that had influenced his intellectual development earlier. Drawing upon these diverse influences, Nehru fashioned his own viewpoints. Critics later pointed to a hazy ideological bent in Nehru's thought, while his admirers saw profundity in his eclectic approach.

To Nehru the implementation of socialist measures appeared to be the best means to reduce the existing inequities within the Indian socioeconomic structure. Yet he remained within the mainstream of the Congress movement, albeit to the left of center, often differing with Gandhi but never leaving him completely. His commit-

32. Nehru, *The Discovery of India*, pp. 16–18.

ment to socialist ideology was not so great that he would risk splintering the Congress. In later years Nehru's adherence to concepts of socialist planning was too far-reaching for such Congress leaders as Rajagopalachari, Prasad, and Patel. But those to the "left" of Nehru were not pleased either.[33]

Nehru was generally willing to overlook those aspects of the USSR which perplexed him. Like many other Indian intellectuals who professed admiration of the USSR, he did not study Soviet society in detail.[34] While holding the general view that Bolshevism had a number of good features in the Russian context, Nehru opposed its transplantation into Indian soil. He held that foreign imperialism and exploitation must end in India, that India's own capitalists had to be sharply restricted, and that widespread land reform measures were necessary. Yet he stopped short of advocating a philosophy of class struggle, the results of which would shake India's caste-ridden society to its very foundations. His emotions called for radical change in the Indian socioeconomic structure by any necessary means. But his intellect—tempered by his aristocratic family background, his education at Harrow and Cambridge, and his exposure to Gandhi—prevailed. He therefore advocated a program which he hoped would bring about basic changes without leading to violent upheaval. Before assuming the mantle of responsibility as prime minister of an independent nation, he was free in his speculation of what might be done within

33. Interpretive articles which discuss some of the points stressed in the above paragraphs include Margaret W. Fisher, "India's Jawaharlal Nehru"; Paul Power, "Indian Foreign Policy"; and Walter Crocker, *Nehru: A Contemporary's Estimate* (Oxford: Oxford University Press, 1966).

34. Writing about the Indian intellectual, Edward Shils noted: "The USSR doesn't attract Indian intellectuals very much. Practically no one reads books about the USSR and certainly practically no one studies it in a scholarly way. Even though he claims that it represents the model for India, the leftist Indian intellectual does not care to learn about it in intimate detail. Even the leftists feel closer to Britain—not least when they deny what they think it stands for." *The Intellectual Between Tradition and Modernity: The Indian Situation* (The Hague: Mouton, 1961), p. 83.

India. But his approach to the transformation of Indian society after 1947 was more akin to that of a British Laborite than a Marxist.

During the 1930s Nehru welcomed the participation of Indian Communists in the common struggle against the British and vociferously opposed the bans imposed on the Communist party of India. But he, like other Congress leaders, opposed the "anti-national" role of the CPI at a time when many Congress leaders were being imprisoned for urging noncooperation with the British. After the close of the war in 1945, the INC reacted by expelling all Communists from its membership. From that time onward Nehru made a basic distinction between Indian Communists and their counterparts in the USSR, as in this October 23, 1945, speech.

When [hundreds of thousands of] Indians staked their all for the country's cause, the Communists were in the opposite camp, which cannot be forgotten. The common man associates the CPI with Russia and Communism. We do not want to spoil relations with Russia, with whom we are looking forward for closer relations when India becomes independent.[35]

The militant disruptive tactics pursued by the CPI from late 1947–50 added to Nehru's disdain for India's Communists. The CPI, like the communalist elements, represented a challenge to his concept of a secular society governed by representative institutions. Nehru believed that it was for the Congress party alone to shape the future destiny of India.

The overriding concern of the Indian government at the time of independence and for several years afterwards was the political and social reconstruction of a partitioned land. Consolidation of statehood, the struggle against communalism, the relocation of millions of refugees, and the adjustment to the reality of Pakistan were top-priority tasks. In the midst of this turmoil Jawaharlal Nehru

35. H. N. Mitra, ed., *The Annual India Register* (Calcutta: Annual Register Office, July–Dec., 1945), p. 120.

also had to shape the direction of his nation's policy toward the world outside the subcontinent.

Nehru had a preeminent role in the formulation of Indian foreign policy. Prior to independence, his interest in international affairs was greater and more sustained than that of anyone else in the National Congress. His outlook represented a blend of both internationalism and committed nationalism. In 1936 he had reestablished within the National Congress a foreign department for the study of world affairs. Nehru never relinquished his hold in this area, and retained for himself the external affairs portfolio in his post-1947 cabinets.

His leadership in the realm of foreign policy (excluding India's relations with her immediate neighbors) was virtually uncontested. While, as Michael Brecher has pointed out, he consulted or accepted advice from close associates on particular issues, the final decisions were his alone. This did not mean that his views on foreign affairs were imposed on an unreceptive party, for the great majority of Congress leaders came to accept and identify with his broad based objectives.[36]

Much has been written about the Indian approach to world politics, the underlying principles of which were first enunciated by Nehru in 1946–47 and elaborated upon at length by Indian spokesmen thereafter. Nehru emphasized India's opposition to colonialism and racialism and to social and economic discrimination. Such aims were consistent with the Gandhian legacy of the independence movement and with recognized humane values. He called for an end to the exploitation of one people by another, and as a corollary, stressed the obligation of former colonial powers to compensate those whom they had previously exploited. A pledge of "unreserved adherence" was given in support of the United Nations' charter.

The "entry" of a newly independent nation into the arena of

36. Brecher, *Nehru*, p. 565 ff.

international politics has been aptly compared with the "entry" of
a previously unenfranchised class into domestic politics.[37] Those
who had previously been excluded from responsible participation
in the political process suddenly acquire a new potential for power.
It is equally true that newly-franchised nations or groups often
become second or third class citizens within the new political
milieu. Nehru, who opposed gradations of citizenship in his own
nation, was quick to project his principle onto the international
scene. India, he maintained, should occupy in the world councils
a place commensurate with her size, population, and "contribution toward peaceful progress." As a leading spokesman for the
struggling mass of colonial (and colored) peoples, India had a
distinctive role in the international forum into which she was
entering.

In this context Nehru reasoned that India's interests would be
best served by charting an independent course in world affairs.[38]
He pledged that India would "keep away from the power politics
of groups aligned one aginst the other." An alliance with Britain
or any other power was out of the question for independent India.

37. Warren F. Ilchman, "The 'Entry' Problem in International Relations:
India," paper delivered at Association for Asian Studies meeting, New York,
April 1966.

38. At various times Indians have described their foreign policy as "independent," "neutral," "noncommitted," "noninvolved," a "positive policy for
peace," etc. The term most commonly used, however, has been "nonalignment."
In the chapter, "Nonalignment: The Expectation," Werner Levi points to nonalignment as having helped to fulfill the psychological needs of the leaders of
many South and Southeast Asian leaders for independence: "It was independence
made operational. . . . It demonstratively distanced the new states from their
old masters. . . ." It allowed free play for the protests of Asian statesman
against the methods of the former rulers and the immorality of the international
system. Another aim of nonalignment was "to give the least possible cause for
outside intervention in internal affairs" of the new states. Levi observed that
"in striking contrast to their global stance was the totally different behavior
within their own region of many nonaligned states, India and Indonesia among
them. To state it briefly, in their own sphere they behaved much like older
nations oriented to 'power politics'." *The Challenge of World Politics in South
and Southeast Asia* [Englewood Cliffs: Prentice-Hall, 1968], pp. 75–91).

In any such alliance India would be a minor partner that could be drawn into an international conflict against her will. India did not wish to entangle herself with "other peoples' feuds and imperialistic rivalries." There was little conceivable advantage in siding with one's former rulers and their allies in a great powers' struggle that was not of India's making or immediate interest.

Nonalignment was also consonant with Nehru's views on Indian national security.[39] Prior to World War II he had held that an independent India would have few defence problems—she would be protected by the international balance-of-power system as well as by the physical distance separating India from the major world powers. The Japanese advance into eastern Assam during World War II weakened the assumption about the invulnerability of India to foreign attack. But after the war Japan no longer remained a threat. None of the states immediately contiguous to the subcontinent posed any defense problems for India. And the possibility of either of the emerging post-war blocs using military force against India was remote.[40] Only in the context of some future global war involving the United States and the USSR might India's territorial integrity be endangered.

The partition of the subcontinent and the ensuing dispute with Pakistan over Kashmir posed an unanticipated problem of another dimension. The tense situation with Pakistan led to escalation of an arms race which had many undesirable consequences for both nations. Eventually the smaller and weaker of the two, Pakistan, obtained Western assistance in order to gain a measure of military parity with India. This in turn brought the subcontinent closer to the Cold War which Nehru had sought assiduously to avoid.

---

39. For further discussion see A. P. Rana, "The Intellectual Dimensions of Indian Nonalignment," *Journal of Asian Studies* 28 (February 1969) ; 299–312. The author notes a "great affinity" between Nehru's approach to the Cold War and the nineteenth-century "balance of power" policy pursued by Great Britain.

40. For an analysis of why nonalignment did not appear to involve many risks see the chapter, "The Origins, Bases, and Aims of Indian Defence Policy" in Kavic, *India's Quest for Security*, pp. 21–45.

Geographically, India was removed from the Cold War which had crystallized in 1947–48. There had been little concern—or even awareness—in India over the imposition of Communist rule upon Eastern Europe. The period of overt Communist expansion in Europe coincided with the momentous events surrounding Indian independence. In no way did the USSR pose a military threat to India. The two nations were separated by the great Himalayan ranges and the buffer state Afghanistan, whose territorial integrity had been respected by the Soviets.

In 1927 Nehru wrote, "it is inconceivable that Russia, in her present condition at least, and for a long time to come will threaten India." Never during his later years as prime minister did he speak of the USSR as a potential aggressor against India. He would have welcomed friendly relations with the USSR, but Premier Stalin did not share his interest in such a development. Several months after India received her independence in 1947, the official Soviet media characterized Congress leaders as "reactionaries" under the influence of "Anglo-American Imperialism." Although dismayed by this verbal assault, Nehru was not too surprised, for over the previous twenty years he had observed the fluctuations of Soviet policy and was accustomed to its abrupt shifts.[41]

In most respects post-independent India remained oriented toward the West. The residue of British law and administration, the retention of Commonwealth ties, and the considerable flow

---

41. Illustrative of Nehru's attitude toward this treatment by the Soviet media is an incident recalled by H. V. R. Iengar. One day he brought Nehru a sheaf of extracts from Radio Moscow broadcasts which had described Nehru as a tool of British imperialism. Nehru glanced cursorily at the extracts, smiled a little wanly, and said, "the heat is not against us though it looks like it. The heat is against the British. The British have always tried to keep the Russians out of this subcontinent and the Russians cannot believe that the policy has changed. Let us wait and see. If we can show the world that we are, in fact, an independent country, the world will change its attitude to us. In the meantime you may study these things, but don't get bowled over by them." H. V. R. Iengar, "Evolution of Soviet Attitude to India," in the *Indian Express*, Jan. 29, 1966.

of commerce all marked the continuing links between Great Britain and India. Before 1947, the National Congress had pledged itself to the severance of close ties with Great Britain. Yet after independence was formally granted, Nehru recognized the advantages of continued close political and economic ties with the British and overcame strong domestic opposition to Indian membership in the Commonwealth. This continuing association with Britain was considered compatible with the principle of nonalignment, as no military ties were envisaged. But from the Soviet perspective, viewing the non-Communist world from the rigid "two camps" theory, it appeared that India's profession of nonalignment was meaningless.

It should be noted that the Indian government did not give very much attention to foreign policy matters until 1950. Most of its energies were understandably channeled into dealing with the domestic problems of communal disorders, Communist insurgency, and the myriad challenges posed by the transfer of power. Only in 1950–51 did Nehru begin to give substance to what he termed the positive aspects of nonalignment. Part of his growing disposition to achieve more balance between the Cold War blocs stemmed from the position taken by the United States and Britain on the Kashmir issue.

Kashmir's original accession to India, as accepted by Nehru, was made subject to a plebiscite. The Western powers wanted to resolve the Kashmir issue on this basis, giving the Kashmiris self-determination of their political fate. A resolution to this effect was passed on April 21, 1948, by the Security Council. India agreed to the resolution, but later insisted that certain preconditions be met before the plebiscite could be held. Continued Western insistence on the plebiscite concept was later viewed by New Delhi as an unfriendly gesture.[42] Assuming a neutral stance on Kashmir

---

42. J. C. Kundra, *Indian Foreign Policy, 1947–54*, and Josef Korbel, *Danger in Kashmir* (Princeton: Princeton University Press, 1954).

for a number of years, the Soviets did not avail themselves of an opportunity to make political capital. In 1952 the USSR gave a first indication that it might favor India's position on the issue, when Y. A. Malik charged that the United States and the United Kingdom were the chief obstacles to a Kashmir settlement, but it was not until 1955 that Moscow declared unequivocal backing for India.[43]

With the unexpected Communist victory in the Chinese Civil War, India also had to come to grips with a new force in the power structure of Asia. Indian nationalism had been influenced by the Chinese Revolution of 1911, and there had been sympathy in India for the subsequent struggles of the Chinese people against foreign imperialism. Independent India maintained good relations with the Kuomintang until Chiang's Government was driven from the mainland. Nehru probably had mixed feelings about the coming to power of Mao's CCP, but his public response was immediate and pragmatic. For him there was no question of approving or disapproving what had happened in China but only "of recognizing a major event in history and of appreciating it and dealing with it." India was among the first non-Communist nations to grant diplomatic recognition to the Chinese Communist regime. Nehru argued that the new government, representing an historic nation which had emerged from a century of European domination, international war, and civil strife, should be granted its rightful place in the world community. He was dismayed when the United States blocked the seating of the Chinese People's Republic in the United Nations.

The establishment of amicable relations with China became the focal point of Indian diplomacy in Asia. New Delhi hoped that gestures of friendliness toward Peking might be reciprocated and that the Chinese would not share the Soviet Union's hostile attitude toward India. But Peking soon ascribed base motives to India's

43. UN *Security Council* O. R., 7th year, 570th mtg., Jan. 17, 1952, pp. 13–18.

profession of good will. The Indian government was described as a "puppet" regime set up and controlled by the imperialists and as a base for the imperialists against the "national liberation movement" of the Asian peoples.[44]

In the months following the outbreak of the Korean War, India was given an opportunity to demonstrate that her commercial and political ties with the West did not govern her foreign policy. At the onset of the war, India supported the United Nation's General Assembly resolution terming North Korea an aggressor. She argued however, that the North Koreans should have been permitted to put their case before the United Nations. With the retreat by the North Koreans across the 38th parallel in September, 1950, Nehru advocated that the conflict be ended on the basis of the *status quo ante bellum*. He strongly opposed the decision by the UN military command to carry the conflict into North Korea. As the American-led forces drove toward the Yalu River, China warned through the Indian ambassador in Peking, K. M. Panikkar, that she would intervene if the advance continued. The warning was not heeded and the Chinese government carried out its threat. The Indian delegation did not support the subsequent UN resolution condemning the Chinese intervention.[45]

Nehru's prime concern was that the Korean War should remain localized and end as soon as possible. He repeatedly called for a negotiated settlement of the conflict. At the United Nations, India abstained on almost all partisan resolutions dealing with Korea. Indian pleas had little if any effect on any of the major powers involved in the conflict, but her impartiality led to her selection to chairman of the important Neutral Nations Repatriation Commission. Although criticized sharply at times, India handled the

44. New China News Agency, Dec. 7, 1949, pp. 124–25.

45. For discussions of India and the Korean conflict see C. N. Satyapalan, "India's China Policy: The first Decade" (Ph.D. diss., University of Pennsylvania, 1964), and Charles Heimsath, "India's Role in the Korean War," (Ph.D. diss., Yale University, 1956).

difficult task of war prisoner repatriation to the general satisfaction of both sides.[46]

New Delhi's position on Korea asserted the authenticity of Indian nonalignment and led to a slight improvement in the heretofore almost nonexistent relationship between India and the USSR. As a starter the Soviets called upon the CPI to work within the parliamentary framework of the Indian system. The Soviets also began to pay some attention to Indian diplomatic personnel in Moscow. Mrs. Vijayalakshmi Pandit, Nehru's sister, who served as India's first ambassador to the USSR, had been ignored by Stalin during her tenure from 1947 through 1949. By contrast, Stalin met with her successor, Dr. Sarvepalli Radhakrishnan, on several occasions.[47] During their second meeting, in April 1952, Stalin assured Radhakrishnan that all major East-West problems could be resolved. K. P. S. Menon, who replaced Radhakrishnan as ambassador late in 1952, was among the last outsiders to see Stalin alive. The talks with the Indian diplomats were among the few granted to any foreigners in 1952. Stalin probably was coming around to the realization that India's foreign policy could be used to further his ends. Had he lived longer, Stalin might have made substantial overtures to win Indian confidence. But even during his talk with Menon he was preoccupied with other matters, far removed from Indo-Soviet relations.[48]

Other perceptible signs of the slight change in their attitude towards India in 1952 included Soviet participation in the International Film Festival and the International Industries Fair held in Bombay that year. The Soviet ambassador to India, Novikov, put forth an offer to increase Indo-Soviet trade. In 1952 a Russian trade union sent India a relief shipment of wheat, rice, condensed

46. Michael Brecher, *The New States of Asia*, pp. 116–20.

47. See *Times of India*, March 5, 1953, and *Hindustan Times*, November 22, 1965.

48. Menon's interesting impressions of the interview are contained in his *The Flying Troika*, pp. 26–32.

milk, and 25,000 rupees during a severe famine.[49] In general, Indian and Soviet delegates at the United Nations consulted with each other more frequently than they had in the past. The major areas of Indian and Soviet concurrence of interests at the United Nations were questions of racialism and colonialism in Africa and Asia. Common cause was made particularly in the denunciation of racism in South Africa.

Yet these cited instances are almost the only examples of relaxation in a relationship that remained on the whole rigid and formal. Soviet media continued occasionally to deride Nehru and the Congress party. Nehru's attitude toward the Korean conflict paved the way for a lessening of tensions, but India was not in a position to do much more than that. Further initiative had to come from the Soviet side.

49. K. P. Karunakaran, *India in World Affairs, 1950–53*, p. 239.

2 The Period of Transition

SEVERAL months after the death of Premier Stalin there were indications that a basic change in the Soviet attitude toward the Nehru Government was in the offing. Over the next two years the USSR made a series of gestures, designed both to gain New Delhi's confidence and to diminish Western influence in India. India's reaction to Moscow's new diplomacy and her assessment of Soviet intentions and actions was somewhat cautious at first, but New Delhi soon recognized that the Soviet cordiality had enhanced the effectiveness of India's mediatory efforts in the East-West conflict, thereby opening up a new dimension for her own international diplomacy.

The Shift in Soviet Policy

It is very improbable that the USSR wanted the direct confrontation with the United States and its allies that developed in the immediate post-war years. Although emerging in 1945 as a strong military power, the USSR was a devastated nation whose vitality had been sapped by the Kafkaesque purges of the 1930's and the privations and heavy casualties of the war with Germany. Stalin's immediate interests were in rebuilding the Soviet economy and securing the Western borders of the USSR against future at-

32

tacks.[1] On the latter point Stalin reflected traditional Russian state interests in demanding that governments friendly to the USSR be established. In reality this meant that in those states occupied by the Red army the postwar governments would be dominated by Moscow-trained Communists loyal to the USSR.

Stalin's territorial ambitions were probably limited to areas over which he could maintain effective control. In dividing respective spheres of influence in the Balkans and Greece he and Churchill were guided by realistic power considerations. The United States acquiesced, albeit somewhat uneasily, to these balance of power considerations. On the whole, President Roosevelt appeared to believe that the situation was manageable and that it would be possible to work things out with his wartime ally.

As the war with Germany drew to a close, however, the tenuous alliance began to disintegrate. It is not the intent of this study to enter into the current debates on the causes of the Cold War. Suffice it to say that the widely accepted approach of Western scholarship for many years focused on the authoritarian nature of the Soviet regime itself as being the sole root of the problem. The guileful Soviet ruler, it was held, simply could not restrain himself from imposing governments created in his own image on the areas occupied by his army and from looking covetously beyond to the war-weary, prostrate lands of Western Europe. The United States therefore was wholly justified in whatever steps it took to meet the threat of Soviet aggression.

In recent years, however, another point of view also has been gaining academic recognition. Looking at events from a different perspective, its exponents stress that the USA as well as the USSR committed acts which contributed to the breakdown of trust between the two sides. The advent of the atomic bomb, it is believed, upset the uneasy balance which had existed between the USA and

1. For an insightful study see Isaac Deutscher, *Stalin: A Political Biography*, 2d ed. (New York: Oxford University Press, 1967).

the USSR and encouraged the USA to use its atomic advantage as a diplomatic foil.[2] America's sidestepping the request for massive financial aid to help rebuild the war-torn USSR, and the concomitant ending of lend-lease aid were also regarded by the Soviets as hostile acts. Whatever American intentions were, they had the effect of causing a reciprocal hardening on the Soviet side and with it the ending of any semblance of representative government for the peoples of Eastern Europe. These criticisms, while sometimes overdrawn, have had a leavening influence in provoking a rethinking of the more simplistic assumptions about American policies.[3]

An action on one side provoked a reaction—often an over-reaction—on the part of the other. As Gar Alperovitz has put it, "the Cold War cannot be understood simply as an American response to a Soviet challenge, but rather as the insidious interaction of mutual suspicions, blame for which must be shared by all." Subsequently the chain of events with which we are familiar unfolded: the Truman Doctrine and with it the formal enunciation of the "containment policy," the European Recovery Program, the formation of the Cominform with its "two camp" thesis, the Communist coup in Czechoslovakia, the formation of NATO, the Berlin Blockade, the Soviet explosion of an atomic device, and the outbreak of the Korean War.[4]

2. Gar Alperovitz has written on this point: "Before the atomic bomb was tested, despite their desire to oppose Soviet policies, Western policy makers harbored very grave doubts that Britain and America could challenge Soviet predominance in Eastern Europe. As Churchill put it in recalling the days prior to the Potsdam Conference, 'We now had something in our hands which would redress the balance with the Russians.'" Alperovitz, *Atomic Diplomacy: Hiroshima and Potsdam* (New York: Vintage, 1967), pp. 228–29.

Others whose writings have challenged conventional thinking on the Cold War include William Appleman Williams, D. F. Fleming, John A. Lukacs, Noam Chomsky, Richard Barnett, Christopher Lasch and Gabriel Kolko.

3. For a critique of both "revisionist" and "moderate Cold Warrior" scholarship see Arnold S. Kaufman, "The Cold War in Retrospect," *Dissent*, November–December, 1967), pp. 775–99.

4. In the words of Arthur Schlesinger, Jr.: "The Cold War . . . was the

In many respects Stalin's diplomacy became self-defeating. The belief that conflict with the West was imminent led to more bellicose Soviet policies in 1948–50, and this in turn provoked a strong reaction in the West. The tension which abounded all along the periphery of the Communist world broke into overt conflict in Korea when the USSR permitted the North Koreans to attempt a forceful reunification of the country.

The Korean War added to the strength of the Western coalition against the USSR. It brought American politics to the fever pitch and made it possible for the Republican government elected in 1952 to launch immediately (with scarcely any domestic opposition) into a program of ringing the Communist world with a series of interlocking military alliances. The Korean conflict also marked the beginning of the self-assertion of a Chinese Communist regime which fought the United States–led UN forces to a military stand-off.

In his last months Stalin himself must have realized that the period of Communist expansion by physical force had ended. He withdrew the doctrinal notion of imminent military confrontation with the West and emphasized instead that the USSR should encourage the inevitable conflicts that were going to occur within

---

product not of a decision but of a dilemma. Each side felt compelled to adopt policies which the other could not but regard as a threat to the principles of the peace. Each then felt compelled to take defensive measures. Thus the Russians saw no choice but to consolidate their security in Eastern Europe. The Americans, regarding Eastern Europe as the first step toward Western Europe, responded by asserting their interest in the zone the Russians deemed vital to their security. The Russians concluded that the West was resuming its old course of capitalist encirclement; that it was purposefully laying the foundation for anti-Soviet regimes in the area defined by the blood of centuries as crucial to Russian survival. Each side believed with passion that future international stability depended on the success of its own conception of world order. . . . Very soon the process began to acquire a cumulative momentum."

While Mr. Schlesinger criticizes some of the "revisionist" writers, his own thinking appears to have been somewhat influenced by their works. Note, for example, the difference in tone between his letter to the editor of the *New York Review of Books*, October 20, 1966, and the above cited quotation from his article in *Foreign Affairs* 46 (October 1967) : 45.

the Western controlled regions of the world. He also noted that Soviet policy would have to become more flexible.[5] But at the time of his passing he bequeathed a stagnant foreign policy featuring exceedingly strained relations with most of the non-Communist nations of Europe and Asia.[6]

During the spring and early summer of 1953 there was little indication that a perceptible change in the conduct of Soviet diplomacy was in the offing. The immediate concern of the new collegial leadership was whether the Western powers would attempt to take advantage of the USSR during the interlude after Stalin's death. It soon became apparent, however, that the West was not united enough to attempt a concerted "rollback" in Eastern Europe.

The necessity to create a more flexible Soviet foreign policy was evident. The Stalinist approach had brought about an anti-Soviet coalition of powers in the West which in turn led to an alliance system encircling the Socialist camp. The possibility had grown of a major war with the West, a war that very few, if any, in the party hierarchy would have welcomed. It was in short necessary to defuse the precipitous international condition which prevailed. Also, if meaningful changes were to occur within the USSR itself, it was necessary to decrease the external pressures. The "stage-of-seige" mentality of the Cold War had been conducive to the Stalinist order of society. Men like Nikita Khrushchev sought to bring an end to the reign of terror within the USSR. Some of the more conspicuous miscarriages of Stalinist justice were dealt with, but the deep resentment which poured forth at the twentieth CPSU

5. J. V. Stalin, *Economic Problems of Socialism in the USSR* (Moscow: Foreign Languages Publishing House, 1952).

6. Studies of Soviet foreign policy in the 1950s in addition to those cited elsewhere include George Kennan, *Russia, the Atom and the West* (New York: Harper and Row, 1957); Zbigniew Brzezinski, *The Soviet Bloc: Unity and Conflict* (Cambridge: Harvard University Press, 1960); J. M. Mackintosh, *Strategy and Tactics of Soviet Foreign Policy* (London: Oxford University Press, 1963); Marshall Shulman, *Stalin's Foreign Policy Reappraised* (Cambridge: Harvard University Press, 1963); and Louis J. Halle, *The Cold War as History* New York: Harper and Row, 1967).

Congress in 1956 was not yet released. A more relaxed relationship with the outside world would minimize the chance for reascendancy of the police-state methods which had for so long burdened the Russian conscience. With the escalation of the Cold War, Soviet military expenditures had grown. The strain of these expenditures was far greater for the Soviet citizen than for his counterpart in the West. The peoples of the USSR had labored for decades without knowing the fruits that Communism was purported to bring. One of the stated features of the Malenkov period was the desire to give the citizenry an improved material standard of living. But for the paramount claims of armaments and heavy industry to be reduced, it was necessary to slow down the pace of the Cold War.

Achievement of the domestic and external objectives of the new Soviet leadership was in large part contingent on a reduction in East-West tensions. A first important step in this direction was the approval of an armistice in July 1953 ending hostilities in Korea. Efforts were made to improve relations with Turkey and Yugoslavia. A foreign ministers' conference with the United States, Britain, and France in January 1954, while producing no concrete results, served to reestablish dialogue with the Western powers.[7] The concept of "peaceful coexistence," previously employed during Maxim Litvinov's years as foreign minister, was refurbished to describe the new direction of Soviet foreign policy.

Gradually Moscow shifted away from the sterile "two camps" approach to a view that recognized the growing "third force" in international politics. The central thesis of the 1947–52 period— "those who are not with us are against us"—gave way gradually to the more flexible position that allowed for a group of newly independent nations not committed to either camp.[8]

7. *Survey of International Affairs* (London) gives a detailed account of the developments in Soviet policy in 1953–54. In particular, see *Survey*, 1953, "The Death of Stalin," pp. 7–48 and *Survey*, 1954, "The Peoples' Democracies," pp. 1–73.

8. On the subject of Soviet policies toward the developing areas over the years, Jan Triska and David Finley wrote: "Soviet goals in the developing areas

By most geopolitical criteria, the significant non-Communist Asian nations are Japan, India, Indonesia, and Pakistan. In 1954–55 Japan and Pakistan were firmly tied to the United States. The Soviet Union began to court India, Indonesia, Afghanistan, Burma and Egypt—those nations which had asserted a preference to remain outside the American-sponsored alliance systems.[9] A focal point of Soviet interest lay in India, the largest and by far the most populous of the nonaligned nations. Led by the world's most influential spokesman for nonalignment, India had demonstrated an independent foreign policy during the Korean War period. It was believed in Moscow that the development of friendly ties with India would help the Communist world's efforts to break out of its diplomatic isolation and to obtain a foothold among the nations of the growing *tiers monde*. Equally important was the Soviet need to counter the Western alliance system around the southern perimeter of the Communist world. Unlike the United States, the USSR sought no formal alliance with India. To neutralize Anglo-American influence in South Asia in itself would be significant. Without India the anti-Communist alliances in Southeast and West

have been formulated within a maximum-minimum range of prospects since the early days of the Russian Bolshevik regime. At the maximum end of the continuum, the optimum outcome for the Soviet Union, stands conversion of the peoples and incorporation of the developing area into the communist party state system. At the minimum end of the continuum stands depriving the imperialists of the assets of those areas. In between are the promotion of socialist political and economic regimes and active support for the Soviet international posture vis à vis the 'imperialist' West. There is nothing new in this continuum of goals. What has changed over the years is the immediate priority awarded them and the strategy and tactics by which they are pursued." See Triska and Finley, *Soviet Foreign Policy*, pp. 254–55.

9. Relations with the nonaligned emerging nations have been discussed in such Soviet publications as E. A. Korovin, *Osnovnye problemy sovremennykh mezhdunarodnykh otnoshenii* [Basic problems of contemporary international relations] (Moscow: Social-Economic Literature Press, 1959), pp. 11–18; and Ia. Etinger and O. Melikian, *Neitralizm i Mir* [Neutralism and peace] (Moscow: Mysl Press, 1964), pp. 31–54. Cited in Norma C. Noonan, "Soviet-Indian Relations, 1953–63," (Ph.D. diss., Indiana University, 1965), p. 5.

Asia would be without the most important geographic linchpin.

The development in 1954 of intercontinental bombers to deliver the nuclear weapons tested the previous year assuaged Soviet feelings of military inferiority. The presence of a formidable Chinese ally and the beginning of contacts with non-Communist nations also helped to lessen the "state of siege" mentality which had previously conditioned the outlook of the Kremlin leaders. Improving relations with the "bourgeois-nationalist regimes" of newly-independent Asian nations created some ideological dilemmas for the Soviets which were (and are) not easily resolved.[10] But this did not deter a distinct shift in Soviet attitude toward the non-aligned nations.

The scope of the foreign policy embarked upon during the Khrushchev era was bolder and more imaginative than in the past. Under Khrushchev, the USSR for the first time became a truly global power. Stalin had pursued a generally probing and cautious course, concerned with defending his holdings and, at propitious moments, expanding them on the periphery of the Soviet-dominated camp.[11] The change in the style and scale of Soviet policy can be clearly seen in Khrushchev's initiatives toward the newly independent nations of Asia and Africa. In contrast to the earlier policy of viewing these nations as appendages of the Western camp, a new assessment took the complexities of the changing world situation more into account. The new policy took advantage of the strong feelings of anti-Western imperialism and the residue of anticapitalism which existed among elitist elements in the emerging nations. The Soviet leaders and media soon began to

10. Philip Mosely summarized the dilemna: "Where should the Kremlin place its main effort: On helping nationalist regimes because they needed Soviet backing in order to resist colonialism and 'neo-colonialism'? Or on helping these non-Communist regimes just enough to demonstrate their ineffectiveness. meanwhile assisting the 'true revolutionaries' to train and marshal their forces for the establishment of Communist rule?" See "Communist Policy and the Third World," *Review of Politics*, 43 (October 1964) : 87–99.

11. See Vernon V. Aspaturian, "Moscow's Foreign Policy," *Survey*, no. 65 (October 1967), pp. 35–60.

refer to a "zone of peace" which included both the Communist
nations and the nonaligned states of Asia.

The first major statement by Premier Malenkov which indicated
that the USSR had become more appreciative of India's nonaligned
foreign policy was contained in an August 1953 address to the
Supreme Soviet:

In the efforts of the peace-loving countries directed towards ending
the Korean War, India made a significant contribution. Our relations
with India are becoming stronger and our cultural ties are growing.
We hope that in the future, relations between India and the USSR
will grow stronger and develop in a spirit of friendly cooperation.[12]

As a harbinger of this desire for "friendly cooperation" with India,
the amiable Mikhail Menshikov was appointed Soviet ambassador
to India on August 31.

The Soviet reappraisal of India's role in international affairs
coincided with an increase in Indo-American tensions. One of
the first times Moscow capitalized on this windfall occurred at
the time of the Korean Peace conference held in Geneva in 1954.
Although India had served as the head of the Neutral Nations'
Repatriation Commission, she was not invited to participate in the
Korean Peace talks. The USSR recognized India's desire to be
included in any conference where the future of Asian peoples was
being discussed. Twenty-seven countries, including the Communist
bloc and Great Britain, voted in the General Assembly Political
Committee to include India in the conference on Korea while
twenty-one nations were opposed. (The United States' negative
vote reflected South Korea's opposition to Indian participation,
and the Latin American nations followed the U.S. lead.) Thus
India did not receive the required ⅔ vote to be seated at the
conference and was excluded from the indecisive discussions on
the Korean issue.

From 1954 onward the USSR also worked for the inclusion of

12. Session of the Supreme Soviet of the USSR, Speech by Comrade Malenkov,
For a Lasting Peace. . . , no. 33 (August 14, 1953), p. 3.

India on all international forums on disarmament. Having achieved a relative military balance with the West, the USSR for the first time gave some serious thought to the arms control issue. Tired of sitting alone at the conference table, the Soviets called in 1954 for the addition of the People's Republic of China, Czechoslovakia, and India to the United Nations' Disarmament Subcommission. Predictably, the four Western nations on the subcommission opposed the proposal, giving the Soviet delegate, Andrei Vyshinsky, an opportunity to chide the British representative, Sir Pierson Dixon, for rejecting India. "After all," said the Soviet diplomat, "India is a member of the Commonwealth. . . . Why do you object to a member of your own family?"[13] The USSR eventually obtained parity for the Communist side on the disarmament Subcommission, but continued to press for the inclusion of India and other nonaligned Afro-Asian nations. In 1962 India was selected as one of the eight "neutrals" in the expanded eighteen-nation commission.

At a time when the United States was sponsoring arms aid to Pakistan and the creation of the Southeast Asia Treaty Organization, Moscow was hailing Nehru's plea for the abolition of nuclear weapons. India was praised as a nation which was "becoming an important factor in the strengthening of peace and security in Asia"—one which would "never join the Americans in the pursuance of their aggressive plans."[14] *Pravda* gave substantial coverage whenever Nehru spoke against the American-directed alliance systems—for example, a December 23, 1953, address to Parliament, in which he termed the impending military aid to Pakistan "a dangerous step for many countries, especially for us and Pakistan."

In July 1953 the Soviet delegate to the UN Economic and Social Council offered four million rubles (about one million dollars) to the Expanded Program of Technical Assistance for use in projects

13. Vyshinsky termed Nehru's plea for prohibition of nuclear weapons a substantial step forward (*Hindu*, April 20, 21, 1954).

14. Radio Moscow broadcast of May 19 as reported in *Hindu*, May 21, 1954.

in underdeveloped areas.[15] Then, at the meetings of the Economic
Commission for Asia and the Far East held in Ceylon in February
1954, the USSR expressed willingness to provide aid "with no
political strings attached" to the Asian nations. There were no
immediate takers of either offer, in part because the USSR placed
barriers in the way of specialized agencies of the United Nations
administering the EPTA aid.

Later in 1954–55 the USSR initiated a program of economic
and technological aid on the basis of bilateral agreements with
several Asian nations that had remained outside the Western
alliance system. Aid was offered to those nonaligned countries
which were "advancing the cause of peace"—primarily India,
Afghanistan, Burma, Indonesia, and Egypt. The potential recipients were at first hesitant over the possible political implication
of accepting the aid, but soon Afghanistan and then India began
negotiations for Soviet aid projects. In September 1954 the USSR
officially offered to build a steel mill at Bhilai in the Indian state
of Madhya Pradesh. Soviet technical experts arrived in November
to discuss the project, and a formal agreement on the Bhilai plant
was signed between the two governments in February 1955.[16]

Reflecting the shift in Soviet policy, the CPI generated support
for the Sino-Soviet "peace" campaign within India. The active
All-India Peace Council enlisted the support of a number of prominent non-Communists in activities which indirectly abetted the
Communist movement. Among the more prominent Indians drawn
into the peace movement were Dr. Saifuddin Kitchlew, a long-
time worker in the Congress movement; Sir Sahib Singh Sokhey,
assistant director of the WHO from 1950–52; and S. K. Patil,

15. UN, *Economic and Social Council Organization Report* (16th session),
p. 142. The Soviet participation in the EPTA and the ECAFE program is documented in Alvin Z. Rubinstein, *The Soviets in International Organization*, pp.
32–61, 138–90.

16. The Soviet economic and technological assistance program to India is
discussed in chapter 7.

president of the Bombay Pradesh Congress Committee.[17] After the Chou En-lai visit to India in June 1954, the Peace Council echoed the communique issued by the two prime ministers calling for a "united campaign for Asia solidarity based on the acceptance of the Five Principles of peaceful coexistence."

The CPI did, however, experience some difficulty in adjusting to the revised Soviet policy towards India. Whenever other considerations took precedence, Moscow did not hesitate to subordinate the immediate interests of the CPI. An example of this occurred in January 1955 when the CPI was campaigning for important state elections in Andhra Pradesh. During the campaign, articles appeared in the major Russian newspapers in honor of India's Republic Day. An editorial in *Pravda* read in part: "The Indian government refuses to participate in aggressive blocs and comes out for peaceful coexistence between various social systems. Guided by peace-loving principles of foreign policy, the Indian government has made a considerable contribution to ensuring peace in Asia and easing international tension."[18] The editorial, which also made some favorable references to Nehru's domestic policies, was widely publicized by the Congress party prior to the election.[19]

During the 1955 state visit of Krushchev and Bulganin to India there was no contact between the Soviet leaders and the CPI. The closest that Khrushchev came to meeting with Ajoy Ghosh, secre-

17. A detailed account of the peace movement in India is included in Overstreet and Windmiller, *Communism in India*, pp. 411–29.

18. *Pravda*, Jan. 26, 1955.

19. The Congress party invested considerable funds and energy into the Andhra campaign. Nehru and other Congress leaders stressed that the Andhra Communists owed their allegiance primarily to the Communist countries. The electorate was reminded of the CPI-led insurgency which had taken place in the Telengana district from 1948 to 1950. The results of the election gave the Congress 61 percent of the seats and the CPI only 8 percent. Details of the election are given in Marshall Windmiller, "The Andhra Election," *Far Eastern Survey*, April 1955, pp. 57–64.

tary-general of the CPI, was a brief handshake at a reception. The Soviet visitors clearly identified with the Congress leadership and in no uncertain terms praised Nehru's policies. Although the seeming snub of the CPI was widely interpreted in the Indian press as a setback for the CPI, the diplomatic success of the USSR later gave more respectability to Communism as an ideology in the "Indian popular mind."

Indicative of Soviet approval of Indian foreign policy were the 1954 slogans commemorating the thirty-seventh anniversary of the Bolshevik revolution. India ranked first among the non-Communist nations receiving greetings. The slogan called for the expansion of friendship and cooperation between the two peoples for the good of world peace. The rank-order and content of the annual greetings sent for the November Revolution and May Day reflect Soviet attitudes toward the recipient nations. Since 1954 India always has been among the first of the non-Commuist nations to follow the "fraternal socialist nations" in the annual slogans.

By the end of 1954 the newspapers and periodicals of the Communist world spoke highly of the Nehru government. Some articles praised the peace-loving nature of the Indian people; others the diversity of Indian culture. Reminders were included that the USSR had played an important role in the transformation of such nations as India, Burma, Indonesia, and Egypt from semi-colonies to truly independent nations. For example, the *New Times* noted: "The fact that there is a socialist world besides the capitalist world, enables these countries to uphold their independence and sovereignty."[20]

On several occasions there were embarrassing time lags before Soviet publications adapted to the new line on India. An illustration of this was the repetition in the 1954 edition of the *Large Soviet Encyclopedia* of virtually the same disapprobation of Mahatma Gandhi's politics that had been printed in the 1952 edition.

20. V. Avarini, "The Twilight of Colonialism," *New Times*, no. 43 (October 23, 1954), p. 5.

The edition obviously had been compiled and had gone to press before the editors adapted to the new line on India. As before, Gandhi was called "one of the initiators of the agreement by Congress leaders with British imperialism in 1947 which led to the division of the country." Gandhism was characterized as "the reactionary political doctrine of Gandhi . . . in the form of religious ethical teaching."[21] In contrast to its extensive comments on Gandhi, the 1954 edition had relatively little on Nehru.[22] Protests by the Indian press and government that the treatment of Gandhi was completely opposed to the professed Soviet friendship and respect for India led to removal and subsequent revision of the offending page.[23]

Soviet historians later altered or eliminated altogether the pre-1953 references to India's leaders and their policies. Reflecting the changed official attitude toward India, the writers A. M. Diakov and V. V. Balabushevich reversed their earlier condemnation of Nehru's policies, and now praised India's "struggle" for peace, its attitude towards the Korean conflict and its support for the seating of the People's Republic of China in the UN.[24]

By 1955 a consistent pattern in Soviet policy began to emerge. Moscow encouraged the concept of an Asian "peace zone," praised India's role in world affairs, increased its trade with India, and pledged economic and technological assistance. The immediate

21. *Bolshaia Sovetskaia Entsiklopediia*, 2d ed., 10: 203.

22. Nehru in 1954 was termed a "prominent Indian statesman" and the "author of several books on international politics and the Indian liberation movement." The only book specifically mentioned was *Soviet Russia* (*Bolshaia Sovetskaia Entsiklopediia*, 29: 486).

23. *Hindu*, Dec. 6, 1954. The Soviet historian Kozhevnikov, on a goodwill visit to India in December, said that the account would be corrected and that "even if the authors of the *Entsiklopediia* did not agree with certain aspects of Gandhi's philosophy, they had no right to make uncomplimentary remarks about him."

24. See, for example, A. M. Diakov, "India v Borbe za Mir" [India in the struggle for peace], *Sovetskoe Vostokovedenie*, no. 1 (1955), pp. 36–43; and Diakov and V. V. Balabushevich, *Nova'shaia Istoriia Indii* [Modern history of India] (Moscow: Eastern Literature Press, 1959).

goal of the Soviets in these gestures seemingly was to reinforce Indian nonalignment in the Cold War with the possibility that in the future Indian support might be enlisted for Soviet policy.

India's Response to Soviet Overtures

As indicated earlier, India had very little involvement with the Cold War in its initial stages, with the exception of the localized civil disorders created by the Communist party of India from 1947 to 1950. India was involved in the many problems surrounding the attainment of independence. A relative lack of serious interest, added to the geographic and psychological remoteness, made it possible for many Indians to develop a "detached" viewpoint of the issues embroiling the United States and the USSR.

Because of latent sympathies for the frequently maligned Soviets Prime Minister Nehru was often willing to give the benefit of the doubt to the USSR. He did not see one side particularly responsible for the outbreak of the Cold War but believed shortsighted and belligerent actions on both sides created the situation. From this perspective, Nehru and such Indian diplomats as K. M. Panikkar and K. P. S. Menon were receptive to any indication of change within the Communist world. Nehru was able to respond quickly to the Soviet initiative in 1955. Being in virtually complete control of Indian policymaking toward the great powers, he was not impeded by the public pressures which would have prohibited a rapid shift in American or British policy toward the USSR in the mid-1950s. Nehru was impatient with the Western leaders for not taking advantage of the openings provided by the Soviets and Chinese at that time. He would have better understood the limitations of Western policymakers had he viewed their situation as analogous to his own with Pakistan.

The death of Stalin provoked widespread comment within India. Speaking in the Lok Sabha, Nehru termed Stalin "a man of great stature who moulded the destinies of his age and proved himself great in peace and war. Whatever else may be said of him, he will

be remembered by the way he built up his great country." Other
Congress party leaders expressed their sympathy in a similar fashion. One commentator termed the "somewhat uncalled-for
effusiveness in condoling the Russian people . . . characteristically
Indian." That India's public leaders should "have hastened to
sympathize with the great dictator's multitudinous admirers in
Russia [without] sharing even remotely Stalin's political theory
and practice is a remarkable tribute to the Indian character."[25]
Among the few public figures who protested the effusive con-
dolences was Praja Socialist party leader, Asoka Mehta. Mehta
called Stalin a "great tyrant" and added that "the deranged,
however diabolical, deserve one's understanding."[26]

There was a wide range of speculation in Indian journals on
the future direction of Soviet foreign policy. We might note here
some of the more perceptive editorial opinions expressed at the
time. Some editorial comment was cautiously optimistic that the
change in leadership might help create a climate in which genuine
settlement of international problems could be achieved. On this
theme, M. N. Roy wrote that the new leadership of the Kremlin
"may be disposed to adopt a more reasonable and less aggressive
policy if they will be given the opportunity to do so [by the Western
powers] without losing face."[27] Several journals predicted that
the USSR would not retain its monolithic control within the Communist world. The *Eastern Economist* noted, for example, that "no
successor to Stalin could command his dominating influence over
Mao Tse-tung who has been a Marxist and a theoretician in his
own right, next only to Stalin."[28] A similar view was expressed in
Thought: "For most of the leaders of the satellite countries it

25. *Thought,* March 14, 1953. Quoted in special section, "Indian Reaction to
the Death of Stalin," of the *Indian Press Digests,* vol. 2, no. 2, (January–March
1953), (University of California, June 1954).

26. *Hindustan Times,* March 10, 1953.

27. M. N. Roy, "The Death of Stalin," *Radical Humanist,* vol. 17, March 15,
1953.

28. *Eastern Economist,* March 27, 1953.

would be psychologically and temperamentally impossible or at any rate difficult to accept the new Russian leadership as superior to themselves in the understanding and application of their particular dogma. A process of silent revolt in those countries was even discernible during the last days of Stalin."[29]

The Indian government watched for indications of the path which the new Soviet leaders would follow. Malenkov had called for a lessening of international tensions, but it remained for the Soviets to demonstrate in practice their professed desire for "peaceful coexistence." The signing of the Korean armistice in July 1953 was regarded by New Delhi as an important step in the right direction.

By late 1953 the United States began to build a *cordon sanitaire* against the expansion of communism in Asia. Of particular concern to India was the American military pact with Pakistan, which in Nehru's words brought the Cold War "to the gates of the subcontinent." A growing divergence between India and the United States on how to deal with the Communist nations was apparent.[30]

Despite his own outspoken opposition to the American-Pakistani pact and later to the Southeast Asia Treaty Organization, Nehru did not publicly mention the acclaim his stand was receiving from the Russians and Chinese. The praise of the Communist nations was probably embarrassing to him, as it nurtured a growing belief in the West that India was moving toward an acceptance of the Communist bloc line in international affairs. Nehru wanted a modus vivendi with the USSR and China, but not at the expense of rapidly deteriorating relations with the United States and the United Kingdom. He was also concerned lest Indian Communists and communalists exploit the growing tensions for their own political advantage.

29. *Thought*, March 21, 1953. Quoted in *Indian Press Digests*, vol. 2, no. 4 (June 1954).

30. See "P" (N. R. Pillai), "Middle Ground Between America and Russia."

Not wishing to create the impression that he was leaning toward the Communist states, Nehru denied that he "criticized only the democratic countries and refrained from criticism of the Communist bloc." On one occasion he reflected: "I have no desire, nor my Government, to sit on a perch and moralize anybody, because we are deeply conscious of our own failings in our own country."[31] Nevertheless, he did indulge in more public criticism of the West than of the Communist bloc. The irony of the situation was that Nehru was personally committed to a parliamentary system, and his government had close political and economic ties with the West. Yet he probably reasoned that the Communist nations, unlike the West, were not doing anything which posed a challenge to India's immediate interests. And after all, were not the Americans and British with their long tradition of open discussion mature enough to take constructive criticism from a friendly people? By contrast, India could not risk such intimacy with her newer Communist acquaintances. Whenever Nehru did permit himself an occasional criticism of the Communist camp, he usually chose the Cominform as the target. He told Parliament in September 1954, for example, that the Cominform was something like the old Comintern, but in "new garb." The activities of those organizations "have caused a great deal of apprehension and disturbance in various countries."[32]

In 1954 Nehru frequently spoke of removing Asia from the Cold War arena. In his statements he denied that India sought a special leadership role among the Asian peoples. Speaking before Parliament in April he emphasized: "We do not seek any special role in Asia nor do we champion any narrow or sectional Asian regionalism. We only seek for ourselves and the adherence of others, particularly our neighbors, to a peace area and to a policy of nonalignment and non-commitment to world tensions and

31. *Lok Sabha, Debates,* vol. 7, no. 5 (August 27, 1954), cols. 592–93; also see M. S. Rajan, *India in World Affairs,* p. 31

32. Ibid., (September 29, 1954), vol. 7, no. 31, col. 3693.

war."[33] Despite such disclaimers, however, Nehru naturally sought a major voice in matters concerned with the disposition of Asian affairs. When he remarked that the United States pact with Pakistan had disturbed the "power balance of the area," one Indian journalist asked perceptively: Which power balance was Nehru referring to? "Was there a power balance before the Pact? If India wants a power balance in Asia does it mean that Mao and Nehru are contending for leadership of Asia, something Nehru has denied?"[34]

A key step toward peace in Asia was to end the long conflict in Indochina and to conclude a settlement guaranteeing the independence and integrity of the Indochinese states. In February 1954 Nehru put forth a plan to the Indian Parliament calling for a ceasefire in Indochina to be followed by direct negotiations among the parties immediately concerned.[35] The whole question would be placed under the jurisdiction of the United Nations. Nehru readily enlisted the support of the Governments of Burma, Ceylon, Pakistan and Indonesia for this proposal.

However, India was not asked to participate in the Geneva Conference on Indochina. The USSR, China, and the United Kingdom all favored India's inclusion in the Conference, but the formal talks were limited to the Great Powers and representatives of those immediately involved in the conflict. Nevertheless an Indian delegation headed by V. K. Krishna Menon had an active role behind the scene.

The British prime minister, Anthony Eden, kept in close contact with Krishna Menon while the meetings were in session. In his memoirs Eden recollected that his strategy and that of Menon was

33. Ibid., pt. 1, vol. 1, no. 6 (April 24, 1954) cols. 5576–82. For a review of Nehru's concept of India's role in Asia see Norman Palmer, "India's Position in Asia."

34. R. L. Nigam, "US-Pakistan Alliance and India," *Radical Humanist*, March 28, 1954.

35. See Lok Sabha Secretariat *India's Foreign Policy:* Selected Speeches, September 1946–April 1961. (New Delhi: GOI Press, 1961, p. 395.

to convince the Communists that "there was a balance of advantage to them in arranging a girdle of neutral states" in Indochina:

I had to describe the situation sombrely and try to convince the Communist nations of the sincerity of my convictions. In this I had an ally, India. That country also had a concern in limiting the onrush of Communist forces. Although Delhi might discount the danger, the protective pad might help. India did not wish to see Burma and Thailand under Communist control.[36]

From New Delhi's standpoint the Geneva Conference provided an opportunity to see if recent Soviet and Chinese professions of goodwill would be carried out in practice. At one point when the proceedings seemed to reach a standstill, Krishna Menon reputedly told the Soviet delegate, V. Molotov, that public opinion in South East Asia would hold the Russians and Chinese mainly responsible if a settlement was not reached. The Indian attitude on the Indochina issue was not among the most decisive factors in the Communist powers' decision to conclude an agreement; yet India's views certainly were taken into consideration. The Communist negotiators at Geneva, in contrast to the Americans present, gave Indian views a careful hearing.

Since she was acceptable to all the nations immediately concerned, India was named the "neutral" member of the three-nation International Control Commission. Shortly after the close of the Geneva Conference, Indo-Soviet contacts increased markedly, and India accepted the Soviet offer of assistance for her Second Five Year Plan. It can be inferred that Nehru attached considerable significance to the Communist nations' behavior at Geneva.

During the Geneva Conference, Chou En-lai, the Chinese foreign minister, accepted an invitation to visit India. Out of the June 1954 meeting between Nehru and Chou, representatives of the world's two most populous nations, came an endorsement of five basic principles which would govern the relationship between New Delhi

36. *The Full Circle: The Memoirs of Anthony Eden* pp. 139–40.

and Peking. These much-heralded principles, first enunciated in
the Sino-Indian Treaty on Tibet two months earlier, soon became
known as the *Panchsheel* or Five Principles of peace. Each signa-
tory agreed to respect the other's territorial integrity and not to
interfere in the other's internal affairs. Observance of these principles would serve as a basis for mutual cooperation and "peaceful
coexistence" between the two nations.

Nehru thought that the Five Principles would serve both as a
statement of ideals and as a means to measure and restrain China's
conduct in foreign affairs. In September he explained to the Indian
Parliament what he had hoped to achieve from meeting Chou and
signing the Five Principles agreement:

The best way is ultimately to talk . . . to any opponent of yours, and
if it is in the interest of both parties, some agreement will be arrived
at. . . . It is not a question of believing the other party's word; it is
a question of creating conditions where the other party cannot break
its word. Maybe the other party breaks its word and it is likely to
find itself in a much worse quandary. These conditions are created
by the joint statement that was made in India and in Rangoon and if
these Five Principles are repeated by the various countries of the
world in their relations to each other, they do create an atmosphere.
That does not mean that all the forces of aggression and interference
and mischief in various countries have been ended. Of course not;
they are there but it means you have made it more difficult for them
to function.[37]

The same rationale could apply equally well for India's formal
agreements with the USSR the following year. Nehru hoped that
mutual statements of good faith might commit the Communist
nations to international responsibilities from which they could not
easily withdraw.

Events moved rapidly in mid-1954, from the conference on Indochina, to Chou En-lai's Indian visit, to the formation of the SEATO.
Concurrent with her growing discontent with Western policy in

37. *Lok Sabha, Debates*, pt. 2, vol. 7, no. 31 (September 29, 1954), col. 3687.

South and Southeast Asia, India developed a growing number of ties with the Communist nations. The USSR under Stalin had not been a contributor to India's First Five Year Plan, but at the Economic Commission for Asia and the Far East (ECAFE) meetings in February 1954, it indicated that economic and technological assistance would henceforth be available. On May 4, D. P. Karmarkar told the Indian lower house that "in a general way Soviet delegates offered technical assistance to India at the ECAFE Conference," but thus far India had not requested such aid.[38] Any Indian reluctance to request Soviet assistance disappeared, however, after the negotiated settlement on Indochina at the Geneva Conference that summer. The atmosphere between Moscow and New Delhi began to clear rapidly, as evidenced by the Russian agreement to build the Bhilai steel plant. Soviet help for the Second Five Year Plan was particularly welcome in that the aid was in the form of heavy industry for the rapidly expanding public sector of the Indian economy.

The improving Indo-Soviet relationship was marked by an increase in the number and variety of contacts between the two nations. While these contacts were closely controlled by the two governments, they did enable an increasing number of Indian and Soviet delegations to visit each other's country. The frequency of the exchange of delegations rose considerably in August and September 1954 and continued high thereafter (see chapter 7). In those two months, groups representing the industrial, agricultural, educational, and cultural sectors of Indian society visited the USSR, and some traveled on to Eastern Europe. In August it was also announced that for the first time military attachés between Moscow and New Delhi would be exchanged.

While Nehru's concept of nonalignment was widely accepted among India's political elite, there was nevertheless some apprehension that India was moving too quickly toward closer ties with the Communist nations. This apprehension was reflected in some

38. *Hindu*, May 5, 1964.

of the queries made to government ministers by members of the opposition parties during the Question Hour in the Indian Parliament. Questions were asked concerning the sponsorship and expenses of Indian delegations going to China and the USSR, the receipt of Stalin Prizes by Indians, the sale of Soviet publications at railway stations, etc. A debate took place over the banning of provocative Soviet literature at government-owned public transportation stations. Commenting on a Communist M.P.'s argument that Soviet literature was inexpensive, the home minister, K. N. Katju, wryly remarked: "We are told, look at these generous people. A book which would cost rupees 5 [U.S. $1.05] for printing and paper is being sold for five annas [U.S. 6–7¢] or nine annas for our spiritual, material and intellectual advancement. I am an old fashioned man."[39] (The proceeds of low-cost Soviet publications sold in India often made their way into CPI coffers.)

The fact that the Parliament always overwhelmingly approved the government's foreign policy resolutions does not mean that there were not doubts about aspects of Nehru's policy. It should be noted that when parliamentary debates on international affairs are closed, the prime minister moves that his overall policy be approved by the House. No Indian M.P. in the mid-1950s, regardless of party, wanted to be marked as an opponent of the government's nonalignment policy. (The bipartisan acclaim for Nehru's policy did not extend to his Government's handling of relations with India's near neighbors.)[40] Misgivings about the

39. Reported in *Hindu*, Sept. 16, 1954. The government's position was clarified by the deputy minister of railways in August 1955. There was no objection, he said, "to books like those of Tolstoi, Marx or Engels, which have now become classics, being sold at railway bookstalls." Books of a "more tendentious or undesirable nature," however, would not be sold. See *Lok Sabha Debates*, pt. 1, vol. 4, no. 14 (August 12, 1955), cols. 3583–84.

40. J. B. Kripalani told the Lok Sabha on Sept. 30, 1954: "Though we have succeeded in easing tensions in the world . . . nearer home, where our interests are intimately and vitually concerned we have invariably failed." He then pointed to the lack of success in India's relations with Pakistan and Ceylon and the Goan and Tibetan problems.

growing rapport between India and the USSR were often sublimated in the Indian press also, but sometimes came to the surface. Such an instance occurred over the treatment of Gandhi in
the 1954 edition of the *Large Soviet Encyclopedia*. Even the ordinarily reserved *Hindu* joined in the wide-spread indignation, commenting editorially: "Anyone who knows the workings of the
Communist mind and the dialectic spirit which informs the Soviet
brand of historian will not be surprised that such an absurd
caricature of Gandhiji has got into a volume which apparently
has all the sanctity of an official reference book."[41]

But, by and large, the section on Gandhi in the encyclopedia was
an aberration from the new Soviet line. Indian politicians began to
note the changing Soviet attitude toward India. For example, Congress party backbencher, S. N. Sinha, gave a brief account of these
changes to the Indian Parliament on Sept. 3, 1954. Sinha at one
time had studied in the Soviet Union. He had since turned against
communism and was an opponent of the CPI within India. While
commenting with sarcasm on the rapid shift in the Soviet treatment
of India he nonetheless called for close intergovernmental relations
with the USSR. Reading from the September 24 issue of *Pravda*
he told his colleagues that "formerly they used to criticize us and
say that our Government was a tool of British imperialism. . . .
After the execution of Beria I do not find these things in the Soviet
newspapers at all." He continued: "Those honorable members
who do not follow Russian at any rate have read in today's newspapers Mr. Menshikov's speech at Naini Tal. Is there any expression there that the Indian Government is the tool of any foreign
government? Any Soviet paper you will find today is all praise
for our culture, for our Government, for our Prime Minister."
He also indicated India's readiness to accept Soviet aid to build a
steel mill whereas "a year and a half back we were not prepared

41. "It is not surprising," continued the editorial, "that even an ostensibly
scientific undertaking like an encyclopaedia, the Soviet compilers are the victims
of the indoctrination and the propaganda they have carried on for years."

to take it."[42] Soviet help would "go a long way in the rapid industrialization of our country." In March 1955 Sinha again read
from *Pravda* to the Lower House, this time recounting part of a
February 8 speech given by V. Molotov to the Supreme Soviet:

Of great historical importance is the fact that there is no more a colonial
India, but an Indian Republic is in evidence. This important change
in events is characteristic of the post-war developments in Asia. The
international authority of India is rising higher and higher as a new
important factor in the task of strengthening peace and friendship
among the peoples.[43]

The Indian ambassador to the USSR, K. P. S. Menon, was
among the more important advocates of Indo-Soviet friendship.
Appointed to his position in Moscow some months before Stalin's
death, Menon had seen first-hand the developments of the Soviet
"thaw." Well accepted by the host country, he successfully implemented Indian policy and served as an on-the-spot observer of
events within the USSR during his lengthy nine year period as
ambassador. There is good reason to believe that Nehru gave more
consideration to Menon's views than he did to most other Indian
diplomats.

Menon returned to New Delhi to confer with Nehru late in
January 1955. Later, in an interview held in Madras, Menon made
a number of references to the good intentions underlying Soviet
policy. He told reporters that "Russia feels that in her interests
it is essential to have a long period of peace; and she is fully
conscious of the dangers of atomic war." There was no doubt, he
said, that Moscow was bent on reducing both internal and external
tensions. It had taken a number of steps toward this end, such as
the settlement of its boundary dispute with Turkey and improvement of relations with Yugoslavia. The Soviet government and
people appreciated India's independent foreign policy and the

---

42. Lok Sabha *Debates*, pt. 2, vol. 7, no. 31 (September 30, 1954), cols. 3828–31.
43. Ibid., pt. 2, vol. 2, no. 30 (March 31, 1955), cols. 3946–47.

role India was playing in the cause of peace. A clear indication of the change in the Soviet attitude toward India had been the acceptance of an Indian-sponsored resolution in 1953 "which eventually formed the basis of peace in Korea." The same resolution had been opposed by the USSR six months earlier. He also declared that the Soviet government was prepared to give assistance to India in the industrial field.[44]

In meeting with the Yugoslav leader, Marshal Tito, in December 1954, Nehru received another first-hand appraisal of recent developments in the USSR. Ousted from the Cominform in 1948, the tenacious Tito successfully withstood Stalin's pressures. The new Soviet leaders had recently put forth the olive branch of reconciliation hoping to bring Tito back within the fold. This reorientation of Moscow's policy toward Belgrade was watched carefully by New Delhi, and considerable significance was attached to the gradual Soviet acceptance of Yugoslavia's "nonalignment" in the Cold War.

The 1954 visit by Tito to India demonstrated the growing links of contact between India, Burma, Indonesia, Egypt, and other nonaligned nations of Afro-Asia with Yugoslavia. Like Nehru, Tito denied that these nations planned to establish a third power group: "Is it not absurd," he asked, "to think that we, who are waging a persistent battle against the division of the world into blocs, should now want to create some sort of a third bloc?"[45] The joint communiqué issued by the two leaders defined their common policy of nonalignment as "a positive, active and constructive policy seeking to lead to collective peace, on which alone collective security can be built."

From Tito, India's prime minister gained insight into the nature and extent of the Soviet "thaw." The Soviet treatment of Yugoslavia provided and would continue to provide Nehru a barometer with which to assess the trends of the USSR's policy over the com-

44. From an account of the interview in *Hindu*, February 3, 1955.
45. *Hindu*, December 22, 1954.

ing years. Shortly after his talks with Tito, Nehru received and
accepted a formal Soviet invitation to visit the USSR.

One of Nehru's few vocal Indian critics in 1953 had contrasted
"Nehru's sympathetic understanding of communism abroad [with]
his Government's treatment of Communists at home":

The indigenous variety appears to irritate Nehru because it disrupts
his regime and challenges his authority. It is . . . difficult to understand
how Nehru, who is so extremely careful about the sensitivity of
Russian and Chinese Reds, treats their satellites and sympathizers in
India with such utter contempt.[46]

The incubation period of improving Indian relations with the
USSR scarcely altered Nehru's attitude toward India's own Communist party. In December 1954 the Preventive Detention Act
(directed against both communalist extremists and the CPI),
which enabled the Indian Government to detain troublesome
individuals without trial, was extended for another three-year
period.[47]

While campaigning in January 1955 for Congress party candidates in the coming national election, Nehru remarked that the
Indian Communists "have no moorings in the land of their birth
but always look to outside countries for inspiration and guidance."
He drew a distinction between the CPI on one hand and the theory
of communism on the other:

In India today there are many types of reactionaries and the biggest
reactionaries of all are the Communists of India. I am not afraid of

46. Karaka, *Nehru*, p. 39.

47. The Preventive Act had been initiated under Sardar Patel's period as
home minister. When the government called for a second extension of the Act
in 1954, several members of the Congress party opposed the measure. Their
opposition, in the words of M. Prasad Singh, was based on the grounds that the
CPI, the Jan Singh, the RSS, etc., were no longer pursuing violent policies as they
had done in previous years. The great majority of the Congress party voted, however, for extension of the Act. Also see David H. Bayley, *Political Liberties in
the New States*.

communism myself, and like the objectives of communism. If any part of the communist economic pattern is good for India, we will adopt it. But our friends, the CPI, have lost touch with all realities. Their slogans are the same which they uttered twenty years ago.[48]

He emphasized, however, that India was "to a large extent" friendly with the USSR and China: "We cooperate with them. We have no grievances against them. Each country should work out its own destiny."

At the Commonwealth Prime Ministers' Conference in London in February 1955, Nehru gave his interpretation of Chinese goals and capabilities, particularly with regard to the Formosan question. The other prime ministers endorsed his proposal for a cease-fire in the Formosan straits to be followed by a "Geneva-like" conference on Formosa.[49] Shortly after the close of the Commonwealth meeting, the Soviet Union put forth a proposal for a ten-nation conference on Formosa. According to the proposal, the USSR, Great Britain, and India would be the host nations. Others to be invited included the United States, People's Republic of China, France, Burma, Pakistan, Indonesia, and Ceylon. The Soviet plan was endorsed by India, but the United States understandably turned it down because the Chiang government had not been invited to participate.[50]

The Afro-Asian Conference held in May in Bandung, Indonesia, symbolically marked the political emergence on the world scene of many peoples who had achieved or were struggling for independence from colonial rule.[51] Soviet praise for the con-

48. *Hindu*, January 15, 16, 1955.

49. See *Economist*, January 28, 1955; and *Guardian* (Manchester), February 5, 1955.

50. *Hindu*, January 15, 16, 1955.

51. Discussions of the Bandung Conference include Mary K. Keynes, "The Bandung Conference," *International Relations* (London, Vol. I, 1954–59), pp. 362–76; George Kahin, *The Asian-African Conference* (Ithaca: Cornell University Press, 1956); Vincent Sheean, *Nehru: The Years of Power;* and Michael Brecher, *The New States of Asia.* Professor Brecher observed (pp. 174–76):

ference stood in marked contrast to the skepticism voiced in many quarters of the West. There was no real problem about whether or not the USSR should participate as an Asian state (one of the critical issues on which the planned second Afro-Asian Conference at Algiers foundered a decade later). At the preparatory conference held in Bogar, Indonesia, the question of Russian participation scarcely arose. Of the Asian nations, all were invited except the two Koreas, Formosa, and Israel. The Soviets themselves did not push the issue at all. It was more advantageous for the USSR to be on the sidelines.

Nehru's sole address at Bandung reflected the prevailing spirit: "For anyone to tell us that we must be camp followers of Russia, America or any other country in Europe is not very creditable to our new dignity, our new independence, our new freedom, our new spirit." Returning to New Delhi, he declared that "Bandung proclaimed to the world the capacity of new nations of Asia and Africa for practical idealism."

The conference was a frustrating experience for Nehru. On several occasions he was dismayed by what he felt to be impeding tactics of pro-Western nations like Pakistan, Ceylon, and Turkey. Nehru had hoped to keep controversy to a minimum and to use the conference as a vehicle for expressing his ideals for international conduct. But after Nehru had called for acceptance of the Five Principles, Mohammed Ali, Pakistan's prime minister, proposed his Seven Pillars of Peace. Out of this came a compromise agreement of Ten Principles, which at the insistence of the anti-Communist states included the right to collective self defence.

Another problem was the difficulty of defining colonialism. India

---

"Disunity was evident throughout the proceedings, even before the assembly convened. . . . Three distinct groups emerged on the communist-colonialist issues. . . . Bandung revealed deep fissures. However, it also expressed one of the fundamental traits of the contemporary global political system—the 'anti-colonial revolution' and the (re)birth of some 60 new states in Asia and Africa with influence in and on the United Nations and the balance of military and political power."

and the other co-sponsors had wanted a mild condemnation of the remaining Western colonialism in Afro-Asia. But the prime minister of Ceylon, Sir John Kotelawala, called for "opposition to all forms of colonialism . . . to Soviet colonialism as well as to Western imperialism."[52] After much argument, an Indian compromise was passed, referring to "colonialism in all its manifestations."

One aspect which has been overlooked by most who have written on Bandung was the duality, even then, of Nehru's attitude toward China. Bandung afforded a chance for some of the small nations on China's borders to voice any fear or misgivings they might have about their large neighbor's intentions. Nehru hoped that China, as a nation seeking respectability, would rectify any such causes for concern. It was China, not India, which gained most diplomatically from Bandung. Nehru probably had mixed feelings about providing Chou En-lai with a forum from which to address the Afro-Asian peoples. While he wanted China to receive its rightful place in the community of nations, Nehru had no desire for Chou to become the leading spokesman for Asian aspirations.

On the whole, though, the events of May augured well for the success of Nehru's forthcoming trip to the USSR. Except for the establishment of the Warsaw Pact, the Soviet countermeasure to West German rearmament, an unprecedented thaw seemed to be taking place in the Cold War. The signing of an Austrian peace treaty, the decision of the Soviet and Western leaders to meet at a summit conference, the notable improvement in Soviet-Yugoslav relations, and "the ever-increasing support everywhere for coexistence" were welcomed by India.[53] Even Sino-American relations took a slight turn for the better with the release of four captive airmen by Peking. An era of peaceful coexistence seemingly was at hand.

52. Quoted by Brecher, *The New States of Asia*, p. 175.
53. An editorial observation in the *Times of India*, May 17, 1955.

3 "Hindi-Russi Bhai-Bhai"
The Affirmation of Goodwill

The Reciprocal State Visits of 1955

AFTER the Bandung Conference had ended, attention focused on Nehru's forthcoming visit to the Soviet Union. One leading newspaper pointed out that the visit would better enable Nehru to "determine how far India can trust the Russian leaders' professions of goodwill . . . and how far it is in India's interests to seek Russian collaboration in the task of executing her development plans. . . ."[1] Among the most skeptical was "Onlooker" in the *Times of India* who reminded his readers that only several years earlier the Soviets had referred to Gandhi as a "bourgeois canaille" and to Nehru as a "running dog of imperialism."[2]

Placing the Soviet trip in perspective as another in the series of Nehru's visits to important world capitals, the *Eastern Economist* noted editorially that all such goodwill missions "provided Nehru ample opportunity to discuss his own point of view on world affairs and to hear those of his hosts." More importantly, the article alluded to the "restraint" shown by the Indian government over the past several years in expressing views on the political situation in the USSR:

1. "Insaf," *Hindustan Times,* June 7, 1955.
2. *Times of India,* June 2, 1955.

If there is still room for goodwill and for good relations, it is because of India's forbearance and universal tolerance. It is too well known that the Government of India had refrained from expressing their views on Russian politics, even when it strongly disapproved of them, in order not to complicate a complex situation.[3]

This assessment was accurate in that public criticism of Soviet policies—restrained even during the Stalin period—was less frequent thereafter and more muted in tone.

At a press conference in New Delhi on May 31, Nehru remarked that "I approach every country, whatever it may be, in a friendly and receptive spirit. Even though I do not agree with it, I want to understand it." As might be expected, he made no specific reference to what his government might elicit from improved relations with the Soviets. He did mention his opposition to the Cominform, recalling that at the Bandung Conference he had said "the functioning of the Cominform in other countries is interference in those countries and is not compatible with the principle of non-interference."[4] The Soviet leaders understood very well the meaning of this and other references relating to the dissolution of the Cominform. It was not the formal structure of the Cominform that concerned Nehru, but the knowledge that the USSR, through Communist parties abroad, had interfered in in the internal affairs of other countries.

While the exact itinerary and date of arrival of the Nehru entourage was not made public until the last moment, the host government had made extensive preparations. In May a large parliamentary delegation from India spent several weeks in Moscow.[5] During the week prior to his arrival, Nehru's public state-

3. *Eastern Economist*, June 10, 1955.

4. *Hindu*, June 1, 1955. In answer to a question on Indian defense against a potential aggressor, Nehru asserted that his nation had the spirit to defend itself with *lathis* and stones if need be. "Therefore," he said, "I am not afraid of anybody invading India from any quarter."

5. *Hindu*, May 30, 1955. Upon his return to India, the leader of the delegation, S. V. Krishnamurti Rao, declared that the Soviet leaders showed "a full appreciation of the efforts of Mr. Nehru to bring about good relations between states. . . ."

ments and sketches of his background were reported extensively
in the Soviet press. An exhibition of Indian art and culture opened
in Moscow during the first week of June. Several thousand copies of
a limited Russian edition of Nehru's *Discovery of India* were
quickly sold by bookshops in several large cities.

A representative editorial in *Pravda* proclaimed that "relations
between our countries have always been friendly, from the fifteenth
century when the brave Russian traveler, Afanasy Nikitin, first
visited India until the present day." While the people of India and
the USSR have different social-political systems, they shared their
desire for peace. *Pravda* continued: "The efforts of the Soviet
and Indian peoples, together with all other peace-loving peoples
. . . are having favorable results. With very active participation by
the USSR and the Republic of India, the flames of war in two
Asian areas, Korea and Indo-China, have been put out. . . . "[6]
Commenting on the *Pravda* editorial, the *Eastern Economist* noted
with irony that the Soviet publicist had gone to some length "to
discover historical and cultural links" to provide bases for friendship and cooperation between India and the USSR. The "method-
ical search for common ties has revealed nothing more striking
than that A. Nikitin visited India in the fifteenth century and that
Karamzin translated scenes from the 'Shakuntala' [a play by
Kalidasa, an Indian writer of the fifth century]."[7] Perhaps the
above observation did not do justice to a long-standing interest in
Indian culture on the part of some Russian scholars, but the skepticism about the recent Soviet effusive praise for things Indian was
understandable.

The Indian prime minister was greeted by large, curious throngs
upon his arrival in Moscow and, for the next sixteen days, he and
his daughter Indira Gandhi received the plaudits of the Soviet
leaders and citizenry. He was hailed "as a man who is doing everything to achieve international brotherhood." India's ambassador

6. *Pravda*, June 7, 1955.

7. *Eastern Economist*, June 10, 1955.

to the USSR, K. P. S. Menon, accompanied the Nehru party in Moscow and on a whirlwind ten day plane trip with stopovers elsewhere in the RFSSR, the Ukraine, Georgia, and the Turkmen, Kazakh, and Uzbek republics. He recalled that:

It would be wrong to attribute the success of the visit merely to the efficiency of the Communist party machine. The reasons lie deeper. India has a quaint appeal to Russia. . . . To them [Russians] steeped in the philosophy of materialism Mahatma Gandhi was a holy puzzle. Jawaharlal Nehru was easier for them to understand. What they admired in him was not that he had merely won India's independence but he was determined to protect it against threats and blandishments.[8]

Menon's belief that Nehru had come to represent for many Russians a symbol of their frequently-expressed yearning for "peace" was undoubtedly true. He might have added, however, that Nehru's enhanced stature in the people's eyes was in large part due to the recent systematic portrayal by the Soviet news media of his and India's increasingly "progressive role" in world affairs since 1953.

One significant aspect of the Nehru visit was that for the first time since 1917 the head of a non-Communist nation was permitted to address audiences in Moscow, Leningrad, Kiev, Tashkent, Alma Ata, Samarkand, Ashkhabad, Sverdlovsk, and other cities. Several non-Communist leaders had in the past come to Moscow for specific purposes (e.g., the Austrian prime minister, Julius Raab, had recently come to iron out details on the Austrian Peace Treaty), but none had been provided a public forum from which to express extensively his views. From this standpoint alone, Nehru's address to an estimated eighty to a hundred thousand people in Moscow's Dynamo Stadium was in itself of historic import.

Nehru praised the economic and social accomplishments of the Soviet state. In a typical address he acknowledged that "today Rus-

8. Menon, *The Flying Troika*, pp. 114–15. One reviewer (in *Survey*, no. 51, April, 1964) points out that Menon's book reveals more of the author's land of origin than of the USSR to which he was accredited from 1952–61. That this critique is probably accurate in no way detracts from its value for this study.

sia is playing a vital part in the cause of peaceful coexistence. . . .
The lessening of the tension is, in large degree, the result of several
steps which your country has taken during the last few months."[9]
In particular Nehru commended the Soviets for coming to an
understanding with Yugoslavia and for agreeing to participate in
the Four-Power Geneva Conference. He "lectured" his hosts on
modern Indian history and the principles underlying India's policies. He pointed out that India, like the Soviet Union, was also
undergoing a great social revolution, but had to follow a path in
accord with her own traditions, ideals, and needs. And he let it be
known that the activities of the Cominform were not always consistent with the policy of peaceful coexistence which the Communist leaders purported to follow.

Before Nehru's departure a joint communiqué was issued by the
Indian and Soviet leaders.[10] It praised the East-West accord on
Austria, the improved Soviet-Yugoslav relations, and the growing
awareness everywhere of the dangers of nuclear war. The communiqué called for the implementation of the 1954 Geneva Agreement on Indochina which had stipulated that nationwide elections
be held in the two Vietnams in 1956. It was the "earnest hope of
the two Prime Ministers that it will be possible, by peaceful means
to satisfy the legitimate rights of the Chinese People's Republic in
regard to Taiwan, and their conviction that the refusal to admit the
People's Republic of China to the United Nations lies at the root
of many troubles in the Far East and elsewhere."

Another significant section dealt with the fear which smaller,
weaker nations have of the larger powers:

Both Prime Ministers recognize that in various parts of the world
there is on the part of the smaller and weaker states a vague and
possibly unreasoning fear of Bigger Powers. They feel it is essential

9. *Hindu*, June 11, 1955.
10. *Foreign Policy of India, Text of Documents, 1947–59.*

to dispel fear in all possible ways. Here again the best remedy is to adhere unflinchingly to the principles of coexistence.[11]

The reference to the fear on the part of the "smaller and weaker states" was prompted by the Indian officials, whereas the disclaimer that these fears are "vague and possibly unreasoning" was clearly a qualification insisted upon by the Soviets.

Both leaders stressed their "profound faith that states of different social structures can exist side by side in peace and work for the common good." The *sine qua non* of peaceful coexistence—the third principle in the Chou-Nehru Agreement of 1954—was expanded to read: "non-interference in each other's domestic affairs for any reasons, economic, political or ideological." In his memoirs, K. P. S. Menon wrote: "The joint statement was entirely Indian in style and in substance. It must be said that at no time did they [Soviet leaders] try to use the slightest influence, let alone pressure to swing India to their side. They made it clear from the onset that they would leave it to us as guests to draft the joint statement."[12]

The Indo-Soviet communiqué received accolades throughout the Communist world and was noted sympathetically by the "non-committed" nations of Afro-Asia. Many in the West, particularly in the United States, believed that Nehru, despite his undeniably good intent, had been "taken in" by the Soviets. At the airport on his departure from the USSR, Nehru reportedly expressed his gratitude to his hosts by saying, "I am leaving my heart behind." It was feared that Nehru had also left some of his common sense behind in Moscow. For example, the *New York Times* had warned earlier that Nehru, in his earnest desire for peace might be "skillfully mousetrapped" in Moscow.[13] A later editorial in the *Times* on

11. Ibid.
12. Menon, *The Flying Troika*, pp. 118–19.
13. *New York Times*, June 11, 1955.

June 24 emphasized that the recently signed Indo-Soviet communiqué would contribute little to the "peace and equanimity of the
world. One cannot doubt that it is his desire to contribute to world
peace and to act as mediator or pacifier, as he sees it, between the
two giant powers, the United States and the Soviet Union. But it
is a pity that Mr. Nehru's contribution to this ideal should have
been a general acceptance of the Soviet policies."

In most quarters within India, Nehru's venture was considered a
success. "Deeds, it is often said, speak louder than words. Yet it
would be unfortunate to underestimate the considerable capacity
for restraint contained in the words of Mr. Nehru and Mr. Bulganin," wrote the usually skeptical editor of the *Times of India*.[14]
In this vein K. Rangaswami of the *Hindu* noted that "the personal
conduct and the manner of approach to problems of the Soviet
leaders profoundly impressed him [Nehru]." Rangaswami, who
had accompanied the Nehru entourage first to Peking and then to
Moscow, was well briefed by high Indian officials on government
foreign policy. He perhaps touched upon one of the key reasons
why the Soviet leaders were able to establish good rapport with
Nehru:

It may be said that the Russians scored where others have failed. Their
study and understanding of India's national sentiments and susceptibilities as well as individual preferences and aversions is almost something uncanny. . . . Never once was there a public mention or private
reference made by the Soviet leaders to their agreement to set up a
steel plant in India. It would have been justifiable if they sought to
make some political capital out of the deal. But they have gained from
the experience of others and have refrained from touching on the
subject.[15]

Amid the speculation over the results of his Russian tour, Nehru
traveled on to Poland, Yugoslavia, Austria, Great Britain, and
made brief stopovers in West Germany and Egypt on his way home.

14. *Times of India*, June 24, 1955.
15. *Hindu*, July 2, 1955.

In each of these countries he mentioned his opposition to the Cominform. Although admitting that the abolition of the formal structure of the Cominform would not guarantee Soviet noninterference in the domestic affairs of other nations, he declared that such a gesture could be interpreted as a welcome sign of Soviet good intentions. He studiously refrained from comment on the "German question" during his one day stops in Vienna and Dusseldorf, but in the latter city he reminded his hosts of the fear of a rearmed Germany which existed in Eastern Europe. It was necessary, he advised, to consider the apprehensions of the Soviet Union, which felt itself to be encircled by hostile bases.[16]

In Belgrade, Nehru received Tito's assessment of recent developments within the Communist bloc. He praised the Yugoslavs for firmly defending their independent policy and not diverging from it "under pressure or from fear of consequences." Although Nehru had not been subjected to the pressures brought to bear on Tito by the Soviets, there could be detected in his praise for the Yugoslavs an implicit reaffirmation of the soundness of his own policy toward the Cold War in general. Addressing the Yugoslav Parliament, Nehru said that it was evil for any country to impose its ideology or pattern of government on others. He spoke against the Communist sponsored "peace movements," and remarked that it was extraordinary that the word "peace" should be used for sloganeering purposes. This allusion was prompted by the convening in Helsinki a week earlier of the World Peace Congress. (A large Indian delegation of ninety members led by Professor D. Kosambi attended the Congress.)[17] Not confining his criticisms to either side in the Cold War, Nehru spoke against the use of the term "iron curtain," remarking that the greatest iron curtain was the one in people's minds, which, like a wall, prevented them from looking at the world as it was.[18]

16. *Hindu*, July 12, 1955.
17. *Hindustan Times*, June 25, 1955.
18. *Hindu*, June 3, 1955.

A last minute but important stop on Nehru's itinerary was in London to confer with Anthony Eden. There he briefed the British prime minister, who was then preparing for the coming Four-Power Conference at Geneva, on his appraisal of recent Soviet policy. Concurrent with Nehru's European tour, V. K. Krishna Menon, Indian ambassador to the United Nations, was putting forth his government's views regarding a settlement in the Far East. Among other things, Menon stressed India's support for the claim of the Chinese People's Republic to Formosa. On his return flight to India, Nehru landed in Cairo where he met briefly with President Nasser. Their talks dealt primarily with the common interests of those Afro-Asian nations which were outside the major powers' alliance structure.

Speaking before the Indian Parliament in September, Nehru attributed the fine receptions he had received in Europe to the widespread "appreciation of India's basic policy." He said that his government was satisfied with the results of the Geneva Conference that had taken place in August. While "the Conference did not produce a blueprint . . . nevertheless . . . it made a tremendous difference to the whole aspect of things in the world." There was "some surprise and great gratification at the melting away to some extent of the high walls and barriers that had existed." Other hopeful signs noted by the prime minister were the Conference for the peaceful uses of atomic energy in Geneva, the visit of Chancellor Adenaur to Moscow, and the successful conclusion of talks between the United States and China for the release of captive American airmen.[19]

Hopes were running high in the Indian press that the Cold War might be coming to an end. "Arguments about whether [the change in Soviet policy] is merely tactical or represents a genuine change of spirit are at this stage futile," declared a *Times of India* editorial. "A reliable answer can be obtained only by proceeding

19. *Lok Sabha Debates*, pt. 2, vol. 7, no. 42 (September 17, 1955), cols. 14197–201.

on the assumption . . . that for reasons of their own, the Communists have no use now for the Cold War."[20]

While in Moscow Nehru had invited the Soviet leaders to pay
a reciprocal visit to India. It was hoped in New Delhi that this
would further commit the Soviets to the path of peaceful coexistence. As one journalist put it, the statements of Bulganin and
Khrushchev in India would "reveal and commit them to an extent
to which no other occasion had ever compelled them," thus acting
as further restraint upon any adventurous Soviet policy.[21]

In November Bulganin and Khrushchev made their historic state
visits to Afghanistan, India, and Burma.[22] The Soviet party included Messrs. Mikhailov, minister of culture; Gromyko, deputy
foreign minister; Kumykin, minister for foreign trade; Rasolov,
deputy minister for agriculture; and Serov, chief administrative
officer. Large Soviet delegations to India and other Asian nations
include, whenever possible, at least one prominent member indigenous to the Central Asian SSR's. Madame Rahimaivena,
Uzbek deputy minister for culture, fulfilled this function in the
Khrushchev entourage.

This marked the first time that any Soviet rulers had ventured
forth in such a manner from the Communist regions. From all
accounts the Russians enjoyed the pomp and pageantry provided
for them during their hectic three weeks in India. Their travels
extended from New Delhi to the Punjab, Jaipur, Bombay, Poona,

20. *Times of India*, Aug 8, 1955.

21. These events dramatized the Soviet resolve to gain influence among the
"bourgeois-nationalist" leaders of the nonaligned Asian nations. For a Soviet
account of the state visit to India see *Visit of N. A. Bulganin and N. S. Khrushchev
to India.* See also *The Awakened East, A Report by Soviet Journalists on the
Visit of N. S. Khrushchev to India, Burma, Indonesia, and Afghanistan* (Moscow, n. d.).

22. The following account of Indian reactions to the Soviet leaders is in
part derived from the author's conversations in various parts of India in the
autumn of 1960 and in 1963–64 with a number of people who recalled the events
of 1955.

Bangalore, Madras, Coimbatore, Calcutta, Srinagar, and else-where.

It is not difficult to raise crowds in India, and throngs of people, the curious and well-wishers alike, turned out. The Communist party of India helped to bring out the masses. Issues of the CPI weekly, *New Age*, and the pro-Soviet tabloid *Blitz* extolled the virtues of Indo-Soviet friendship. The Indian government itself provided special buses in New Delhi and several other cities to bring in villagers from the outlying countryside. But by and large, the Indian public turned out spontaneously to get a glimpse of the Russians. More than five hundred thousand assembled at the Ram Lila grounds in Delhi, and millions in the largest center of CPI strength, Calcutta, watched the Russians being driven through the streets. In Calcutta the Khrushchev limousine broke down amid the swirling mass of humanity, and the Soviet leaders were whisked safely away in a police van.

According to K. P. S. Menon's account, the Indian people saw in the Soviet Union "a friend, who to all appearances, demands nothing from them except friendship." He tells also of how the "resilient" Soviet leaders responded by taking to "native food, customs and costumes . . . with gusto." As headdress is an impor-tant symbol of identification in India, Khrushchev and Bulganin at the appropriate times donned everything from Gandhi caps to Rajput turbans. In Madras they permitted young girls to adorn their foreheads with *kumkum*. They greeted people by folding their hands in Indian fashion and saying *namaste* and concluded a number of speeches with the Hindi expression, "Hindi-Russi bhai-bhai," Indians and Russians are brothers.[23]

It was, however, the support for the Indian positions on the emotionally charged Goa and Kashmir issues that most endeared Khrushchev and Bulganin to the Indian polity. The timing of their statements on Goa was particularly opportune as they came directly before and after the meeting between American secretary of state

23. Menon, *The Flying Troika*, pp. 130–31.

Dulles and the Portuguese foreign minister Cunha. It was rumored that Dulles had publicly referred to Goa as a "Portuguese province" and that the United States might even consider the defense of Goa as part of its NATO obligation. In contrast, on November 27 Bulganin had declared that "there is no justification for the Portuguese colony of Goa to exist still on the ancient soil of India. It is a shame on civilized people."[24] In his own colorful idiom Khrushchev three days later compared the Portuguese reluctance to let go of Goa to the "reluctance of a leech to part from the body whose blood it is sucking."[25]

A controversial press release of December 2 on the Dulles-Cunha talks included an obvious though not explicit reference to Goa. While Dulles, in part, clarified his position a few days later by saying that Goa was definitely not covered under the NATO Agreement, the damage had been done insofar as India was concerned. The India press was quick to compare the Soviet and alleged American outlook on Goa.[26] Khrushchev added more fuel to the fire by reiterating that "the Portuguese forcibly occupied Goa and perpetrated atrocities and cruelties on the Goan people." As an advocate of the "third principle of peaceful coexistence," he added, "I want to make it clear that it is not our purpose to antagonize one country against another. But I strongly believe that no country has any right to dominate over another country and interfere in her internal affairs." Khrushchev also used the "noninterference" theme in dealing with the Kashmir question. "It was not necessary," he said, "to make any changes in the borders of India and Pakistan as some other countries wanted to do."[27]

Located in the heartland of Asia, Kashmir touches upon remote frontiers of the USSR and Afghanistan and has extensive borders

24. *Times of India*, November 28, 1955.

25. *Times of India*, December 1, 1955.

26. On December 8 the *Times of India* commented, "indeed if Bulganin and Khrushchev were looking for an ally to foster their plans, they have found one in a totally unexpected quarter."

27. *Hindu*, December 11, 1955.

with the Tibet and Sinkiang regions of China as well as contiguity with Pakistan and India. During the fighting that accompanied the partition of the subcontinent in 1947, Indian troops occupied the valley. While this is not the place to discuss the relative merits of the rival claimants, it should be noted that the Indian government held any political solution to the Kashmir question other than the *status quo post bellum* to be unacceptable. Although Nehru had almost unlimited freedom of action in formulating his nation's policy toward the Communist and Western powers, he seemingly had much less flexibility in handling the potentially explosive relationship with Pakistan. He was therefore very averse to foreign criticism directed against India's stance on Kashmir and welcomed Soviet support for his Government's position.

Khrushchev refused to comply with the Pakistan request that he and Bulganin not visit Kashmir. His strongest pronouncements on Kashmir were made in Srinagar itself, the capital of the disputed valley. There he was housed in palatial style on a hillock overlooking beautiful Dal Lake. His hosts were not disappointed when Khrushchev declared: "the question of Kashmir as one of the states of India has been decided by the peoples of Kashmir."[28]

While their effusive support for the Indian position on Goa and Kashmir was more than welcome, Bulganin and Khrushchev caused uneasiness for their hosts on several occasions. Their behavior in those instances was a far cry from the deference they had shown to Indian "sentiments and susceptibilities" earlier that year during Nehru's Moscow visit. Perhaps the enthusiasm of the Indian welcome, as one British writer put it, "led them to misjudge the temper and outlook of informed Indian opinion."[29] Heavy-handed attempts to impress Indians with Soviet military might, to discredit Britain and the United States, and to give the impression of Indo-Soviet solidarity embarrassed the Indian leadership.

28. *Times of India*, December 12, 1955.

29. J. M. Mackintosh, *Strategy And Tactics of Soviet Foreign Policy* (London, 1963), p. 131.

Speaking to a joint session of the Indian Parliament on November 21, Bulganin stated that the "people of the USSR deeply appreciate the Indian Government's view on military aggressive alignments." This obviously anti-Western remark made on a forum provided by a nonaligned government provoked dismay in India and abroad. Not to be outdone, Khrushchev on his return to Moscow declared that "370 million Indians as well as the peoples of Burma and Afghanistan are our allies in the struggle we are waging for peace." Recalling Disraeli's quip about an opponent, Walter Lippman wrote: "Is Khrushchev inebriated with the exuberance of his own verbosity?"

Disturbed by the crude anti-British remarks of Khrushchev, the *Times of India* on November 23 commented that those who "failed to grasp the spirit" of nonalignment mistakenly identified the anti-colonialism of Asian nationalists to be hostility toward the West. Yet there was little public reaction against their lack of restraint while the Soviet leaders remained in India. The same newspaper attributed this to the Indian code of hospitality and to the stand on Goa taken by John Foster Dulles midway during the Russian visit:

As the shower of bricks fell all around, the Indian public began to feel a vague sense of uneasiness, which yielded place to bewilderment and then to embarrassment, annoyance and indignation. These sentiments were beginning to get vocal in political circles and the press of the country when Mr. J. F. Dulles stepped in like an answer to a prayer to divert to America the piling up Indian ire. The Kremlin should award to Mr. Dulles the Stalin Prize for the signal service rendered by him to the USSR and world communism.[30]

After the Soviet leaders returned home, however, even the well-modulated *Hindu* editorialized against their representation of India as an ally of the Soviets against America, the "prime enemy of peace."[31]

30. *Times of India*, December 14, 1955.
31. *Hindu*, December 25, 1955.

Despite this criticism of the conduct of the Soviet leaders, almost all shades of Indian opinion accepted and many praised the overall results of Nehru's diplomacy toward China and the USSR in 1954–55. Few were the articulate voices that suggested that Indian neutrality in the Cold War was developing pro-Soviet leanings. One such voice, the *Eastern Economist,* recommended that "positive measures" be taken "to recover the position of greater neutrality that we seemed to occupy three years ago." The editorial noted that official statements by government officials in India are overly critical of the West while "criticisms of the Communist world are held in abeyance for considerations—Panchshila or otherwise. . . . To the extent that Panchshila imposes silence on us not to criticise the tyranny exercised behind the Curtains, it is a positive denial of our Gandhian faith."[32]

Sensitive to any suggestion that India was at best fence-sitting and at worst moving into the embrace of the Soviets, Nehru gave the following explanation of the Indian Cold War position after the Soviet leaders had departed:

Some people in the West are very angry that we gave them a warm welcome. People in many parts of the world seem to think that if you are friendly with one person that means you are hostile or inimical to another. . . . The area of friendship should not be confined by a wall of hostility to others. . . . This is our national and international outlook.[33]

Nehru was naturally pleased with the stand taken by the Soviets on Goa and Kashmir. While he had not solicited Bulganin's and Khrushchev's remarks, he nonetheless felt that they had said "the correct things." The Soviet leaders, said Nehru, had "expressed their opinion after due consideration and great deliberation."[34]

While in India Bulganin and Khrushchev avoided public contact with leaders of the CPI, although the Indian Communists indirectly benefited from the publicity generated by the presence of the

32. *Eastern Economist,* December 30, 1955, pp. 984–91.
33. *Hindu,* December 27, 1955.
34. *Hindu,* January 4, 1956.

Soviet leaders. Good relations with the Soviets in no way diminished Nehru's rancor for the CPI. Electioneering in Trichur on December 27, Nehru criticized the slavish way in which the CPI sought to "copy" a revolution that had taken place 5,000 miles away. We wished the Soviet leaders well, he declared, "but wishing them well does not mean that we should lock up our own mind and intelligence and forget our own experience and our own country."[35]

We should mention here the CPI's difficulty in adjusting to the revised Soviet line on India. The CPI was considerably slower than the Soviets in acknowledging the "positive elements" in India's foreign policy, and in 1954–55, was sharply divided on how to view the Nehru government. In July 1954, Politbureau member and editor of the CPI weekly, P. Ramamurti, wrote a controversial article which termed Nehru an opponent of American imperialism. As such Nehru deserved CPI support.[36] This position was at first attacked by the majority of the party leaders, but it became more acceptable after several articles in international Communist publications took a similar position. In December 1955, after returning from a trip to Moscow, the secretary-general of the CPI Politbureau, Ajoy Ghosh, made a clear distinction between "the peaceful aspects of Nehru's foreign policy" and the "reactionary" elements of his domestic policies.[37]

After Nehru had proclaimed that India's goal was the creation

---

35. *Hindu*, December 27, 1955.

36. In putting forth a slogan calling for "a national platform of peace and freedom," P. Ramamurti wrote: "All peace-loving mankind, and our people are enthused by the fact that Nehru . . . has today taken a stand against many of the US machinations in Asia and against its threat to India.

"The more Nehru takes a forthright stand against the imperialists and by the side of the forces of peace . . . the more enthusiastic will be the support of our millions." "Drive US Out of Asia!" *New Age*, July 18, 1954, p. 14. Quoted in Marshall Windmiller, "Indian Communism and the New Soviet Line," *Pacific Affairs*, December 1956, p. 349. (The account in the next few paragraphs is derived mainly from the Windmiller article and several other writings on the same period.)

37. Ajoy Ghosh, "Communist Answers to Pandit Nehru," *New Age*, December 5, 1955.

of a "Socialist pattern of society," the Soviets more strongly urged
the CPI to support his policies. By mid-1956, the CPI had reached
the position adopted by the USSR two years earlier in strong support of Nehru's international role. There was never a common
agreement, however, on how the party should react to Nehru's
domestic policies. The party was never monolithic in practice—
those who had control of the Politbureau at any given moment
could not control debate or prevent factionalism. The "Rightist"
leadership scored an argumentative point over those urging a more
militant policy when the CPI in 1957 won an electoral victory in
the state of Kerala. It seemed then that the party might begin to
enlarge its areas of support beyond the narrow confines of Kerala,
Bengal, and Andhra. But the prospects for enlarging the electoral
base of the CPI diminished with the surfacing of the Sino-Indian
dispute in 1959.

Aftermath of the Visits

In the West it was generally believed that India was moving
closer to the Soviet outlook on international affairs. The opposition to military pacts cited in the joint Indo-Soviet communiqué
of December 13 was interpreted by some to mean a condemnation
of NATO and SEATO, even though the Soviets themselves were
signatories to several such pacts. A month after the Russian leaders
had returned home, an unidentified spokesman for the Indian
government attempted to balance the picture by letting it be known
that "if one chooses he could interpret the communique as self-
condemnation by the Russians."[38] It would remain, however, a
major task for Indian diplomacy to demonstrate after the events
of 1954–55 that the government was not being unduly influenced
by China and the USSR and had not abandoned its capacity for
critical judgment.

The Soviet courtship of India continued into 1956 with an
admixture of promises, praise, and economic assistance. In Jan-

38. *Hindu*, January 11, 1956.

uary the Russian writer, Ilya Ehrenburg, engaged in political as
well as literary pursuits when he visited New Delhi. He repeated
the pledge that India would be given strong backing by the Soviets
in the United Nations on the Kashmir and Goan issues. At the
ECAFE Conference in February, held in Bangalore, the Soviet
delegate, P. A. Maletin, termed Nehru "the outstanding statesman
of our epoch." On more tangible matters he revealed that beginning in 1956–57 the USSR would offer scholarships to students
from the ECAFE nations.[39]

 During late 1955 and early 1956 a substantial number of Soviet
specialists came to India to discuss with their Indian counterparts
additional Soviet aid for developmental projects within the Indian
public sector and to offer to share with India the Soviet experiences
in the construction of industrial enterprises, electrical power stations, and even in the utilization of atomic energy for peaceful
purposes. The Soviets apparently had encouraged their Eastern
European colleagues also to give assistance to India, for in short
order Czechoslovakia, Hungary, Poland, East Germany, and
Rumania all indicated their willingness to undertake projects. For
example, it was announced on November 12 that the Soviets and
Rumanians had offered to assist the Indian government in prospecting for and refining oil products. Shortly thereafter five Soviet
technicians arrived in New Delhi to discuss the matter. The subject
of oil had been a sensitive one between India and the Western
nations, and the suspicion (whether or not justified) existed in
some quarters that Western oil companies were not overanxious
to find susbstantial oil fields in India. The Indian government,
which had to spend valuable foreign exchange to import oil products, understandably welcomed the Soviet offers of assistance.[40]

 In March 1956, Anastas Mikoyan set out for India, primarily
to work out the details of the Indo-Soviet Trade Pact signed during

39. *Hindu*, February 7, 1956.

40. Information in this paragraph compiled from secondary accounts and
interviews with several Government of India officials.

the Bulganin-Khrushchev visit. On the way to New Delhi, Mikoyan made a one day stopover in Karachi, Pakistan. Relations between the USSR and Pakistan had fallen to a new low as the result of the outspoken Soviet support for the Indian position on Kashmir. Mohammed Ali, the prime minister of Pakistan, had been angered by Khrushchev's insistence that "the people of Kashmir themselves had decided to become part of India." These, said Ali, were "extraordinary statements coming from leaders of a country which denounces colonialism. . . . " However, despite their mutual grievances, neither the Soviets nor the Pakistanis wanted to alienate the other irrevocably. With this in mind, Mikoyan and Mohammed Ali concluded a brief discussion by agreeing in effect that "mutual misunderstanding should not be permitted to run riot."[41]

It had been announced in December 1955 that the volume of Indo-Soviet trade had surpassed the level set by the 1953 agreement. A new pact was drawn up calling for the USSR to supply India with one million tons of steel and steel products, mining and oil drilling equipment, etc., over the three-year period.[42] In turn India would increase its shipments of raw materials and light manufactures to the USSR. It was again stipulated that over the three years the value of India's imports from the USSR was to equal that of its exports. While the total volume of Indo-Soviet commerce remained comparatively small, the percentage increase as compared to the 1953 level was impressive. The value of India's imports from the USSR rose from $.9 million in 1953 to $31.3 million in 1956, while exports to the USSR increased in value from $.7 million in 1953 to $26.2 million in 1956. In discussing the nature of the new agreement, Mikoyan stressed that "the USSR is trying hard to avoid casting a burden on India's balance of trade

41. An observation made after the Mikoyan-Ali talk by Pakistan's foreign minister, H. H. Chowdrey.

42. Joint Communiqué on Economic Relations, Dec. 13, 1955. For discussion on the significance of the agreement see Wilfred Malenbaum, *East and West In India's Development* (1959), pp. 38–39; and Joseph Berliner, *Soviet Economic Aid*.

and payments." The USSR, he said, would buy those goods which India wished to export and would offer India goods that would benefit the development of the economy.

Mikoyan's hosts were very interested in the events that had occurred during the recently ended Twentieth Party Congress of the CPSU held in Moscow. It was Mikoyan who, in his address to the Congress on February 16, had made the first sharp indictment of certain aspects of Stalin's policies. Khrushchev probably used Mikoyan's address as a trial balloon to test the Congress' reactions before launching his own "secret speech" of revelations about Stalin.) Word of the dramatic nature of the CPSU Congress had leaked out, and Indian journalists pressed the reticent Mikoyan for clarification. His only public comment on the matter was that the "cult of personality" was being done away with as a "safeguard for the future successes" of the party.[43]

While the Twentieth Party Congress of the CPSU was still in session, Nehru told the lower house of the Indian Parliament that "it is an important matter not only for the USSR but for all countries in the world at large to understand these great changes that are taking place." These changes are "taking the USSR more and more towards one kind of normalcy which is to be welcomed in every way."[44] Parenthetically Nehru expressed the wish that those (meaning the Communists of India) "who sometimes looked up to them" would follow the Soviet example. He then went on to criticize, the CPI's part in the violence and bitterness which had followed the recent Indian States Reorganization Act.

The apparent results of the CPSU Twentieth Congress seemed to vindicate Nehru's belief that there was a strong trend toward liberalization within the USSR and that this trend should be welcomed and encouraged. On March 20 he told the Lok Sabha that

43. *Hindu*, March 28, 1956.
44. Lok Sabha, *Debates*, vol. 1, no. 8 (February 23, 1956), col. 817.

"there can be no doubt that the CPSU Congress has developed a new line and a new policy." His appraisal continued:

This new line, both in political thinking and in practical policy, appears to be based on a more realistic appreciation of the present world situation and represents a significant process of adaptation and adjustment. According to our principles we do not interfere in the internal affairs of other countries, just as we do not welcome interference of others in our country. But any important development in any country which appears to be a step toward the creation of conditions favorable to the pursuit of a policy of peaceful coexistence is important for us as well as others.[45]

Implicit in Nehru's position was that the "process of adaptation and adjustment" was a continuing one, having the cumulative effect of further relaxing Soviet relations with the non-Communist nations.

Dr. S. Radhakrishnan, India's vice-president, who had served as Nehru's ambassador to Moscow from 1950–52, carried this line of reasoning one step further to its logical conclusion. He intimated that if the non-Communist world continued its distrust of the USSR, then "we shall be held responsible for the continuation of the Cold War."[46] Upon his return from a state visit to the USSR in June 1956, Radhakrishnan declared that "the present hatred of dictatorship, the emphasis on collective leadership, and the freedom of discussion within the Party may well be regarded as the first step towards the liberalization of the Soviet state."

New Delhi viewed the abolition of the Cominform on April 18 as a symbolic gesture by the Soviets to further ease international tensions. Nehru, who had spoken out strongly that past year against the Cominform, welcomed this move. It was by no means believed in New Delhi, however, that the CPI had been orphaned by Moscow. Like its predecessor, the Comintern, the formal ap-

45. Lok Sabha, *Debates*, vol. 2, no. 27 (March 20, 1956), cols. 304–48.

46. From an address to the Indian Council of Public Affairs in Patna, *Hindu*, March 22, 1956.

paratus of the Cominform had been dissolved to meet Soviet policy needs in the context of a changing world situation.

It was not until June that Khrushchev's secret speech of February 24 to the closed session of the CPSU Party Congress was brought to the world's attention. In India, as elsewhere, there were reactions to Khrushchev's charges. Many Indian newspapers pointed to the obvious fact that he and other detractors of Stalin had, themselves, participated in the actions that were now being condemned. Nonetheless, a widely held point of view was that regardless of Khrushchev's own past actions, the denunciation of Stalin's excesses was both necessary and courageous.

Nehru apparently believed that domestic reforms within the USSR would indirectly contribute to an easing of international tensions. He now sought to persuade others to accept his basic approach in dealing with the Russians (and Chinese). At the Commonwealth Prime Ministers' Conference in July 1956, his position was reflected in the resultant joint statement which indicated the prime ministers' "willingness to facilitate increased contacts" with the USSR.

Only two years had elapsed since late 1953, when the Soviets had launched their efforts to win India's confidence, until the mutual state visits of 1955. During this interval Nehru at first had reacted somewhat cautiously to the Soviet overtures, looking all the while for overt signs of change in Soviet practice. It was suggested in the previous chapter that he was favorably impressed by the direction of Soviet policies in 1954. By the end of 1955 his government's implicit assumption was that the Soviets were genuinely willing to practice coexistence, at least insofar as Indo-Soviet relations were concerned.

When did Nehru decide that it was safe for India to become closely involved with the Soviet Union? No precise answer can be given, but Indians in a position to have a reasoned opinion almost invariably cite sometime within the twelve month period beginning June 1955 as the time when Nehru became firmly convinced that the Soviets were genuinely willing to coexist peacefully in all aspects of Indo-Soviet relations. For example, in reviewing the significance of the Bulganin-Khrushchev grand tour of 1955, Sisir Gupta listed "the promise of Soviet aid; the endorsement of India's unity; the acceptance of its national leadership as a progressive and desirable phenomenon; the promotion of India's status in the world; . . . and the use of Soviet influence to prevent the irresponsible functioning of its followers in India as providing the bases for India's friendly relations with the USSR in the following years."[47] An official in the Indian External Affairs Ministry emphasized to the present writer that the results of the Twentieth Party Congress "confirmed" the belief that there was a permanent basis for good Indo-Soviet relations.

In any event an increasingly cordial and cooperative relationship with the USSR had become, by mid-1956, a cornerstone of Indian foreign policy. The relationship between the two governments had reached a point where neither could withdraw from its growing commitments to the other without strong repercussions.

47. Sisir Gupta, "India and the Soviet Union," p. 145.

4 Peaceful Coexistence in Practice, 1956–58

THE dimensions of an increasingly cordial Indo-Soviet relationship were rather well defined by mid-1956. On some matters the two governments found grounds for mutual cooperation in the immediate years that followed. In 1957, for example, India called upon the USSR to veto a Western-sponsored resolution on Kashmir in the UN Security Council. On the other hand, India indirectly lent its support to most Soviet proposals on arms control.

Yet the professions of goodwill made during the halcyon days of 1955 were not always observed in practice. Old strains reappeared from time to time. In 1957–58 there were several occasions when the Soviets felt sufficiently provoked to rebuke the Indian government.

India and the Hungarian Revolution

The reactions of various nations to the Suez and Hungarian crises reveal much about their international orientation and general outlook at the time. For the emergent nations of Asia and Africa the Suez situation was obviously of greater import. They identified with a fellow non-Western nation struggling against an apparent attempt by imperial powers to reassert their former influence. To most Afro-Asians the conflict in Hungary was psychologically as well as geographically remote. The Western nations, in turn, were chagrined by what appeared to be a "double standard" by certain newly-independent nations in their stance on the Suez and Hungarian crises. India, in particular, received the brunt of this criticism.

Prime Minister Nehru's views on the Hungarian revolt and its aftermath provide an interesting case study of his thoughts about and policy toward developments in the Communist world. Most assessments of the Indian government's reaction to the Hungarian Revolution have centered on the extent to which India's position was consistent with her professed nonalignment policy. That there were several rather distinct phases to the Indian stance on Hungary is often overlooked. In the following section we will examine these phases and attempt to chart Prime Minister Nehru's interpretation of the tragic events as they unfolded during November 1956.

Preoccupation with the dispute over the Suez Canal dominated India's attention for several months prior to the outbreak of the Suez and Hungarian crises. At the London Conference in August 1956, India's representatives put forth several proposals purported to meet "all requirements of the users and international community without prejudice or derogation to the sovereignty of Egypt."[1] The Indian resolutions were supported by the USSR, Ceylon, and Indonesia but were not acceptable to the Western powers. Other Indian efforts to serve a mediatory role were unsuccessful. When the crisis erupted on November 1, Nehru immediately declared: "in all my experience of foreign affairs I have come across no greater case of naked aggression than what France and England are trying to do."[2] Indian sympathies were entirely with the Egyptians, as government officials and newspaper editorials alike denounced the action of the former colonial powers.[3]

1. *Lok Sabha, Debates*, pt. 2, vol. 8, no. 45 (September 13, 1956), cols. 6964–65.

2. Supplement "War in Egypt" in *Hindu*, November 2, 1956.

3. An extensive although somewhat uncritical account of the Indian position on the Suez and Hungarian crises is included in M. S. Rajan, *India in World Affairs*, p. 151 ff.

Events in Hungary developed more rapidly. India's ambassador K. P. S. Menon, accredited to both the USSR and Hungary, had visited Budapest for a few days in mid-October without sensing that a revolt would take place soon after he returned to Moscow.[4] But in the last week of October the latent unrest in Hungary rapidly turned into spontaneous workers' demonstrations which brought changes in the government leadership. On October 31, a week after his installation as prime minister, Imre Nagy announced that Hungary was withdrawing from the Warsaw Pact and called for the removal of Soviet troops from the country. The sordid details of the next few days—temporary withdrawal of Soviet troops from Budapest, their reentry to "restore order," the removal of Nagy— need not be recounted here.[5]

According to K. P. S. Menon's interpretation of events, the Soviets had been sincere in their end-of-October pledge to leave Budapest. He noted that there was, however, a good deal of pressure on Khrushchev at the time. Molotov and other powerful rivals had blamed the uprisings in Eastern Europe on Khrushchev's de-Stalinization policy. His opponents anticipated that Khrushchev would fall if matters worsened. Khrushchev himself knew this and therefore had to order the intervention when the Hungarian Communists lost control of the situation.[6]

4. See Menon, *The Flying Troika*, pp. 163–80.

5. For a comprehensive account see the section "Poland and Hungary" in *Survey of International Affairs, 1956–58*, pp. 72–138. Paul Kecskemeti wrote about the outbreak of the insurrection: "Looking at the climax of October 23, 1956, one has the impression of a sudden jump from political stability to chaos. On closer inspection, however, it becomes apparent that the political situation had been in flux for a number of years before the final explosion. Indeed, in Hungary, as well as in the other countries of East Central Europe that passed into the Soviet orbit, political and social changes of the greatest moment had been compressed into a decade. . . . With Stalin gone, the inevitable relaxation of his system in the Soviet Union released a number of centrifugal, disruptive tendencies in the dependent territories. . . . Perhaps the most extraordinary aspect of the Hungarian revolution was the rapidity with which a national consensus crystallized after the outbreak." Paul Kecskemeti, *The Unexpected Revolution* (Stanford, Cal.: Stanford University, 1961), pp. v, 6.

6. Interviews with K.P.S. Menon in New Delhi, February 1964.

The critical nature of the Hungarian situation was not immediately recognized in India. The reasons for this were in part historic. To Indians the events of the immediate post-war years in
Europe were of relatively little significance compared to their own
immediate experiences surrounding the attainment of independence. There was little awareness or concern about the imposition
of Russian will by force on Eastern Europe. The period of overt
Communist expansion coincided with the turbulence of partition
in the Indian subcontinent. Later, when the Indian government
gave more attention to the East European scene, it assumed that
the Communist regimes there were firmly consolidated.

Perhaps the first leading statesman to sense that the new leaders
of post-Stalinist Russia wished to ease Cold War tensions, Nehru
sought to persuade the Western powers that the USSR should be
given the opportunity to liberalize its regime without outside interference. He began to promote the notion that the two opposing
blocs should accept the political and territorial status quo in
Europe. Many international developments from 1954 through
mid–1956—an end to the fighting in Korea and Vietnam, the
markedly changed Soviet attitude toward India and other nonaligned nations and the subsequent growth of cordial Indo-Soviet
relations, Khrushchev's condemnation of Stalinist practices, the
disbanding of the Cominform—all gave support to Nehru's contentions about the positive change within the Communist world.

The uprising in Poznan, Poland, in June 1956 was disquieting
to those who hoped for a peaceful transformation within the Communist countries, but the Indian government apparently viewed
the Polish situation as an aberration rather than as a portent of
things to come. But in Poland, and particularly in Hungary, change
did not come gradually and without violence. As the nature of
events in Hungary became clearer, Nehru undoubtedly felt an urge
to speak out as he had done on Suez; yet for the most part he remained silent as Soviet troops crushed the revolution. During the
Tibetan uprising of 1951, Nehru had refrained from criticizing

the Chinese in an effort not to antagonize a large and potentially friendly neighbor. Similarly in the case of Hungary he did not think it in the interest of India or of world peace to bring strong pressures on the USSR.

The Indian government and public media were far more involved emotionally with Suez than with the Hungarian situation. Upon learning that the West was bringing the Hungarian matter before the Security Council, the *Hindu* correspondent at the United Nations wrote on October 30 that "Russia was in a damnable corner.... [The] main object seems to be to extract the maximum propaganda advantage out of it and expose Russia to the world as militarily intervening to suppress a popular revolution."[7]

Only on one recorded occasion did Prime Minister Nehru publicly express his views while the fighting was going on in the streets of Budapest during the first week of November. Addressing a UNESCO Conference meeting in New Delhi on November 5, he sadly observed: "We see today in Egypt as well as Hungary both human dignity and freedom outraged and the force of modern arms used to suppress peoples and to gain political objectives." Referring indirectly to the Soviet Union, he noted that the spirit of the Five Principles Agreement had been violated.[8]

Later, in answer to criticism that his government's reaction to the Hungarian situation was both delayed and tepid, Nehru contended that there was little reliable information available as to what was happening in Budapest. He told Parliament on November 16 that "the situation was obscure for some days, and it was only gradually the story of the tragic events that had taken place there had become known."[9] Along the same line, he reiterated three days later that "the broad facts were not known to us" for some time. There is reason to believe, however, that New Delhi had not been

7. K. S. Balaraman in *Hindu*, October 30, 1956.

8. *Hindu*, November 6, 1956.

9. *Lok Sabha Debates*, pt. 2, vol. 9, no. 3 (November 16, 1956), col. 265.

entirely unaware of the "broad facts." It is true that no senior diplomat was present in Budapest, but one member of the Indian Embassy managed to get several well-written and detailed reports out of Hungary via the Austrian border not long after the fighting broke out.

Prime Minister Nehru did reveal that in forming his initial opinions he attached considerable importance to the Yugoslav assessment of the Hungarian situation. It should be remembered that Yugoslavia, despite its own history of defiance of Soviet authority, did not wish to see an open revolt in Hungary. The fear that the conflict might spread into a conflagration involving all of Europe led Tito to back the Soviet explanation that the revolt was inspired by reactionaries. Nehru told the Lok Sabha on November 20 that "historically, linguistically, and geographically, Yugoslavia is in touch with developments in Eastern Europe. Tito is a leader of great experience and great ability. I am free to confess that we have to some extent been guided by their appraisal of the European situation. So far as Asia is concerned, we presume to know a little more than they do. . . . In regard to the European situation we certainly attach value to what they say."[10]

During the emergency session of the UN General Assembly the Indian delegation abstained on most of the Assembly resolutions concerning Hungary. India abstained on the resolution (1004) passed on November 4 which condemned the Soviet intervention, called for immediate withdrawal of Soviet troops, upheld the right of the Hungarian people to select their own form of government without external interference, and instructed the UN secretary-general to set up a committee which would thoroughly investigate the situation within Hungary. The chief Indian delegate, Krishna Menon, objected to several parts of the resolution, particularly those condemning the Soviet action and calling for an investigation under UN auspices into Hungary's internal affairs. He attempted to explain that while India "was not neutral where hu-

10. Ibid., (November 20, 1956), col. 381.

man freedom is concerned" the tone and content of the resolution required that India abstain.[11]

Then on November 9 came the controversial vote by the Indian delegation which provoked the most anger in the West and criticism at home. On that day the General Assembly passed another resolution (1005) calling for the withdrawal of Soviet troops and the subsequent holding of elections in Hungary under the auspices of the United Nations. The vote was 48 nations in favor of this resolution, 11 opposed, and 16 abstentions. All of the non-aligned Asian and Middle Eastern nations abstained with the exceptions of India and Ceylon which joined the Communist bloc in casting negative votes. [12] In explaining his vote, Krishna Menon told the Assembly that "we cannot subscribe to the idea that any sovereign state can agree to elections under the UN Organization." Considerable controversy exists as to whether or not Krishna Menon consulted with New Delhi before casting his negative vote on the November 9 resolution. It has been strongly suggested by several who were members of the Nehru government during that period that Krishna Menon acted on his own initiative. In any event, Nehru came to the support of his UN delegate in the face of criticism. Whether or not he had any personal reservations, Nehru later endorsed Menon's vote as being "entirely in consonance with our general policy and instructions."[13]

The considerable opposition to the government's stand on Hungary marked the first time Nehru's foreign policy had ever been subjected to serious, sustained criticism within India. It was not the principle of nonalignment as such that was challenged but its implementation. Speaking in Madras on November 17, the highly respected J. P. Narayan remarked: "I am concerned over our foreign policy. We are following a double standard—one standard

11. *UN General Assembly, Official Records*, Second Official Emergency Sess., 569th mtg., pp. 44 ff.

12. Ibid., 571st mtg., p. 79.

13. *Lok Sabha Debates*, pt. 2, vol. 9, no. 3 (November 16, 1956), cols. 265–66.

of measurement for Egypt and another for Hungary. That is why I am opposing it."[14]

In the Parliamentary debate of November 19–20 on Hungary, opposition to Nehru's policy was voiced by the Praja Socialist party leaders, J. B. Kripalani, A. Mehta, and H. Kamath, and the appointed representative of the Anglo-Indian community, Frank Anthony.[15] Leaders of the right-wing Hindu Mahasabha urged that India should withdraw from the Commonwealth because of Suez and sever relations with the USSR. Even H. N. Mukherjee, spokesman for the Communist members of Parliament, conceded at one point that the Soviet action in Hungary was "clumsy and sometimes nasty on account of a certain panic." And from the Congress party backbench, S. N. Sinha, among the first to herald Indo-Soviet friendship in 1954, now recommended: "As a friend of the USSR we can advise that country to pull out not only from Hungary itself but from the whole of Eastern Europe." Somewhat to Nehru's embarrassment the only full support for his policy outside the Congress party came from the CPI. Toward the end of the sessions, however, Nehru's explanations began to mollify his critics. Resentment became more focused thereafter on Krishna Menon and the way he had presented India's position before the United Nations. From that time forward Krishna Menon became a more frequent target than the prime minister himself when members of opposition parties wished to criticize the government's foreign policy.

Actually the Indian government's position on the Hungarian tragedy had passed gradually into a second phase before the above mentioned debates in Parliament took place. This second phase of Indian policy began several days after the Anglo-French expeditionary force had ended its Egyptian venture. India and other non-Western nations were then able to look at the European scene with a cooler perspective. More importantly, the inception

---

14. *Hindu*, November 18, 1956.

15. For text of speeches by opposition leaders see *Lok Sabha Debates*, pt. 2, vol. 9, no. 4 (November 19, 1956), cols. 390–510.

of the phase coincided roughly with the end of effective resistance by the Hungarian insurgents against the Soviet troops. Nehru's reaction prior to this time was indicative of his primary concern that the conflict in Hungary should remain localized and not spread. By November 10 the question of whether Hungary would withdraw from the Warsaw Pact had been decided by force of arms. With this matter resolved, Nehru's concern centered on how the suffering of the Hungarian people might be relieved. He strongly supported food and medical shipments and other relief measures sponsored by the UN. He also began to consider ways that the Soviets might be gradually induced to withdraw their armed forces from Hungary.

After two weeks of indecision Nehru called for the eventual withdrawal of Soviet troops from Hungary. This change was evidenced in a joint statement issued by the prime ministers of India, Burma, and Indonesia after their November 12–14 meeting in New Delhi to discuss Suez and Hungary. The statement expressed regret for the reentry of Soviet troops into Budapest and called for their speedy removal from the country. The Hungarian people should then be permitted to determine their own form of government, free from external interference.[16]

Rankled by the criticism from abroad and at home, Nehru now felt the necessity to explain the earlier position his government had taken. At times his strained logic, and that of Krishna Menon, had reflected the dilemma of how India might help ease the situation in Hungary without bringing undue pressure on the USSR. On November 15 he told the Parliamentary Consultative Committee on Foreign Affairs (undoubtedly with the Kashmir problem in mind) that the holding of an election in Hungary under UN auspices might create a bad precedent. During the subsequent debates in Parliament, he said that India had opposed only one—the phrase calling for elections in Hungary "under United Nations

16. See Government of India, *Foreign Policy of India: Text of Documents, 1947–59*, p. 257.

auspices"—of the four major points in the controversial November 9 General Assembly resolution. Referring to another resolution (1006) on which India had abstained, he reasoned: "when India abstained she stood for withdrawal."[17] In her own way India was attempting to get the Soviet troops out of Hungary: "What was proposed in the resolution would have come in the way of that withdrawal."

In Parliament on November 19 Nehru pointed out that "the majority of the people in Hungary wanted a change . . . and rose in insurrection to achieve it, but ultimately they were suppressed." Despite some "Fascist elements" a very large majority of the Hungarian people "claimed freedom from outside control, objected to Soviet troops coming, wanted them to withdraw, and wanted some internal changes in their Government." In the end the Hungarian people were "bound to triumph."[18] Nehru's feelings about the Hungarian situation were mixed. He objected to a member of his own Congress party referring to Kadar as a Russian quisling and puppet:

Mr. Kadar, I am prepared to say, does not perhaps command the allegiance of the majority of the Hungarian people. That is a different matter. But to run down an individual whose whole life has been one of fighting for freedom, who had been sent to prison by the Communist Government [during the Rakosi era] . . . is irresponsible thinking and speaking.[19]

Nehru felt that the great tragedy of Hungary was that events "moved too far too fast." If, like the Poles, the Hungarians had moved through a Titoist stage, they might have secured the substance of their demands and Soviet intervention might have been avoided. On December 4 he told the upper house that the processes of liberalization and democratization might have occurred peacefully in Hungary, as they did in Poland, if the Hun-

17. *Lok Sabha Debates*, pt. 2, vol. 9, no. 4 (Nov. 19, 1956), col. 391.
18. Ibid., cols. 378, 384–85.
19. Ibid., cols. 583–84.

garian leadership had handled the situation prudently. He also associated the Soviet intervention in Budapest with the Suez question: "I imagine that in Hungary they would have escaped that danger also if exactly at that time the Anglo-French invasion had not come in [Suez]. This is quesswork, of course, I do not know. It is a possibility."[20] The possible disintegration of the Warsaw Pact without the simultaneous breakup of NATO and SEATO was undesirable so far as India was concerned. Among other things such an occurrence might lead the Soviet leaders to revert to their pre-1953 "stage of siege" mentality and be provoked into taking steps that would further endanger world peace.

Along this line an officially approved article written by "X" in 1957 reflected the Indian government's outlook at the time of the Hungarian revolt. "X" recalled that the repercussions of the Twentieth Party Congress of the CPSU were felt throughout Eastern Europe. Uprisings occurred, first in Poland, then in Budapest. When Imre Nagy took over at the height of the crisis, there were hopes that a settlement on the Polish lines would be possible in Hungary also. Mr. Nagy, however, was not made of the same stuff as Mr. Gomulka, and the situation in Hungary got out of hand. The USSR was in a difficult position, continued "X," noting the rationale for Soviet intervention. If it failed to crush the "counterrevolution" in Hungary, other countries might similarly try to unilaterally leave the Warsaw Pact. "The Anglo-French adventure in Egypt left no alternative; with a world war possibly looming, it felt unsafe to leave Hungary in chaos."[21]

In December 1956 during the eleventh regular session of the UN General Assembly, India abstained on most of the resolutions which dealt with Hungary. According to Krishna Menon, India supported the substance but opposed the condemnatory tone of the resolutions: "Although the adoption of resolutions might sometimes be a tribute to our sense of morality and satisfy us that we

20. *Rajya Sabha Official Record*, vol. 15, no. 12 (Dec. 4, 1956), col. 1534.
21. "X," "Destalinization."

have done our duty, it is not sufficient to derive a subjective satisfaction; it is also necessary to take some effective steps which would alleviate the sufferings of the Hungarian people. . . ."[22] Menon, however, did convey the changed Indian attitude when on December 10 he declared that the "overwhelming majority of the Hungarian people" wanted the USSR to withdraw its forces. He tried also to persuade the Soviet and Hungarian governments to permit UN observers to enter Hungary. Nehru personally made the request that Dag Hammerskjöld be permitted to inspect the situation there. The requests were refused.

Pleased with India's original reaction to the Hungarian situation, the Soviets became rather irritated when India later called for the entry of UN observers into Hungary and self-determination for the Hungarian people. Thereafter the Soviet leaders were not reluctant to drop hints in private that India also had a goodly number of problems including Kashmir. Yet the Soviets on February 20, 1957, vetoed for the first time a Western-sponsored resolution (S/3787) on Kashmir.[23] The vote on Kashmir restored much of the recently-diminished Soviet prestige within India.

Throughout 1957 Nehru emphasized that what had already happened in Hungary, however tragic, could not be undone. He told Parliament in September that his concern was to help the Hungarian people. This could not be done "by loudly condemning the things we do not like."[24] He opposed any move to block Hungary's representatives from attending the 1957 autumn session of the General Assembly. What could be gained, he asked rhetorically, if India joined "in some kind of repudiation of the Hungarian representation in the UN? How exactly do we help the Hungarian peo-

22. *UN General Assembly, Official Records*, 11th sess., 608th mtg. (December 4, 1956), pp. 521 ff.

23. *UN Security Council, Official Records*, 12th sess., 773rd mtg. (February 20, 1957), p. 31.

24. *Lok Sabha Debates*, pt. 2, vol. 6, no. 37 (September 2, 1957), col. 11323–24.

ple by not recognizing the present Government there?"[25] (New Delhi, unlike some Western nations, maintained its diplomatic ties with Hungary after the Kadar regime came to power.)[26]

In December 1956 Nehru had termed the imprisonment of Imre Nagy "most unfortunate." When asked in the Indian upper house of Nagy's whereabouts, the prime minister replied. "I believe he is in the Carpathian Mountains. He is being kept in a very healthy spot—one of the health resorts of Rumania."[27] Needless to say Nehru was shocked when he learned of Nagy's execution in June 1958. He strongly implied that the USSR was responsible for Nagy's death. Nonetheless Nehru retained the belief that the gradual processes of liberalizing change would again resume in Hungary and throughout Easten Europe.

Aspects of Indo-Soviet Diplomatic Relations, 1957–58

Despite minor irritation with India's position on Hungary early in 1957, the Soviets continued their cordial gestures toward India throughout the year. Setting the tone was a lead article in *Pravda* marking the seventh anniversary of India's Republic Day. The article emphasized: "India has become a great power now playing an important role in the international arena. Pursuing their peace-loving policy the great Indian people are striving for friendship with all countries. . . . During the troubled days of the imperialist aggression against Egypt, India consistently came out on the side of the Egyptian people."[28] Marshal Zhukov, on a brief visit to India in late January, visited a number of Indian military establishments.

25. *Rajya Sabha Official Records*, vol. 18, no. 18 (September 9, 1957), col. 4197.

26. A statement on Indo-Hungarian trade, Hungarian collaboration on industrial projects within India, and other aspects of the relationship is contained in *India and Foreign Review*, (March 15, 1966) : 5–7.

27. *Rajya Sabha Official Records*, vol. 15, no. 2 (December 3, 1956), col. 1335.

28. *Pravda*, January 25, 1957.

His major theme was that "if India, China, and the USSR remain united there would be no occasion for any world wars."

Kashmir

The Soviet leaders in 1955 committed themselves to support India's position on the Kashmir issue in its entirety. In the UN Security Council in February 1957 the USSR was called upon for the first time to veto a Western-sponsored resolution on Kashmir. A brief review of the 1957 Security Council proceedings on Kashmir follows.

On February 14 Great Britain, the United States, Australia, and Cuba co-sponsored a draft resolution (S/3787) which was unacceptable to the government of India. The resolution noted that "demilitarization preparatory to the holding of a free and impartial plebiscite under UN auspices has not been achieved in accordance with the resolutions of the UN Commission for India and Pakistan." It called for "the use of a temporary UN force in connection with demilitarization" and authorized the president of the Security Council, Gunnar Jarring of Sweden, to visit the subcontinent for the purpose of discussing the resolution with representatives of India and Pakistan.[29]

The USSR delegate, Sobolev, on February 18, proposed amendments to the above resolution. He argued that "the situation in Kashmir has changed considerably" since 1948 when the Security Council had first called for a plebiscite. The people of Kashmir had settled the question themselves and now considered their territory an integral part of India. Sobolev called for continued bilateral negotiations on Kashmir by India and Pakistan "without outside intervention of any sort." In a counter resolution (S/3789) and the Soviet delegate deleted reference to "the use of a temporary UN force in connection with demilitarization" in Kash-

29. *UN Security Council, Official Records*, 12th sess., 768 mtg. (February 14, 1957).

mir.[30] After his amendments were rejected by the other Council members, Sobolev, on February 20, vetoed the Western-sponsored resolution (S/3787). He justified the veto by alleging that the resolution, as it stood, favored Pakistan.[31]

Prime Minister Nehru was displeased with the proceedings on Kashmir. He termed "deliberately hostile" the attitudes toward India of some countries in the Security Council:

The resolution came specifically from the side of Britain although a few other countries also sponsored it. We did not like it because these countries brought forth the resolution without giving any thought to the naked invasion of Kashmir.[32]

The belief prevailed in New Delhi that the West provoked a Soviet veto in order to embarrass India.

In its autumn session the Security Council again debated the issue. The Soviet delegate attempted to link up the intensification of Western pressures on Kashmir with Pakistan's membership in SEATO:

It would be hard to disagree with the statements by Mr. Nehru, P. M. of India, on March 4 in which he said that certain Powers which do not like his country's independent foreign policy are seeking to exert pressures from within and without to induce India to change it.

He continued:

The Soviet delegation for its part shares the concern caused in peace-loving circles in Asia and throughout the world by the policy of organizing politico-military blocs and establishing military bases on foreign soil. . . . The fact that Pakistan has allowed itself to be drawn into the [Western] orbit . . . has left its mark on the Pakistan Government's policy with regard to the Kashmir problem as well. As a result of Pakistan's policy, which has found support among that

30. Ibid., 770th mtg. (February 18, 1957), pp. 38–40.
31. Ibid. 773rd mtg. (February 20, 1957), p. 31.
32. *Hindu*, February 22, 1957.

country's partners in SEATO, the situation in the Kashmir area continues to be strained.[33]

In closing, Sobolev warned that the authority of the Security Council must not be used to impose "alien rule" on the people of Kashmir.

The 1957 debates served notice that the Soviet veto or threat of veto would be readily available to check Security Council resolutions on Kashmir unfavorable to the Indian position. The Soviet position could be summed up briefly in the words of a *Pravda* editorial of March 13, 1957, which declared: "the Kashmiri people themselves decided the question . . . , *de facto and de jure*."

Arms Control

After 1955 Soviet and Indian representatives consulted more frequently on matters dealing with arms control. Whenever their approaches seemed to coincide, they coordinated their policies.

The USSR called for Indian participation in all major conferences on disarmament. In June 1957 for example the Russians backed India's unsuccessful bid to send a delegate to speak at the forthcoming Five-Power Disarmament Commission in London. For some time India had favored the enlargement of the United Nations Disarmament Subcommittee, contending that Indian representation on committees discussing disarmament would give a voice to the vast majority of nations who neither have nuclear weapons nor wish to make them.[34] The Government of India regretted that the Western Powers were unwilling to accept an Indian delegate to the London Conference, and spokesmen for several

33. *UN Security Council, Official Records*, 12th sess., 799th mtg. (November 5, 1957), pp. 1–4.

34. Prime Minister Nehru told the upper house that "disarmament is perhaps the basic issue which governs other matters. The Disarmament Commission of the U.N. faces deadlock. India is prepared to assist the Commission if called upon to render its services." *Rajya Sabha Official Records*, vol. 18, no. 18 (September 9, 1957), cols. 4193–94.

opposition parties in the Indian Parliament registered protests.[35] The Soviet delegate to the UN Disarmament Subcommittee revealed that he had raised the issue of India's participation fourteen times.[36]

The USSR appeared to be attentive to what India and the other nonaligned nations had to say on arms control questions.[37] On November 28, 1957, Nehru made an appeal to both the USSR and the United States, calling for an end to the armaments race. Moscow newspapers published Nehru's appeal on December 11, and a reply by the Soviet leaders declared they would observe a moratorium on atomic testing beginning January 1, 1958, if the United States and Great Britain would agree to do likewise. Nehru was gratified by the Russian and American response, which he held to have much in common.[38]

Needless to say, the USSR did not consult India before renewing nuclear testing in October, 1958. Speaking in the UN Political Committee after the USSR had begun a new series of tests, Krishna Menon expressed his dissatisfaction:

When the USSR suspended tests five months ago, not only my country, but a great part of the world, particularly Asia and Africa, responded very generously. It would be wrong . . . to disguise our feelings of disappointment that these tests have been renewed. That the USA and

35. A CPI spokesman, Bhupesh Gupta, asserted: "The Western Powers refused to hear India on the UN committee. Why? Because they know that once India's voice is heard on the committee the case would be stronger for disarmament and the voice of the Asian-African people would be heard with logic, force and reasonableness. . . ." (Ibid., col. 4223.)

36. Reported from London by K. S. Shelvankar in *Hindu*, September 6, 1957.

37. For a discussion of the Soviet outlook on disarmament see M. Mackintosh and H. Willetts, "Arms Control and the Soviet National Interest," in *Arms Control: Issues for the Public*, ed. L. Henkin (Englewood Cliffs: Prentice Hall, 1961), pp. 141–74.

38. Nehru expressed gratitude for the attention paid by Bulganin and Eisenhower to his proposal and noted how much there was in common in their replies. See *Lok Sabha Debates*, pt. 2, vol. 10, no. 28 (December 17, 1957), col. 5888.

UK have not discontinued the tests is in our opinion no justification for renewal by the USSR.[39]

Disengagement in Europe, as proposed by the Polish foreign minister, Adam Rapacki, was more acceptable to the Warsaw Pact nations than to the NATO nations. Nehru welcomed such proposals for the neutralization of central Europe in principle, although he always qualified his remarks. "Anything that lessens tension and fear, I think should be welcomed," answered Nehru when asked about the Rapacki Plan. He indicated, however, that the plan should be considered only as part of a larger scheme of disarmament. Commenting on George Kennan's lectures in Britain on disengagement, Nehru observed:

It is interesting that a very eminent American expert has come to that view and has advocated [disengagement]. But it is not only Mr. Kennan. The realization is coming more and more to people's minds, even though many of them may not say so because they have the feeling that "if we say this we might be weakening our country's policy, and making the other country think we are weakening."[40]

In his commentary on the European scene, Nehru sought to pursue a course of strict neutrality, but his remarks inadvertently benefited Soviet diplomacy more than the West's.

Middle-East Crisis, 1958

Towards the end of 1956 Nehru felt the need to clear up a number of misunderstandings between India and the United States. His trip to the United States in December made a start in this direction. One contentious point that cropped up shortly thereafter was the post-Suez "Eisenhower Doctrine" towards West Asia. At

39. Extracts from the verbatim transcript of the General Assembly Political Committee (*Hindu*, October 19, 1958). For the rapporteur's summary see *UN General Assembly, Official Reports*, 13th sess., 1st comm., 952 mtg. (October 17, 1958), pp. 48–50.

40. *Rajya Sabha Official Reports*, vol. 19, no. 19 (December 12, 1957), cols. 2349–50.

an All-India Congress Committee meeting on January 7, 1957, and in the Lok Sabha on March 25, Nehru decried the idea of a "power vacuum," which served only to encourage Big Powers to cut out "spheres of influence" and subvert the independence of other countries.[41]

In July 1958 American and British troops entered Lebanon and Jordan to prevent possible uprisings similar to that which had recently overturned the Iraqi government. A spokesman for the India External Affairs Ministry declared on July 18 that members of the United Nations observer team who had been present beforehand in Lebanon should be "allowed to continue their functions. This would be a safeguard against the infiltration of foreign elements, and the presence of American troops against any threat from outside is therefore not necessary." Addressing the Indian Parliament in mid-August, Nehru declared:

We do not accept that foreign troops should be used in any territory [in West Asia] in the circumstances prevailing there. We are convinced that there can be no settlement and no return to normality until foreign troops are removed.[42]

India welcomed the end of the crisis when the United States and Great Britain agreed to the Arab nations' resolution of August 21 calling for the restoration of stability to the area and withdrawal of foreign troops. India's delegate to the UN assembly, Arthur Lall, emphasized then that "we have no doubt, whatsoever, that there will be an early withdrawal of troops from Lebanon and Jordan."

While both India and the USSR called for the withdrawal of American and British forces from West Asia, the rationale behind their positions varied in part. One of India's main considerations was that the crisis should remain localized and that a confrontation of the United States and the USSR should be avoided. Nehru

41. *Lok Sabha Debates*, pt. 2, vol. 1, no. 7 (March 25, 1957), col. 657.
42. *Lok Sabha Debates*, pt 2, vol. 18, no. 4 (August 14, 1958), col. 865.

wanted the situation resolved speedily and, as at the time of Suez, wished to stop the situation from deteriorating to the point where Soviet "volunteers" might come on the scene. Unlike the USSR, India had little to gain from the general turmoil and anti-Westernism generated by the crises.

New Delhi was pleased, though, with a Soviet proposal during the height of the crisis that a five-nation conference be convened to resolve the issue. On July 19 Khrushchev called for a summit meeting with the Western Big Three, the USSR, and India as participants to be held a few days later in Geneva. Earlier in the year Nehru had expressed India's willingness to attend high-level conferences. On April 9 he told Parliament: "Always our answer has been that we do not wish to push ourselves into any conferences, but if our presence is wanted by the principal parties concerned and we feel that we can help we want to be of help."[43] Khrushchev's message to Nehru pointed out that "history says that any local war can easily turn into a world conflagration. . . . The Soviet government considers that the conferences should work out concrete recommendations for ending the conflict in the . . . Middle East and submit them to the Security Council and that body should consider them with the participation of the Arab countries." In his reply to Khrushchev, Nehru gladly offered his services to resolve the conflict along the lines of the Soviet proposal. The Western Big Three were in no mood for such a confrontation, however, and the conference did not take place.

Nehru's remarks about the USSR in late 1957 were made in a variety of contexts. When asked at a press conference, "How is India's self-interest served by comforting Communists abroad and fighting them at home?" he replied:

> We try to comfort every suffering mortal. . . . We do not understand this passionate crusading spirit of Communism or anti-Communism. . . . Internally we pursue certain policies and if anybody opposes [them] we argue with him, but if the opposition is one of violence,

43. *Lok Sabha Debates*, pt. 2, vol. 15, no. 42 (April 9, 1958), cols. 9054–55.

then it becomes a different matter. I do not agree with the Communist theory. Part of it may be true, but the essential parts have been proven by experience to be wrong.[44]

On another occasion he was called upon to explain the "pro-American" remarks made by India's finance minister, T. T. Krishnamachari, during a visit to the United States in the autumn of 1957. Nehru compared Krishnamachari's admiration of Washington, Jefferson, and Lincoln and America's democratic traditions with his own remarks when visiting the USSR in 1955: "I go to the USSR and I am received with the greatest friendship and cordiality. It touches my heart and I thank them for it in appropriate language. But there are people in America and maybe . . . some people here who think I have sold my conscience to the USSR." Nehru went on to say that some had interpreted his parting repartee, "I am leaving part of my heart here," as meaning that India had some secret pact with the USSR. "I said this only because I was moved by what I saw and the reception I got there."[45]

India's policy towards China and the USSR was not adopted out of fear, reassured Nehru. "I can assure this House," he told the Lok Sabha on November 28, 1957, "that there was not the slightest element of fear or apprehension in . . . our policy with regard to China or Tibet or the USSR." On the same theme he asserted to the Rajya Sabha in December:

I can say with complete honesty that there is not the remotest chance . . . of India being afraid of Russia or China, or India having any conflict with Russia or China. I am not saying that on any kind of sentimental or even an idealist basis but purely on practical grounds. Even if we differ, if we are opposed in various policies, nevertheless there will be [no conflict].[46]

44. *Hindu*, October 22, 1957.

45. *Lok Sabha Debates*, pt. 2, vol. 9, no. 14 (November 28, 1957), cols. 2740–41.

46. *Rajya Sabha Official Reports*, vol. 19, no. 19 (December 12, 1957), col. 2476.

In his view India remained outside the Great Power conflict both ideologically and geographically.

Irritants in the Relationship

In 1958 Nehru's public remarks irritated the Soviet leaders on several occasions. As a reaction to the uprisings in Eastern Europe, the Soviets had tightened their stand on "revisionism" and pressured Yugoslavia to conform to the Soviet line on world affairs. Yugoslavia refused to be intimidated, and as a result relations between Moscow and Belgrade worsened. Before an open session of the All-India Congress Committee early in May, Nehru referred to Soviet intervention in Yugoslav affairs and complained about the pressure tactics employed against the Yugoslavs.

Khrushchev was displeased over India's interference in his dealings with Tito. From his standpoint their differences were an internal affair between two Communist parties. He told India's ambassador to Moscow in polite terms that India should observe the Khrushchev-Nehru joint communiqué and not interfere in the internal affairs of others. The *Hindu* correspondent, K. Rangaswami, wrote shortly after the incident:

It has been noted in Delhi that the Russian reaction to Indian criticism of any kind has always followed the line of dropping a broad hint about the numerous problems confronting India, particularly Kashmir. This happened once before during the Hungarian trouble when India was severely critical of the Russian intervention. On that occasion, while the Western Powers were bitterly hostile to India for not having instantaneously condemned the USSR, it was the turn later of the Russians to direct their guns against India.[47]

The Soviets, further annoyed by Nehru's comments on the execution of Imre Nagy in June, also did not allow an article written by Nehru entitled "The Basic Approach" to go unanswered. In the article Nehru stressed that "India has to do its own thinking, profiting by the example of others, but essentially trying to find

47. *Hindu*, May 27, 1958.

a path for ourselves suited to our own conditions." Then, pointing out the inadequacies of the capitalist and communist "solutions" to social and economic problems, he reiterated at some length his basic criticisms of communism in practice: "We see the growing contradictions within the rigid framework of Communism itself. Its suppression of individual freedom brings about moral reactions. Its contempt for what might be called the moral and spiritual side of life not only ignores something that is basic in man, but also deprives human behavior of standards and values. Its unfortunate association with violence encourages a certain evil tendency in human beings."[48] Nehru then went on to cite his admiration for many of the positive achievements of the USSR, but deplored the fact that communism had become associated with practices of violence and that the means employed often distorted the ends. He agreed with the communist charge that the capitalist structure of society was based on violence and class conflict. But the Communists themselves were guilty of defending their views with a "language of violence and condemning those who do not accept it." Nehru found the approach of Communists and anti-Communists alike, when they attempted to force their views on others, to be "wholly unscientific, unreasonable, and uncivilized, whether it is applied to the realm of religion or economic theory or anything else."[49]

Ironically, Nehru's remarks had been addressed primarily to those Indians who had been awed by the impressive advances of the Communist countries, particularly China. Nonetheless, the aspersions made by the Indian prime minister against communist practices prompted a reply.

This reply was given by academician Pavel Yudin, the Russian ambassador to China, in the December 1958 issue of the *World Marxist Review*. Yudin began by asserting that Nehru did not discuss contemporary social phenomena and world problems in

48. Nehru, "The Basic Approach."
49. Ibid.

the "sound way" that he had assessed the historical forces that shaped Indian and world history prior to Indian independence. He then got down to answering the particulars of Nehru's complaints against the Communist methods, beginning with the use of violence as a means to implement state policy:

While speaking about violence in the USSR and other socialist coun-tries, Mr. Nehru conveys the impression that there is no such thing in India. It almost appears as if the Indian state organs—police, courts, prisons and the army—are in no way associated with exerting violence in respect to the people. Is this really the case? Let's recall a few facts. . . .[50]

So far as Nehru's concept of socialism was concerned, it had "very little real likeness to real socialism," charged Yudin. For Nehru:

the antagonism between capitalism and socialism is wearing thinner and thinner. In his conception of socialism for India, Nehru does not say anything about land ownership, about what socialism implies for the landlords, Indian and foreign capitalists, how the poverty of the peasants and the workers will be ended, how exploitation will be abolished, etc. . . . India has still much to do to abolish the remnants of feudalism from the countryside.[51]

India as yet had not gained full economic independence from the colonialist nations, as had China: "The question of India's eco-nomic independence, her freedom from imperialist influence, is an acute one, and will have to be solved if the National Congress intends to pursue a consistent policy of making the country in-dependent of the former colonialists." Yudin then compared India's slow rate of progress with the more rapid steps that China was making to develop its economy, abolish feudalism and all its survivals and create a new social order.

Significantly, after Yudin had delivered his sharp critique on

50. P. Yudin, "Can We Accept Pandit Nehru's Approach," *World Marxist Review*, vol. 1 (December, 1958).

51. Ibid. The quotations in the following paragraphs are from the Yudin articles.

India's domestic shortcomings, he closed by praising Nehru's foreign policy. "The progressive people of the world highly appreciate the noble and historic role of Pandit Nehru as the leader of the national liberation struggle of the Indian people. They value Nehru as an outstanding leader of the world against the warmongers of today." He then spoke of the feelings of "sincere friendship and fraternity" felt by the "great Indian people" towards the USSR. The USSR and other socialist countries had every confidence that "the great Indian people are capable of and will be working miracles in transforming India into a modern industrial power," and would assist India in achieving the goal of economic development.

Yudin concluded: "As to the ways and methods which the Indian people may adopt to achieve this noble goal, that is a matter for the Indian people alone to decide." The meaning of this concluding remark was clear; the USSR was willing to accept the Congress government's handling of India's domestic affairs, but only on the condition that Nehru did not interfere with or adversely criticize conditions in the Communist world.

Yudin's article reflected more the post-1957 Chinese viewpoint of India rather than the general Soviet line. After the Sino-Soviet differences hardened in 1959, he was removed from his post as ambassador to China. (An immediate cause for his recall in November 1959 stemmed from his open support of the Chinese on the Sino-Indian border dispute.) His reply to Nehru's "Basic Approach" cannot be dismissed, however, as being the aberrant view of a Sinophile. His thoughts about India undoubtedly were shared by Russian leaders, although political considerations had since 1954 muted the expression of misgivings about India's domestic policies. Khrushchev gave top priority to Nehru's foreign policy (which for the most part abetted his own policy goals), and was thus willing to overlook the Indian domestic scene. From time to time since 1959, Soviet writers have leveled criticism at Indian policy, but nothing comparable in tone to Yudin's remarks.

Taken somewhat aback by the Yudin article, Nehru intimated

that his intent had been misunderstood. Thereafter, the events of 1959 had the sobering effect of bringing his theorizing on the nature of communism to an end. After the flareups on the Indian border, Nehru began to distinguish quite sharply between communism as practiced by the USSR and by China.

5 Indo-Soviet Relations Amid The Sino-Soviet-Indian Triangle, 1959–61

DESPITE pledges of mutual friendship in the mid-1950's, differing approaches to the political and economic problems of their massive populations created a natural rivalry between China and India. Several incidents along their lengthy border in the Himalayas brought the smouldering friction between the two governments into the open in 1959. In that same year the increased discord in Sino-Soviet relations also began to reach serious proportions. From that time onward a common concern over China added a new dimension to the New Delhi–Moscow relationship.

The questions dealt with in this section include the following: How did the problem of dealing with India exacerbate the already strained Peking-Moscow alliance? In what ways did the Indian Government attempt to use the Soviets as a restraint upon Chinese ambitions in the Himalayas and elsewhere? And how were the Soviet reactions to the Sino-Indian border clashes viewed by India?

Deterioration of Sino-Indian Relations, 1957–59

The origins of the Sino-Soviet and Sino-Indian disputes are extremely complex and not within the scope of this study.[1] It can

---

1. For differing interpretations of the causes underlying the Sino-Indian conflict see Alastair Lamb, *The China-India Border*; P. C. Chakravarti, *India's*

be said, however, that Chinese policy toward both India and the USSR hardened after 1957. Before then the Chinese need for a strong Russian ally took top priority. But from February 1957 onward the Chinese launched an attack against Yugoslav 'revisionism,' and later directed the message at those who gave comfort to the 'revisionists.' Chinese discontent further stemmed from the belief that Khrushchev was attempting to reach an understanding with the United States at the expense of China. The Soviets also had been most reluctant to share their knowledge of nuclear weapons and did not fully support Chinese aims during the Formosa crisis in 1958.

While the Chinese had been amicable toward India in 1954–55, their attitude soon stiffened. By the end of 1957 Chinese and Indian interests generally began to work at cross-purposes. Peking then became displeased with the premium that Premier Khrushchev continued to place on close ties with India. It was one thing for Khrushchev to deflect India from the West, but another matter altogether for him to lavish praise and substantial economic assistance on New Delhi. To the Chinese the Indian National Congress represented a classical example of a 'bourgeois-nationalist' movement which had served the purpose of expelling the British colonial rulers, but had long since outlived its usefulness. The CCP complained further that the unwarranted Soviet acclaim for the Nehru government was making it impossible for a genuine Indian revolutionary movement to develop. Moreover, Soviet aid on easy terms to India stood in contrast with the more businesslike terms

China Policy; George Patterson, *Peking versus Delhi*; Gunnar Myrdal, *Asian Drama*, 1: 192–208; Government of India, Ministry of External Affairs, *Notes, Memoranda, and Letters Exchanged between the Governments of India and China* (about fifteen Indian White Papers have been published) ; and *Documents on the Sino-Indian Boundary Question* (Peking: Foreign Language Press, 1960).

Books dealing with Sino-Soviet dispute include Donald Zagoria, *The Sino-Soviet Conflict*; Klaus Mehnert, *Peking and Moscow*; Edward Crankshaw, *The New Cold War*; and Alexander Dallin, ed., *Diversity in International Communism* (New York: Columbia University Press, 1963).

of Soviet assistance to the fraternal socialist nations.[2] Nehru's implied criticism of the Chinese abrogation of the "Hundred Flowers" campaign, and his open distaste for the coercive aspects of China's developmental programs all contributed to Peking's ire.

The Tibetan problem brought Sino-Indian differences into the open for the first time. In 1950–51 the Indian government, despite some initial protests, had acquiesced to the military "liberation" of China's Tibetan region. Subsequently the 1954 Sino-Indian accord (which incorporated the Five Principles of Peaceful Co-existence) subjected any remaining Indian contacts with Tibet to Chinese approval. But China was unable to end the smouldering discontent among the Tibetans. In July 1958 the frustrated Chinese accused India of permitting "American and Chiang Kai-shek special agents [and] Tibetan reactionaries to carry out subversive and disruptive activities in Tibet." Some weapons and supplies most probably were smuggled across the Indian border into Tibet, but there is no evidence of any official Indian governmental col-lusion in such activities. (It should be noted also that the areas in Tibet where the Khampas were in rebellion are very inaccessible from India.)

Early in 1959 widespread revolt broke out in Tibet.[3] At first Prime Minister Nehru was reluctant to discuss the situation as he did not want to open himself to charges of interference in China's domestic affairs.[4] But Peking did not appreciate Nehru's stance. Also the Chinese were annoyed by the criticism levied against Peking by the Dalai Lama after the Tibetan spiritual leader and his entourage were given political asylum in India. Left with no other recourse, Nehru pointed out that the magnitude of the Tibetan uprising "reflected a strong feeling of nationalism." He urged that

2. The above complaints were made to the Soviet government at appropriate times in the late 1950s but did not appear openly in the Chinese press until the early 1960s.

3. For an account of the Tibetan situation in its historic context see George Patterson, *Tibet in Revolt* (London, 1960).

4. *Lok Sabha Debates*, vol. 29, no. 35 (March 30, 1959), cols. 8514–25.

the fighting cease and that the Chinese respect the earlier autonomy which was promised to the Tibetans. He then expressed his hope that China and India should not develop "feelings of hostility towards each other" over the issue.[5] But hostility did exist and Sino-Indian relations continued to deteriorate. On April 2 Nehru enigmatically warned the Indian Parliament (as yet uninformed about the possibility of a major Indian border conflict with China) that "behind all these minor matters lie much bigger matters which we have to face today, tomorrow and the day after."

In their first announcement (in March) of the Tibetan revolt the Russians backed the Chinese contentions,[6] but thereafter the Russian press remained silent when the Chinese intensified their reproaches against India's alleged role in the upheaval. It can be assumed that the Kremlin derived a modicum of satisfaction from China's problems in Tibet, as Khrushchev recalled Peking's criticisms of his handling of the Eastern European situation after the debunking of Stalin in 1956. Khrushchev's reluctance to support China's accusations against India reflected the increasing friction in Sino-Soviet relations, as well as his reluctance to jeopardize his carefully-nurtured friendship with India. From that time onward the Soviets refrained from supporting any Chinese polemics directed against the Nehru government.

In 1956–57 the Chinese had taken possession of the undemarcated, uninhabited Aksai Chin area of Ladakh.[7] There

5. Ibid. vol. 30, no. 55 (April 27, 1959), col. 13499.

6. "Twice in early April Moscow repeated in radio commentaries Peking's claim that Kalimpong, in northern West Bengal, had been used as a base for the Tibetan rebels, despite Nehru's denial of the charge. Subsequently, however, the USSR suppressed from its public coverage all such charges against India and excised hostile references to India from reports on CPR articles and speeches carried in Soviet media." See Harry Gelman, "The CPI: Sino-Soviet Battleground," in A. Doak Barnett, ed., *Communist Strategies in Asia* (New York: Praeger, 1963), p. 111.

7. An historic background of Ladakh is provided in Fisher, Rose, and Huttenback, *Himalayan Battleground*. For an analysis of the politics surrounding the Aksai Chin dispute see G. F. Hudson, "The Aksai Chin," *St. Anthony's Papers*, no. 14, Far Eastern Affairs, no. 3 (London: Chatto and Windus, 1962).

(allegedly unknown to the Indian government until the summer of 1958), the Chinese built a motorable road linking Sinkiang with Tibet. The road had the immediate value of enabling the Chinese to send more troops and equipment from Sinkiang across the narrow Aksai Chin salient into rebellious Tibet. Since coming to power, the Communist regime occasionally had published maps showing China's historic claims to parts of Ladakh and the North East Frontier Agency. It was contended that the borders imposed on a weak China under duress by imperial Britain were subject to renegotiation. These claims were reiterated in September 1958.[8] Early in 1959 Chou En-lai let it be known that his nation would forego its recent claims and accept the MacMahon Line as the boundary in the eastern sector if India would recognize China's claim to the Aksai Chin area. In reality Chou was asking for Indian acceptance of a *fait accompli*. Nehru rejected this precondition for a settlement as unacceptable, and moved to step up Indian defenses in the remainder of Ladakh.[9] Several skirmishes took place in mid–1959 between Chinese and Indian patrols in the area, and the border conflict was brought to the world's attention.[10]

8. The Chinese "announced anew their claims over Indian territory by re-issuing an old map of China in July showing large areas of NEFA, Ladakh, and parts of Bhutan and Uttar Pradesh as parts of China. The border situation (in Ladakh) which had remained quiescent since late 1956 suddenly took a serious turn. . . . The first Chinese incursion into NEFA also occurred in September, 1958." See C. N. Satyapalan, *India's China Policy: The First Decade* (Ph.D. diss., University of Pennsylvania, 1964).

9. It has been strongly suggested that Krishna Menon in 1957-58 favored ceding the Aksai Chin region with its important roadbed linking Sinkiang with Tibet. Nehru considered this view as an alternative, but finally decided not to make any territorial concession to the Chinese. Had the Chinese requested permission to build the road in Aksai Chin *before* it was a *fait accompli*, Nehru probably would have given his consent without having to lose face. The writer, however, is not in a position to verify this plausible contention.

10. In September 1959 the Indian government released its first White Paper: *Notes, Memoranda and Letters Exchanged and Agreements signed between the Governments of India and China, 1954–59*, which revealed the heretofore secret exchanges of letters on the contentious border issue. For an analysis of the Indian position see Palmer. *South Asia and United States Policy*, pp. 248–66.

The first official Soviet comment on the border flareups sounded innocuous enough. After a clash occurred near Longju in the North East Frontier Agency in late August, a Radio Moscow broadcast and subsequent TASS bulletin on September 9 called on the two Governments to resolve their border problems:

> The incident on the Chinese-Indian border is certainly deplorable. . . . The Chinese and Soviet peoples are linked by the unbreakable bonds of fraternal friendship. . . . Friendly cooperation between the USSR and India is successfully developing in keeping with the idea of peaceful coexistence. . . . Its [the dispute's] inspirers are trying to discredit the idea of peaceful coexistence between States with different social systems and to prevent the strengthening of the Asian people's solidarity in the struggle for consolidation of national independence.[11]

The Russian statement on the border incident received little attention in the Western press. Most noted were the phrases "unbreakable bonds of fraternal friendship" between the Chinese and Soviet peoples, and "friendly cooperation" with India. From these phrases the inference was drawn that Russia leaned toward China on the issue.

The Chinese themselves knew better than this. An article entitled "The Truth About How the Leaders of the C.P.S.U. Have Allied Themselves With India Against China" (*Peking Review*, November 8, 1963) asserted: "On September 6, 1959 the Soviet *chargé d'affaires* in Peking was told that India's regime was provoking a Sino-Indian border conflict. The Soviets were warned not to be taken in by Nehru, who was seeking to use the Soviets for his own ends. The Soviets, however, did not accept the Chinese plea; against Peking's objections, the TASS statement of September 9 was published." Their only public acknowledgment in 1959 of the TASS bulletin reported that the Soviets had found the border incidents "deplorable." No criticism was made of the seemingly neutral stand the Soviets had taken. But the Chinese were

11. *Pravda*, September 10, 1959.

rankled by the Soviet stand, although their displeasure was not revealed to the world until late 1960, and they did not put forth their side of the story fully until November 1963.[12] The CCP leaders correctly read into the statement that the disputes inspirers (i.e., themselves) "are trying to discredit the idea of peaceful coexistence between states of different social systems." (During the exchange of polemics in 1963, the Chinese directly linked the beginnings of their differences with the USSR and other socialist nations with the failure of the USSR and other socialist countries to support unconditionally China's stand in the border conflict with India.)

The Government of India also saw the significance of the Soviet statement. At a press conference in New Delhi on September 11, Nehru reflected on the meaning of the TASS statement. "Considering everything, the statement was a fair one and an unusual one for the Soviet Government to sponsor."[13] Krishna Menon was more precise. It was the first time, he noted, that the USSR has ever come out "speaking about peaceful settlement between Communist and non-Communist parties." When probed about the possibility of Russian mediation in the dispute, the Indian defense minister replied that China and India could settle the matter themselves.[14]

It was hoped in New Delhi that Krushchev could exert some restraint on his Chinese comrades. In October, the Soviet premier flew to Peking shortly after his September meeting in the United States with President Eisenhower. He tried to persuade the Chinese that improved Soviet-American relations did not imply that he was truckling under to the "imperialists." The CCP leaders, however, were not impressed with Khrushchev's explanation of his

12. In his speech on November 14, 1960, to the delegates at the World Conference of Communist Parties in Moscow, Teng Hsaio-ping recalled that the "tendentious" TASS communiqué had "revealed our differences to the world." Cited in Crankshaw, *The New Cold War*, p. 87.

13. *Hindu*, September 12, 1959.

14. *Hindu*, September 21, 1959. A remark made by Krishna Menon in the United States on "Meet The Press."

recent conduct. The content of the private talks has not been revealed, but it can be surmised that among the Chinese grievances was the preferential treatment accorded by the Russians to the Nehru government. We can speculate on what the Chinese may have asserted: For the Soviets to have called for the inclusion of India at the proposed Summit Conference in July 1958 was bad enough. But the Soviets did not even acknowledge Indian encouragement of the Tibetan "counter-revolutionaries" after mid-April, 1959. Furthermore, the Russians along with the Americans were shoring up a "reactionary" government which lacked the support of the Indian people. While begrudging aid to fraternal socialist nations, the Russians authorized in September 1959 a loan worth $378 million for projects in India as part of its pledge to India's Third Five Year Plan. As a final provocation the USSR had refused to support the Chinese position on the border dispute; and against Chinese wishes, had permitted a statement to be published which revealed Sino-Soviet difference openly to the "imperialist camp."

Khrushchev's plea that "disputes should be settled by negotiations" evidently did not impress the Chinese. Shortly after his return from Peking, a border incident occurred in Ladakh in which nine Indian policemen were killed. The first reaction in the Soviet press to the incident was an article in *Pravda* on October 29, six days after the news was released by New Delhi. The *Pravda* account printed both the Indian and Chinese versions of the incident. All the essential facts and contradictions of the two conflicting accounts were included, but no commentary was given. Then on October 30, in a major policy speech to the Supreme Soviet, Khrushchev made extensive reference to the incident. After repeating that the USSR was "bound by unbreakable bonds of friendship" to the Chinese People's Republic and also to India, "with whom we are successfully developing friendly relations," he continued:

We are especially sorry that these incidents have resulted in loss of life to both sides. Nothing can make up for the loss of the parents and relatives of the victims. We would be happy if there were no more incidents on the Sino-Indian frontier [and] if the existing frontier disputes were settled by way of friendly negotiations to the mutual satisfaction of both sides.[15]

A week later Khrushchev called the whole dispute "sad" and "stupid," inasmuch as the area under contention had no strategic importance, nor was it even habitable. He recalled the Soviet cession of "a few kilometres of land" to Iran after World War II in order to preserve the peace.[16] On December 19 a high ranking Soviet diplomat openly spoke of his government's "embarrassment" over the border situation. "It is more than untimely," he said, " it would be inopportune at any time."[17] And on December 22 the Soviet press departed from its normal procedure and for the first time published an Indian charge against China without waiting for the Chinese rebuttal.[18]

Nehru's Reaction to the Soviet Position on the Himalayan Dispute

It is interesting to note the means by which Nehru conveyed his displeasure with the Chinese to the Soviet premier. After the incident in NEFA in late August, India's ambassador gave Khrushchev the Indian version of the clash. The TASS statement issued thereafter expressed distress over the incident. Shortly after the Indian government made public the news of the Ladakh clash on October 23, a personal message was sent by Nehru to Khrushchev. The message was carried by the Chairman of the Foreign Relations Committee of the Soviet Council of Nationalities, N. A. Mukhitdinov,

15. *Pravda*, November 1, 1959.

16. A remark reportedly made by Khrushchev to the Moscow correspondent of the *New Age* on November 7 (*New Age*, November 15, 1959).

17. *New York Times*, Paris ed., December 20, 1959.

18. H. Gelman observed: "On December 22, the Soviet press departed from its previous practice of delaying reportage on Indian notes to Communist China until they could be balanced by a C.P.R. reply; now Moscow promptly reported Nehru's letter to Chou of December 21, reiterating Nehru's preconditions for a meeting. Thus for the first time the Soviet press gave currency to non-Communist criticism of a Communist power without simultaneous rebuttal." (*Communist Strategies in Asia*, p. 116.)

who had been conferring with Indian officials in New Delhi. Mukhitdinov met Nehru on Tuesday, October 27, and returned to Moscow on Wednesday. On Thursday, the 29th, *Pravda* published an account of the incident, and on the next day Khrushchev addressed the Supreme Soviet.[19]

Had Sino-Soviet relations been on an even keel generally, the chances are that Moscow would not have responded to New Delhi's plea. But the combination of Sino-Soviet disagreement on a number of other issues apparently tipped the balance in India's favor insofar as the USSR's stand on the Himalayan border question was concerned. Moscow was not concerned with the merits of the disputants' claims as such, but with the timing and the means employed by the Chinese. The incidents were viewed as a challenge to Khrushchev's policy of "peaceful coexistence."

The reaction within official New Delhi circles was that the Soviet attitude was indirectly helpful to India. While the Soviets had not expressed any opinion publicly on the merits of the dispute, they had not supported the Chinese. By October's end, Nehru appeared to be losing hope for a "reasonable negotiated settlement" with China. He sent a "confidential memorandum" to Indian diplomats abroad, preparing them for the eventuality of India using armed forces to push the Chinese from occupied territory in Ladakh.[20] Henceforth in his public statements he drew a clear distinction between the conduct of the Soviets and the Chinese. On October 21 he told a Calcutta press conference that Khrushchev was eager and anxious for an East-West settlement, "but the same eagerness for peace is not there" in China's case. Nehru then asserted: "I consider the USSR first of all as having reached

19. Reported by K. Rangaswami in the *Hindu*, November 4, 1959. Rangaswami enjoyed the confidence of official New Delhi circles. He was among the first Indian journalists to understand the implications of the Sino-Soviet rift for India. His coverage of Mukhitdinov's role as courier between Nehru and Khrushchev in late October was not mentioned elsewhere in the Indian press.

20. The memorandum also said that the Chinese had threatened to create incidents in NEFA unless India recognized China's claim to the disputed area in Ladakh (*New York Times*, November 12, 1959).

normalcy after a revolution. Secondly, I consider the USSR as a territorially satisfied power. Of course, they might have a desire for supremacy in economic and other fields. But China has not gotten over the first flush of its revolutionary mentality." The USSR, as Nehru had pointed out on an earlier occasion, adapted itself to changing realities. "In other countries where Communist parties function without that touch of reality and a sense of responsibility, they become much more rigid."[21]

On the same theme Nehru told the Lok Sabha in November:

There is a marked difference between the broad approach of the USSR to world problems and the Chinese approach. I do not think there is any country in the world . . . which is more anxious for peace than the USSR. And I think that is the general view of people—even of their opponents. But I doubt if there is any country in the world which cares less for peace than China today.[22]

The USSR was characterized by Nehru as working for a peaceful settlement of world problems, while China was characterized as caring little for peace and as being opposed to any constructive moves by the Soviets in this direction.

Part of Nehru's effusiveness about the USSR in speaking to the Indian Parliament has to be viewed in the context of the debates themselves. The long-frustrated non-Communist opposition parties were given an opportunity to criticize the government's foreign policy.[23] Nehru sought to counter the suggestion that the USSR, being a Communist nation, was unreliable and might turn against India in the future as China had already done. It was necessary to dispel rumors that some high-level members of the CPSU leader-

---

21. *Rajya Sabha Debates*, vol. 26, no. 12 (August 25, 1959), col. 1776

22. Ibid., pt. 2, vol. 25, no. 10 (November 27, 1959), col. 2206.

23. The Indian Parliament had not been informed of the border dispute until mid–1959. Nehru argued that he had not ignored the defense of India in his enthusiasm for *Panchsheel* and termed his past policy "vigorous and watchful." Of the opposition parties, only the CPI commended Nehru's past efforts toward peaceful negotiation with the Chinese. See, e.g., *Rajya Sabha Debates*, no. 12 (December 8, 1959), cols. 1705–21.

ship supported the Chinese view on the border issue,[24] and to explain the position that the CPSU had actually taken on the dispute. In answer to those in his own Congress party who thought that India should make basic changes in its defense policy, Nehru cautioned that if India were to enter into an alliance with the Western powers, Russia would then be forced to support China. Nehru felt that the USSR was the only country which could possibly restrain the Chinese, but as early as November 5, 1959, he voiced some doubt whether China would heed the USSR.[25]

Indo-Soviet Relations in General, 1960–62

The growing tensions between India and China on the one hand and the USSR and China on the other came to the suface in 1959. Therefore until the autumn of 1962 both relationships were marked by a pattern of slowly intensifying hostility. Let us first digress for a moment from the interplay of the Sino-Soviet-Indian triangle to consider some of the particulars of Indo-Soviet relations from 1960 until the crisis of October, 1962.

Khrushchev's Second Visit to India

The first months of 1960 were marked by the state visits of a host of Soviet dignitaries to India. On January 20 a seventy-four member delegation headed by President Voroshilov, Frol Kozlov, V. Kuznetsov, and Madame Furtseva arrived in New Delhi as a prelude to Khrushchev's appearance. In a division of labor, Voroshilov concentrated on speeches extolling India's effort in consolidating

---

24. A Soviet Minister allegedly said at the Inter-Parliamentary Union Meeting in Moscow shortly after the Longju incident that India, not China, was on the offensive. Nehru, in speaking before the Rajya Sabha early in September 1959, commented that the Russian had undoubtedly been misinformed by the Chinese.

25. *Hindu*, November 5, 1959. On November 4 a Soviet diplomat in New Delhi reportedly said that Khrushchev's October 30 speech to the Supreme Soviet was the most that could be done by the USSR to relieve tension between India and China. There was no question of Khrushchev personally intervening in the matter for the present.

world peace, while the other Soviet ministers went afield to meet with various groups of Indians.[26] A few weeks later Khrushchev, en route to Indonesia, made a hastily-scheduled visit to India. Among other things, he sought to counterbalance the favorable impression made by President Eisenhower two months earlier, when the American president had been met by record throngs. He was also interested in bringing an end to the Sino-Indian border dispute.

The public enthusiasm for the Soviet premier in India did not compare with that of his 1955 visit. Taya Zinkin summed up the lack of interest: "To add insult to injury Nehru fell asleep while his guest spoke at the civic reception in Delhi to an audience half the size that greeted him last time and one-fifth the size that cheered Eisenhower a short time ago."[27]

As before, Khrushchev created a few moments of embarrassment for his hosts. After receiving a lengthy standing ovation in the Indian Parliament, he proceeded to extol the virtues of a single-party state like the Soviet Union, as opposed to the evils of the multi-party bourgeois state. He also made a jocular reference to India taking a food "dole" from the West. Before the same Parliament in December 1959, Eisenhower had given full backing to India in her dispute with China, and had given assurance that the United States would stand behind India. Khrushchev made no mention of the Sino-Indian differences, but praised the "wisdom and strength" of India's nonaligned foreign policy.[28]

At no time during his several day visit did Khrushchev discuss the removal of the Communist government from power in Kerala by the Indian central government in July 1959. Nor did he comment on the election which was being held at the time in Kerala

---

26. Kozlov visited Bhilai and the Soviet-equipped model irrigated farm at Suratgarh, Rajasthan. Madame Furtseva spoke to women's groups on such subjects as the contribution women could make to the abolition of war.

27. *Guardian* (Manchester), February 16, 1960.

28. *Hindu*, February 12, 1960.

that February.[29] He was apparently determined not to do anything that could be construed as interfering in India's domestic affairs. While the Soviet leaders may have welcomed a CPI victory in Kerala, their thoughts on the subject were completely muted.

Khrushchev apparently urged Nehru to enter into negotiations with Chou En-lai on the border question. It is unlikely that he exerted pressure as such, but he held that it was in the interest of all concerned to have a negotiated settlement. Khrushchev wished to see the matter resolved quickly. From his standpoint any future outbreaks would be nothing but troublesome to the USSR. Sino-Indian talks would also contribute to a "relaxation of international tensions" prior to the summit meeting scheduled in Paris that summer.

After speaking with Khrushchev on February 12, Nehru told the Rajya Sabha: "As things stand now I see no ground for a meeting, no bridge between the Chinese position and ours. There is no room for negotiations on that basis and there is nothing to negotiate now. But it may arise later."[30] Nehru probably told Khrushchev that the next move must come from Peking if there were to be any negotiations. Such a Chinese move would have to be conciliatory enough to inspire the confidence of the Indian government and people that the Chinese really desired a peaceful settlement of the dispute.

Yet Khrushchev's request that India try to reach some settlement with China on the border probably influenced Nehru's decision several weeks later to meet with Chou in April. Continued rejection of Chou's offer to confer would have created the impression that the Indian government was adopting an unreasonable

29. The Communist government in Kerala had been removed from office and the state placed under the rule of the central government in mid–1959. In the February 1960 election the CPI won a slightly greater percentage of the popular vote than that received in 1957, but their number of seats in the Kerala Assembly decreased from 60 to 26. A summary of the Keralan situation is included in Palmer, *The Indian Political System*, pp. 232–33.

30. *Hindu*, February 13, 1960.

attitude. The Soviet request that Sino-Indian talks be held could not be regarded lightly. In April Chou came to Delhi and held talks with Nehru, but the positions of both countries on the border issue had become so rigidly set that there was no basis for compromise. A statement issued by the two leaders patched over the disagreement somewhat. It was agreed, for instance, that officials of the two governments should meet and "examine, check and study all historical documents, records, accounts, maps and other materials relevant to the boundary question." In accordance with this plan, there was an exchange of letters, documents, etc., over the next two years, but no meaningful dialogue took place. During this period India put forth a more concerted effort to document its position than did China. The real nature of the problems between China and India, however, were political, not cartographical, and the official meetings came to naught.

The USSR displayed continued willingness to assist India's economic growth in spite of Peking's displeasure. Among the Khrushchev entourage was A. Mikoyan, who examined the plans to utilize the $378 million aid pledged by the USSR for India's Third Five Year Plan.[31] Also, talks were held with the Indian Atomic Energy Commission on possible Indo-Soviet collaboration in the development of peaceful uses of atomic energy.[32] In the succeeding months a number of delegations made visits between India and the USSR to discuss trade, Soviet economic aid, and similar matters. On August 30, 1960, the USSR offered an additional sixty crores rupees (about $122 million) for India's Third Five Year Plan, making a total commitment of 240 crores ($500 million) to the Plan. In vivid contrast to this increased aid to India,

31. The Soviet projects for India's Third Five Year Plan are listed in chapter 7, pp. 175–77.

32. An agreement calling for Indo-Soviet "cooperation in research connected with the development of atomic power reactors" and for the "reciprocal exchange of scientific information and for visits of specialists in the various aspects of the peaceful uses of atomic energy" was subsequently signed in October 1961. *Statesman*, October 7, 1961).

many Soviet technicians were withdrawn from China in the autumn of 1960 and many Chinese trainees departed from the USSR. Extensive Soviet aid commitments to India were being fulfilled on schedule, while the projects envisioned under the Sino-Soviet Agreement of 1959 lagged seriously. In 1961 the supply of Soviet military equipment to India added a new complexity to the Sino-Soviet-Indian triangle. In April 1961 the Indian Defense Ministry purchased eight Antonov-12 turboprop transport planes, which were put to use immediately in the Ladakh area. Later, 24 Ilyushin-14 transports were acquired. Then in mid-1962 it was announced tha the USSR would sell India two squadrons of MIG-21 fighters and would subsequently build several factories in India to manufacture MIG's.[33]

The Nehru-Khrushchev communiqué contained no mention of the Sino-Indian dispute. Nehru recognized the recent reduction in the troop level of the Soviet armed forces and repeated "his appreciation of Khrushchev's proposals for total disarmament." They were, in essence, a call for the application of the principle of nonviolence to the solution of international problems.[34] The identity of view of the two countries on problems of world peace, and the common allegiance to the principles of peaceful coexistence, were repeated. An unprecendented reference was also made to President Eisenhower, when it was suggested that the lessening in world tensions was "due in no small measure to the personal initiative and coordinated effort of the leaders of the Great Powers, notably Mr. Khrushchev and Mr. Eisenhower." Paradoxically, Khrushchev's visit to India coincided with the date of the tenth anniversary of the 1950 Sino-Soviet Treaty.

India, An "Area of Agreement" for the United States and the USSR

The possibility of conflict with China gave the Indian government additional reason to be on good terms with both superpowers.

33. See chapter 7, pp. 205–7.

34. Complete text of communiqué reprinted in *Hindustan Times*, February 17, 1960.

For the most part Indo-American misunderstandings had lessened since 1956.[35] President Eisenhower in late 1959 had declared that the United States backed India in its dispute with China, and he had intimated that the USA would come to India's assistance in the event of military emergency.[36] It is doubtful whether Nehru in 1960 (or for that matter in 1962) anticipated anything much more than Soviet moral support in the event of an overt conflict with China. He nonetheless had reason to believe that the USSR viewed the Sino-Indian dispute with a pro-Indian "neutrality."

It was in India's interest to see a rapprochement between her Russian and American benefactors. Nehru wished to convince the United States of the Soviet determination to come to a mutual understanding, and he contrasted this with the Chinese intransigence. In an interview in December 1959 he told an American reporter:

The USSR seems to be . . . almost determined to come to a settlement with the West. They are very keen on this for reasons one can understand. I mean selfish reasons, not humanitarian reasons. . . . Russia with its vast expanse isn't short of territory. They want to show that they can progress economically at a rapid pace and impress the world. . . . China is somewhat different. At the present moment their mentality does not fit into this Russian mentality.[37]

When the proposed summit meeting between Khrushchev and Eisenhower was called off in the aftermath of the U-2 incident, Nehru was sorely disappointed. Several months afterwards he told the Indian upper house that "on the whole the general attitude of

35. See P. Talbot and S. Poplai, *India and America* (New York: Harper, 1958).

36. During their August 1959 talks Eisenhower and Prime Minister MacMillan had discussed Sino-Indian relations. After that time the Western allies indicated they would not tolerate any Chinese aggression against India. An understanding apparently was reached between Nehru and Eisenhower (and later the Kennedy administration) that Anglo-American aid would be forthcoming in the event of an emergency situation.

37. Quoted in the *Hindu*, May 22, 1959.

the great countries is so rigid now that all the previous flexibility has gone."[38] But even the summit breakdown did not change his appraisal "that both Khrushchev and Eisenhower are anxious for peace, desire peace."

There was little reason, maintained Nehru, for the two Cold War antagonists to be at loggerheads. The USSR and the United States had so much in common that their dispute was artificial and unrealistic. Once the fear and suspicions had been cleared away, an area of agreement might emerge between the two nations. On the same theme Nehru told the upper house of Parliament on August 18, 1960, that "it is a remarkable thing and it is worth considering how these two tremendous protagonists of the Cold War can yet have this friendly feeling for India. We have not tried to buy their friendship by any weakness of ours or by any subservience to anybody."[39]

Nehru was prone to emphasize the similarities which he observed in American and Soviet societies. In his *Discovery of India*, written during the latter stages of World War II, he had made the comparsion:

All the evils of a purely political democracy are present in the USA; the evils of the lack of political democracy are present in the USSR. And yet they have much in common—a dynamic outlook and vast resources, a social fluidity, an absence of medieval background, a faith in science and its applications, and widespread education and opportunities for the people. (p. 553)

Both countries had the "basis for a progressive, democratic society," he observed, and in neither could a small elite long dominate over an educationally and culturally advanced people."

Nehru understood the influence exerted by the USSR and the United States in the contemporary world. On one occasion in Parliament he quoted the prophecy made by Tocqueville in 1835

38. *Rajya Sabha Official Reports*, vol. 30, no. 7 (August 17, 1960), cols. 1128–29.

39. Ibid., vol. 30, no. 8 (August 18, 1960), col. 1353.

on the unheralded rise of Russia and the United States to world prominence.[40] Both of these nations were now friendly to India and assisting in her development. India appreciated the help of both nations, given without political strings attached. Nehru was able to take pride in emphasizing that the USSR had given aid "not to a country that was subservient to them, but to a free country which had an independent policy."

Concern about Indian Over-involvement with the USSR

Some Indian politicians understandably were concerned lest the government, in its desire to pursue its policy of "peaceful cooperation," move too close to the USSR. They therefore urged that appropriate caution be exercised. An expression of this concern was made by Sudhir Ghosh (Praja Socialist party) in the upper house in August 1960. After praising Nehru for having developed good relations with a country like the USSR, which "has an entirely different political system from India's," Ghosh suggested that the USSR was perhaps too deeply involved in India's economic activities and planning:

Russia today is more deeply involved in the economic activities, economic plans and programs of India than in any other country outside the Communist camp. Her participation in our activities extends over a very wide field: steel . . . , oil drilling and refineries, pharmaceuticals, . . . atomic energy, heavy machine building.[41]

The non-Communist opposition parties in Parliament did not recommend that the government drastically alter its basic policy towards the USSR. The fear nonetheless was privately expressed by some that the USSR, like China, might someday "betray" India's good faith.

During the question hour in Parliament, opposition members sometimes asked the government questions about the USSR's

40. *Lok Sabha Debates*, pt 2, vol. 46, no. 24 (September 1, 1960), col. 6216.
41. *Rajya Sabha Official Reports*, vol. 30, no. 7 (August 17, 1960), cols. 1241–42.

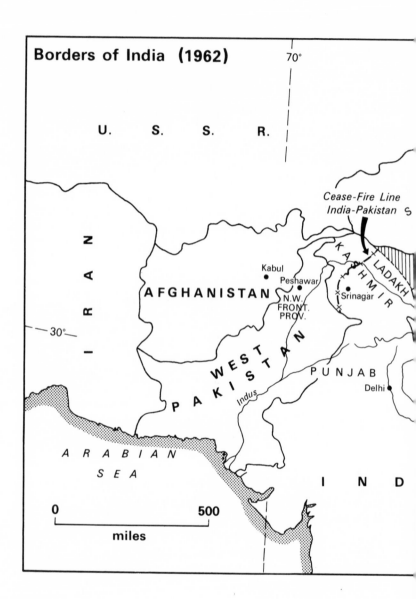

Borders of India (1962)

70°

U. S. S. R.

Cease-Fire Line
India-Pakistan

IRAN

AFGHANISTAN

Kabul
Peshawar
N.W.
FRONT.
PROV.

KASHMIR

LADAKH

Srinagar

30°

WEST
PAKISTAN

PUNJAB

Delhi

Indus

ARABIAN
SEA

IND

0   500
miles

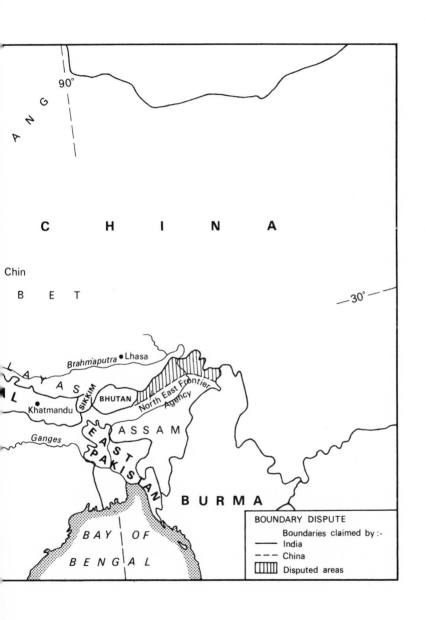

90°

ANG

CHINA

Chin

BET

30°

Brahmaputra • Lhasa

LAYAS

SIKKIM

BHUTAN

North East Frontier
Agency

L

• Khatmandu

Ganges

EAST PAKISTAN

ASSAM

BURMA

BAY OF
BENGAL

BOUNDARY DISPUTE

Boundaries claimed by :-
——— India
- - - China
Disputed areas

policy. One such question dealt with Soviet maps of the Himalayan areas, which from the Indian standpoint were incorrectly drawn. These maps, most of which had been drawn up before the Sino-Indian border had come into the open, often depicted territory in the disputed areas to be Chinese.[42] The fact that the Soviet maps seemingly reinforced the Chinese claims was deplored in New Delhi.

In April 1959 Mrs. Lakshmi Menon, deputy minister for external affairs, reported that the Indian government had already drawn the attention of the respective governments to the "discrepancies" in Chinese and Soviet maps depicting parts of India as part of China.[43] It was later revealed that the 1959 edition of the *Soviet World Atlas* (*Atlas mira*) showed India's international border as south of Sikkim and Bhutan instead of to the north as depicted by Indian maps.[44] The 1959 *Atlas mira*, like the 1955 edition, showed the Aksai Chin area of Ladakh, South East Bhutan, and NEFA as Chinese. (It should be remembered that the Soviet maps, like the *Large Soviet Encyclopedia* and other such publications, are compiled many months before they are published. That the maps should have coincided with the Chinese claims as late as 1961 did not mean that the Soviet government supported Chinese claims to the area, let alone any military effort to establish supremacy in the disputed areas.)

The Indian government was sensitive to criticism that its close dealings with the USSR might endanger Indian security. When a minor espionage scandal broke out in January 1961 involving several junior members of the Soviet embassy, Nehru was very reluctant to discuss the matter publicly. It was rumored that three employees of the embassy had been passing on information to the

42. An evaluation of the respective Indian and Chinese claims to the disputed areas of Ladakh is made by Fisher, Rose, and Huttenback in *Himalayan Battleground*.

43. *Lok Sabha Debates*, pt. 2, vol. 30, no. 52 (April 22, 1959), cols. 12715-21.

44. An article in the *Times of India*, March 3, 1961, called attention to the Russian maps.

Chinese about Indian roadbuilding activities in the Himalayan regions. Nehru dismissed the matter by disclosing on March 3 that the Soviet ambassador to India had apologized for the espionage activities and that those members of his staff that had been involved were dismissed.[45] On March 30, 1962, Nehru told the Rajya Sabha that "adequate precaution had been taken to see that no secret information could leak out" to Russian pilots who were flying training missions in the Ladakh area. The Russians were instructing Indian pilots and crews in the use of the transport planes recently purchased from the USSR.

Nehru at the United Nations (October, 1960)

A glimpse into the nature of Indo-Soviet relations on the international scene in 1960–61 is afforded by Nehru's participation in the turbulent session of the UN General Assembly in the autumn of 1960. Before arriving at the UN session, Nehru revealed that for the first time India would not sponsor the resolution calling for the seating of the Chinese People's Republic in the world organization. Public opinion in India, he explained, was opposed to India taking such an active part on China's behalf. India would nonetheless vote for a Soviet-sponsored resolution supporting Communist China.[46] From 1960 onwards India continued to vote for the seating of the Chinese People's Republic, but with little enthusiasm.

Nehru was unwilling to accept Khrushchev's call for a reorganization of the UN Secretariat. He told the Assembly on October 3 that while he did not rule out future changes in the structure of the UN, he was opposed to the "troika principle" or "any change in the UN structure at present."

India and four other nonaligned nations put forth a proposal in the Assembly which was unacceptable to the United States. The

45. *Hindu*, February 24, March 1, 3. 1962. It was reported in several other newspapers that Khrushchev was embarrassed by the incident and had given orders for the Soviet and East European embassies to cease espionage activities in India.

46. *Hindu*, September 26, 1960.

resolution in effect called for an Eisenhower-Khrushchev meeting as soon as possible to ease the tensions created by the U-2 incident. (The USSR neither opposed nor accepted Nehru's proposal, but Eisenhower made it clear that he did not want to be pressured into such a meeting.) A counter-resolution, termed "absurd" by Nehru, was then sponsored by Australia. This resolution in substance said that Big Four relations were the concern of the parties immediately involved; namely, the USSR, USA, Great Britain, and France. In exasperation Nehru withdrew the resolution of the five-neutral nations following the adoption of an Argentinian amendment which deleted the names of Eisenhower and Khrushchev and in Nehru's view divested the original resolution of its sense of urgency.[47]

Nehru was rankled that the United States had apparently given its blessings to the Australian amendment which "cut the uncommitted nations down to size." Upon returning to India he still seemed preoccupied over the matter. He told some members of Parliament that he had liked the attitude of the Communist leaders at the UN. They had kept in constant contact with him, trying to convert him to their viewpoint and to convince him that they respected his views. He contrasted the Soviet attitude with that of the West towards the uncommitted nations. He had met with Eisenhower and Macmillan for only one hour each, and that had been his sole personal contact there with the Western leaders.[48] (His experience at the UN had evidently given Nehru an additional reason for which to welcome the victory of the Democratic candidate, John F. Kennedy, in the American presidential election that November).

When the Congo issue was brought up at the autumn session of

47. *Hindu*, October 5, 1960.

48. See *Hindu*, October 19, 1960. Several speakers from the Swatantra, P.S.P. and Jan Sangh parties were critical of Nehru's conduct at the UN. They felt the prime minister had given the impression that he was inclined to minimize the shortcomings of the Communist nations. See *Lok Sabha Debates*, pt. 2, vol. 47, no. 7 (November 22, 1960).

the General Assembly, India and the USSR were in agreement only on the point that the Belgian forces should be withdrawn from Katanga. The Soviets wished to oust the UN command in the Congo and tried to enlist support for the Lumumba government. To solidify Lumumba's position, the Soviets threatened to give unilateral aid to his government. On its part India held that all financial, technical, and military aid to the Congo must be channeled through the United Nations.

Disagreement between India and the USSR on how to handle the Congo situation increased after the assassination of Lumumba in 1961. Nehru denounced the murder of Lumumba, but expressed disagreement with the Soviet contention that the UN should immediately withdraw its forces from the Congo. Such a withdrawal, warned Nehru, would lead to civil war and large-scale intervention by outside powers that could develop into a conflict of world-wide involvement.[49] When several African nations (Ghana, Guinea, the UAR, and Morocco) did withdraw their forces from the Congo, Nehru quickly responded to Hammerskjöld's request for Indian replacements, even before he asked the consent of the Indian Parliament. Needless to say the Soviets were disturbed by Nehru's action. Their displeasure was reflected in an article written for Pravda by Ajoy Ghosh, secretary-general of the CPI,[50] and in the resolution passed by the Sixth Party Congress of the CPI held in April 1961.[51]

Like the USSR, but not so vehemently, Nehru criticized the ill-fated Bay of Pigs invasion of Cuba. Nehru told the lower house of the Indian Parliament on April 21, 1961, that there should be no interference in Cuba by outside countries. "If the Cubans themselves want either to do something to their present government or not," he declared, "it is up to them to decide. Others should not intervene."

49. *Hindu*, February 16, 1961.
50. *Pravda*, April 5, 1961.
51. *New Age*, May 7, 1961.

The Belgrade Conference (September 1961)

Despite its own nonaligned stance in the Cold War, the Indian government had some reservations about holding a conference of nonaligned nations. Nehru did not want to be identified with any anti-Western resolutions that such a conference might adopt. At a preliminary meeting held in Cairo in June 1961, the Indian representative opposed the seating of the Stanleyville government of Antoine Gizenga, whereas 14 of the 20 representatives present voted to seat the Gizenga regime.[52] India also questioned the neutral status of such countries as Cuba and Liberia.[53]

In a letter to Tito, Nehru opposed the concept of a "neutralist bloc." He also expressed concern that the Belgrade Conference might be dominated by some of the smaller, more radical nations. Tito in reply did his best to mollify India's prime minister, for without Nehru's participation the conference would lack the most universally respected leader of the *tiers-monde*.

India definitely was a moderating force at Belgrade.[54] Whether or not the conference would nonetheless have developed strong anti-Western overtones must remain unknown, for on the very eve before the meetings began the delegates were startled by the resumption of Soviet nuclear testing. The concern over the unilateral abrogation of the testing moratorium did not lead to a condemnation of the Soviet action. Tito, Sukarno, and Nasser referred to

52. A number of African countries, notably Ghana, Guinea, and Mali, were dubious of India's position on African affairs. President Kennedy's statement that American views on the Congo were essentially the same as India's led them to think that India was working for a "Western-type solution" to the Congo problem. These African nations were also dissatisfied with India's "soft" stand on Algeria.

53. At the Cairo preliminary meetings the representatives of the nations present decided by unanimous vote which other nations should be invited to Belgrade. To Nehru the role of Cuba in excluding a number of nonaligned Latin American countries, Cyprus, and Tanganyika was far out of proportion to her size and importance.

54. A senior Yugoslav delegate who attended the conference told this writer that it was extremely difficult to get the Indian delegates to agree on anything. In this regard he mentioned Tito's exasperation in trying to obtain India's acceptance of the final commuiqué.

the Soviet tests only in passing. Nehru, however, termed the present situation the most dangerous crisis which had arisen in fifteen years and said it would be a "tragedy" if the delegates parted without making their voices heard. He advised that the conference should not condemn one side or the other, but should emphatically stress that East-West negotiations had become imperative.[55]

The conference designated Nehru (who had previously scheduled a short tour to the USSR on his way back to India from Belgrade) and Kwame Nkrumah of Ghana to convey the concern of the nonaligned nations to the Soviets. In Moscow Nehru told Premier Khrushchev that the resumption of atomic testing retarded disarmament talks and aggravated international tensions. With implicit reference to the Soviet nuclear testing, Nehru told his hosts on September 7 that "everything that may lead to war causes us the greatest concern. . . . Respecting all countries as I do, I still have to say that in our time, in our era, to start a war against anyone is ultimate folly." Khrushchev told Nehru in return that the USSR had resumed testing "with heavy hearts and deep regrets." On the day following his talks with Khrushchev, Nehru remarked to a group of Indians: "Once again the foul winds of war are blowing. There are atomic tests and the world grows fearful." The gravity of the talks on the East-West situation did not constrain Nehru from thanking the Soviets for their economic aid. "I am afraid," he told a luncheon group at the Indian embassy, "that after we receive this assistance [for India's Third Plan] my appetite will grow and I will ask for more."[56]

If Nehru had any inkling as to why the Soviets chose the eve of the Belgrade Conference to begin the tests, he said nothing publicly on the subject. In Moscow he emphasized India's past and present opposition to nuclear testing. When he was later criticized by some quarters in the West for not speaking out as strongly as

55. *Hindu,* September 4, 1961.

56. *New York Times,* September 8, 1961. See also *Hindustan Times* and *Statesman,* September 9, 1961.

he might have against the Soviet action, Nehru was "puzzled and somewhat distressed." He said as if in reply that "we were shocked and grieved by the resumption of nuclear tests by the Soviet government. I have laid stress on that whenever I have had occasion to talk."[57] In principle Nehru supported Khrushchev's proposal for general and complete disarmament, but more realistic first steps to arms control had to be taken before such a sweeping proposal could be seriously considered.[58]

The Annexation of Goa (December 1961)

In December 1961 the unfavorable Indian reaction to Soviet nuclear testing was more than compensated for by the immediate and favorable Russian response to India's military annexation of Goa and the tiny enclaves of Daman and Diu.

Since the early 1950's Nehru had resisted domestic pressures to resolve the Goan question by force, hoping that the Portuguese might follow the precedent set by the French in the peaceful withdrawal from Pondicherry. It became apparent, however, that the Portuguese were determined to retain their Indian enclaves. Among the factors which influenced Nehru to give in to the demands for the military "liberation" of Goa was mounting public opinion. All of the opposition parties and several of Nehru's close associates within the Congress party called for action. The fact that 1961 was a pre-election year increased the clamor. Nehru probably reasoned that India could bolster her diminishing stature in the eyes of Afro-Asians by action against the Portuguese. The sub-Saharan Africans in particular would applaud any measure directed against Portuguese colonialism. It might also have been rationalized that a swift military maneuver would produce fewer casualties (it did) than the frequent clashes between Goan police and Indian groups along Goa's borders.

57. From a report by Paul Grimes in the *New York Times*, October 31, 1961.

58. India's role in the atmospheric test-ban agreement of 1963 is discussed by Homer Jack,"Non-Alignment and the Test Ban Agreement: The Role of the Non-Aligned States," *Journal of Conflict Resolution*, 7, no. 3; pp. 542 ff.

In the Indian Parliament on December 7 Nehru gave a hint that firmer steps would be taken on the Goan issue:

We have always been reluctant, as the House knows, to solve problems by application of force. . . . But I must say that the Portuguese attitude [on Goa] has been exasperating in the extreme. It has been difficult for us to restrain our feelings or the consequent actions. . . . Therefore we felt that we should be perfectly prepared for any developments and consequences, and we have taken some steps to that end. What exactly will happen, I cannot say at the present moment, because it depends on circumstances, on developments. . . . But the present position is not to be tolerated.[59]

The next day Portugal protested the massing of 30,000 Indian troops and air and naval units on the borders of Goa. Ten days later the Indian forces crossed the Goan borders and occupied the enclave within 36 hours.

It remains a moot point whether or not the Soviets were informed beforehand of the Indian plan to annex Goa. Several days before the military move took place, the president of the USSR, Leonid Brezhnev, arrived in India on a goodwill tour. He reassured a meeting of the Indo-Soviet Cultural Society on December 17 that "the Soviet people regarded with full understanding and sympathy the desire of the Indian people to achieve the liberation of Goa, Daman, and Diu."[60] That evening at midnight the military operation began. On December 18, the day that the Indian public and the outside world learned of the takeover, Brezhnev assured a civic reception in Bombay of firm Russian support for the action. He noted the recent Khrushchev statement at the twenty-second Congress of the CPSU which called for the elimination of Portuguese colonialism from India.[61]

In the UN Security Council the USSR vetoed a resolution sponsored by the United States, the United Kingdom, France, and

59. *Lok Sabha Debates*, pt. 2, vol. 40, no. 15 (December 7, 1961), col. 3864.
60. *Hindu*, December 18, 1961.
61. *Statesman*, December 19, 1961.

Turkey calling for an end to the hostilities. The Soviet delegate, V. Zorin, said his vote represented a victory for the "true principles" of the UN Charter: "Today saw . . . the expression of the will to defend colonial countries and peoples and their right to life, freedom, and independence."[62]

The Indian news media and general public alike were pleased and excited by the Goan adventure. Angered by the firm language of Adlai Stevenson and other delegates from Western nations, the Indian government was comforted by the words of the Russians. Some organs of the Indian press, usually more circumspect about Indo-Soviet relations now, defended their nation's policy in a surge of chauvinistic vigor. One of the more frank appraisals of India's attitude towards the USSR appeared in the *Times of India:*

Since New Delhi's foreign policy is not ideologically determined, its friendly ties with the USSR contain no element of hypocrisy or make believe. It is a straightforward relationship unaffected by different and even inconvenient social and economic systems and uncomplicated by any desire to convert each other to a different point of view. . . . Not every aspect of Soviet policy regarding Berlin, disarmament or nuclear control is acceptable to New Delhi, but Moscow's recognition of the fact that any complete identity of views is unnecessary is most encouraging.[63]

Moscow was willing to give New Delhi unequivocal support in defending its Goan venture, whether or not there had been prior consultation between the two governments on the issue. Unaccustomed to being reproached for its international conduct, the Indian government was appreciative of the "profound sympathy and understanding of its aspirations" shown by the Soviets.

62. *UN Security Council, Official Records,* 16th sess., 987th mtg. (December 18, 1961), pp. 21–26.

63. *Times of India,* December 20, 1961.

6 The Himalayan Confrontation, 1962-64

NEW Delhi was in large measure satisfied that the Soviets had not supported China's position on the Sino-Indian border flareups of 1959. While the Soviets did not say anything publicly on the merits of the dispute as such, the Chinese viewed the Soviet statements as provocative and unfriendly. It was the first time that any Communist nation had ever taken a neutral stance in a dispute between another Communist nation and a non-Communist state.

Nehru hoped to maintain and, if possible, strengthen his bonds of "friendly cooperation" with the USSR, particularly in the event of continuing Sino-Indian hostilities. Undoubtedly he had ambivalent feelings about the increasing strain in the Sino-Soviet alliance. Presumably their mutual disagreements with China gave India and the USSR an additional common interest. However, the chances of the USSR being able to exercise some restraint on Chinese policy towards India lessened as Moscow and Peking grew further apart.

The deep rift between the CPSU and the CCP was further exposed at the Third Conference of the Rumanian Communist party held in Bucharest in June 1960. There Premier Khrushchev and his colleagues, and the Chinese delegation led by Marshal Peng

139

exchanged recriminations against each other's ideology and recent conduct in world affairs.[1] Having arrived from Paris after the aborted Summit meeting Khrushchev was incensed that the Chinese had reproduced a private letter from the CPSU to the CCP for the conference's edification. He delivered an impromptu attack on China's post-1957 domestic policies and on the way the Chinese were trying to force their views on other Communist nations. He even touched upon the recent strain in Sino-Soviet military co-operation. In answering the Chinese charge that the USSR had not supported them in their border conflict with India, Khrushchev in turn said that it was China that had let the cause of socialism down by quarreling with India.[2] The Sino-Indian dispute itself was purely nationalist in origin, having nothing to do with ideology.

At the Moscow conference of eighty-one Communist parties in November, 1960, the Soviets and Chinese put their respective cases before the assemblage.[3] Teng Hsaio-ping, the leader of the Chinese group, rebutted Khrushchev's remarks at Bucharest against intemperate Chinese conduct towards India. The border dispute, explained Teng, was deliberately engineered by the Indian government to help postpone its overthrow by the "people." To expose the plot of the "Nehru clique" the CCP was entitled to call on the support of the CPI and other Communist parties. But the USSR,

1. See Zagoria, *The Sino-Soviet Conflict*, pp. 319–39.

2. Khrushchev's remarks about the Sino-Indian dispute are paraphrased by Edward Crankshaw, *The New Cold War*, p. 108: "By quarreling with the Government of India they had not merely failed to work with the Russians towards the socialization of India; they had worked against it. Of course, Nehru was a capitalist. But the Chinese dispute with him had nothing to do with capitalism and Socialism: it was a purely nationalist dispute and it had done the Socialist cause untold harm, quite apart from such details as losing Kerala to Communism. What right had Peng to complain of lack of support in such circumstances, especially when anyway it was impossible to get at the rights and wrongs of the dispute?"

3. For a discussion of the Moscow conference see Zagoria, *The Sino-Soviet Conflict*, pp. 343–69.

by its actions, was helping to shore up the "reactionary" Indian government.[4]

The joint communiqués of the Bucharest and Moscow conferences concealed for the most part, the real nature of the Sino-Soviet rift, and the proceedings were not publicly revealed until early 1961. It can be assumed, though, that the Government of India was reasonably well-informed of what had occurred. India had informants among the East European Communist parties, and in New Delhi there were few secrets between the "left wing" of the Congress party and the "right-wing" of the CPI. Insofar as the dialogues between Khrushchev and Marshal Peng at Bucharest and the Soviet premier and Teng at Moscow represented their respective parties' viewpoints toward India, they were of extreme interest to New Delhi.

The Chinese were "stepping in where Russia feared to tread," recognizing the Algerian rebel government, openly supporting the unrecognized Communist party of Iraq, and giving encouragement to exiled Communist leaders from the United Arab Republic.[5] In 1960–61 the Chinese also tried to lessen somewhat the strong Soviet influence over the CPI. The Central Executive of the CPI supported both the Bucharest and Moscow resolutions while the Russian position on peaceful coexistence and support for Nehru's government was reflected in its official declarations. An important minority of the CPI, however, particularly the "leftist" faction of West Bengal, was very reluctant to endorse any resolution which sided with the CPSU at the expense of the CCP. Encouraged by the way in which the Chinese withstood the criticism levied against them at the Moscow Conference, the "leftists" intensified their criticisms of the Dange-Ghosh leadership for the latter's compromising attitude towards the Nehru government.[6]

---

4. Crankshaw, *The New Cold War*, p. 127.

5. *London Times*, June 13, 1960.

6. In October 1960 the West Bengal party sharply criticized the Central Executive Committee for having sided with the Russians without having fully

Indirectly the Government of India gave its backing to the "moderate" faction of the CPI in the party's internecine struggle. A manifestation of this governmental policy was in the decision to grant visas to a delegation of five Soviet observers, headed by M. Suslov, to attend the Sixth CPI Congress in April 1961. A group of Chinese observers were refused visas.[7] The appearance of Suslov at the congress and his basic endorsement of the program being pursued by the CPI helped to bolster up the "moderate" Ghosh faction in the face of increased criticism of his program by the Andhra and Bengali groups.

While the differences between Peking and Moscow were obviously of utmost importance to him, Nehru restricted his public commentary on the matter to a few generalizations. On one of the infrequent occasions when he did discuss the subject before Parliament, he described the "ideological conflict" within the Communist world as a "fairly big one" in which the Chinese and Russians were thinking and pulling in different ways. His own interest, said Nehru, was "not from the point of view of which ideology is correct," but stemmed from the effect which the dispute was having on world problems. The Chinese thesis that war is inevitable would mean "our living in a state of semi-war all the time, intense cold war, some time or other breaking into full war. As I understand it, that is not the attitude of the Soviet Government. So it is a very vital difference."[8]

In 1957–58 Nehru had been criticized by the USSR for commenting on Russian relations with the Eastern European nations. In the 1960's he was subjected to much more intense fire from the Chinese for trying to foment and exacerbate the differences between Peking and Moscow. The Indian government stressed the

"acquainted itself with the views of the Chinese." (Gelman, *Communist Strategies in Asia*, pp. 117–24.)

7. A few weeks earlier New Delhi had refused to grant a Chinese delegation permission to attend a meeting of the World Peace Organization being held in India.

8. *Lok Sabha Debates*, pt. 2. vol. 47, no. 8 (November 23, 1960), cols. 1956–57.

importance of Indo-Soviet friendship and cooperation to both countries. Whenever possible, Indian diplomats (some more subtly than others) would drop hints that the combined danger or hostility from China and Pakistan might cause New Delhi to reconsider its nonaligned policy. It was known to the Indian External Affairs Ministry that Khrushchev had a continuing interest in Indian non-alignment. In 1961 Khrushchev had raised his commitment to India's Third Five Year Plan by 60 crores rupees and had for the first time provided New Delhi with some military equipment. In addition, Indian officials were always given a ready hearing when-ever they had occasion to make a complaint against Chinese con-duct. In this light, it would have been superfluous, as well as inopportune, for the Indian government to interfere openly in the Sino-Soviet rift. Hence the relative restraint in New Delhi's efforts to exploit Moscow-Peking differences.

China was portrayed as the ingracious recipient of Indian good-will. Lal Bahadur Shastri, in moving the resolution on foreign policy at the annual All India Congress Committee (AICC) meet-ing in May, 1961, summed up this sentiment. He pointed out that besides Russia, India was the only country which had given the utmost support to China. India had tried to maintain friendly rela-tions, supported China's cause in the United Nations, and so forth. He then noted: "Russia and China differed in their approach to world problems. While the USSR and most of its supporters be-lieved in the policy of coexistence and building a socialist or Com-munist society by peaceful methods, the Chinese and their sup-porters thought that society could be built up only through class conflict and violence."[9]

The Sino-Indian Border War, 1962

There are some aspects of the Sino-Indian relationship that are still shrouded in uncertainty. From what is known, however, it appears that China bore a large share of responsibility for

9. *Hindu*, May, 1961.

making the border question with India a serious issue between the two countries. She had occupied the Aksai Chin salient between Tibet and Sinkiang during the days of cordial relations, and in 1956–57 had built a strategically important roadway there. During those days it is possible that the Chinese might have successfully negotiated a settlement on the Aksai Chin, but if they ever attempted to do so it is not a matter of record. As Sino-Indian relations worsened, the Chinese began to encroach into uninhabited areas of Ladakh claimed by both countries and to set up a number of guardposts.

The appointment of V. K. Krishna Menon as defence minister in 1957 roughly coincided with the Indian government's decision to build up defences along the borders adjoining Chinese territory. Previously India had concentrated practically all of its forces along the frontiers with West Pakistan. (Even at the outbreak of major Sino-Indian fighting in 1962 the bulk of Indian forces were still keyed on Pakistan.) The 1959 skirmishes at several points along the borders in Ladakh and the North East Frontier Agency suddenly made the border question a highly volatile political issue in India, particularly since almost all information on the matter had previously been withheld from the Indian populace. Opposition party leaders seized upon the opportunity to attack the long-dominant Congress party, and the press, both responsible and otherwise, kept the matter in public focus. The Indian populace had not been informed that there was a border problem with China until September 1959; thereafter the pressures of public opinion inhibited New Delhi's diplomatic flexibility in dealing with China. By the autumn of 1961 New Delhi had committed itself to matching China post for post in the disputed territory, and had launched what came to be known as a "Forward Policy" in Ladakh by outflanking the Chinese posts.[10] Some leading Indian army

10. B. M. Kaul, *The Untold Story* (Bombay, 1967), p. 280 ff. Lieutenant General Kaul, who was strongly attacked for his role in India's military setback, has written an autobiography in which he lashes back at his critics. The book is marred by some of the authors personal vendettas, including an almost paranoic

officers made the point, although not very forcefully, that India
was undermanned in Ladakh and NEFA, numerically, logistically,
and in the quality of weaponry. But Nehru and presumably Krishna
Menon made the calculated assumption that China in any event
would not wage war with India over the matter, and that a pro-
fusion of Indian posts, however undermanned, would deter the
Chinese. "In the spring of 1962 Nehru sanctioned a more provocative policy in Ladakh, involving direct attempts to cut the lines of
communication to the Chinese forward posts."[11] Peking's reply in
turn was to set up more forward posts and to warn India in increasingly sharper diplomatic notes of the possible consequences
of the course it was pursuing. India continued its buildup along
the borders, although Nehru and Menon were both opposed to
taking an American offer of weapons which, while strengthening
the defences, might have compromised the nonalignment policy.

In July 1962 the Chinese surrounded a small Gurkha post in
the Galwan River Valley in Ladakh, leaving the personnel there
a path of retreat. But the Indians held their ground and the Chinese eventually withdrew. Lorne Kavic has surmised that

In retrospect, this incident in the Galwan River Valley appears to
have been of great significance. To Peking, it must have indicated
that the Indian Government was now prepared to risk an armed clash
to maintain its positions and the Chinese posts would either have to
be abandoned as the supply lines to the individual forward posts were
cut, or be secured through offensive action against the Indian forces.
From the standpoint of New Delhi, the Chinese withdrawal was seemingly interpreted as confirming the view (hitherto held with less conviction) that China would not risk an open clash but would respect
demonstrations of India's determination to maintain its territorial
integrity by force of arms if that was required. Thus emboldened, the

obsession with General J. N. Chaudhuri, and by his prescription that India can
resolve all her external problems by a strong show of force to her opponents.
Nonetheless, there is much to commend his analysis of India's China policy from
1959–62. His treatment of Nehru and Krishna Menon on the whole displays
insight into their thought and actions.

11. Lorne Kavic, *India's Quest for Security*, p. 170.

Indian authorities decided on an even more resolute course of action in NEFA, where Chinese occupation of Longju remained an open challenge. The scope of the challenge was considerably broadened when Chinese forces seized the Dhola post and Thag La ridge in the Kameng Frontier Division [of NEFA] on 8 September.[12]

New Delhi then decided to move against the Chinese in the Dhola area. The decision to do so was allegedly made despite declarations by Generals Sen and Daulet that the Chinese would overrun the Indian defences if they attacked in force. On October 5 Lieutenant General B. M. Kaul was appointed commander of a new corps to be formed in NEFA, an indication that a get-tough policy was now operative. Then, just before leaving for a trip to Madras and Ceylon on October 12, Nehru told reporters that he had given orders to the army to drive the Chinese from NEFA.[13] Krishna Menon made a similar remark on October 15 in Bangalore. The prime minister's remark apparently was a theoretical statement of intent rather than an immediate directive to the regional commanders. But the stage was now set for a confrontation for which the Chinese were well prepared militarily and the Indians were not. On October 16 India charged that the Chinese forces had fired on their Dhola post, and the Chinese counterclaimed that Indian troops were attacking all along the Kechilang River and driving northward. It can be assumed that the Chinese, who were by now preparing their attack, welcomed this "provocation." On October 20 the Chinese launched a massive "defensive action" both in NEFA and in Ladakh. At this point the question of which side had initiated the firing became irrelevant.[14] Although Indian govern-

12. Ibid., p. 172.

13. *Hindu*, October 13, 1962. General Kaul maintains that Nehru's careless remark was contrary to a Cabinet subcommittee decision not to reply to Chinese probings of a minor kind on the NEFA frontier (Kaul, *The Untold Story*, p. 387).

14. For the official Indian view of the 1962 conflict see Government of India, Ministry of External Affairs, *Notes, Memoranda, and Letters Exchanged between the Governments of India and China*, White Paper, no. 8 (New Delhi; January 20, 1963). The Chinese position is contained in *The Sino-Indian Boundary Question*, 2d enlarged ed. (Peking: Foreign Language Press, 1962).

ment press releases during the first days spoke of the invaders being repulsed with heavy losses, the military situation in fact rapidly deteriorated for the Indian forces. Within a month's time the Chinese occupied the eastern and western extremities of NEFA and were poised to drive on Assam. Their advance forces outflanked the Indian defenses and drove almost to the north bank of the Brahmaputra River. In Ladakh the Chinese captured all of the Indian posts on territory which Peking had claimed. Then on November 20, a month after their offensive had begun, the Chinese suddenly announced they would unilaterally initiate a ceasefire and would begin withdrawing their troops from the occupied territories on December 1. Indian officials and the Indian press saw treachery in Peking's move, but the Chinese carried out their withdrawal as announced. By around January 15, 1963, their troops were withdrawn from Ladakh to the "line of actual control" which existed on November 7, 1959, and from NEFA to a position twelve and one-half miles north of the MacMahon Line.[15]

There had been considerable speculation about the motives behind the Chinese actions in October–November 1962.[16] We might briefly mention some of the more important considerations which most probably influenced Peking's decisions. One was the immediate military situation in the border regions. Realizing that their comparative advantage along the NEFA and Ladakh frontiers was decreasing as time passed, the Chinese probably felt it best to strike a decisive blow as soon as possible. Such a victory would put the "pretentious" Indians in their place, convince the peoples of the border regions of China's supremacy, and impress Pakistan and the neutral nations of Asia.[17] By humiliating Khrushchev's Indian

15. An account of the fighting is contained in Kavic, *India's Quest for Security*, pp. 174–87.

16. See William E. Griffiths, *The Sino-Soviet Rift* (Cambridge: Massachusetts Institute of Technology Press, 1964), pp. 6–7, for an interpretation of China's minimal and maximum objectives.

17. There appears to be little substance to the contention put forth by a number of commentators that China was jealous of India's economic successes

friends, China could further assert its independence of the USSR. Furthermore, with the deepening Cuban crisis, the USSR could ill-afford to act in any way on India's behalf. The Chinese had limited territorial goals, and they stopped after driving the Indians from areas in Ladakh to which they claimed historical rights. Had the Chinese gone beyond NEFA, they would have overextended their lines of supply, an act that would have had serious consequences when winter closed the mountain passes. Extending the fighting into the plains would have meant encountering better trained and better equipped Indian divisions. Also the Indians would then have a chance to employ the military equipment sent by the Americans and British during the first weeks of the war. The panic-stricken Indian government on November 19 had even requested Anglo-American air strikes against advancing Chinese troops; Washington and London were studying the request when the Chinese cease-fire occurred the next day.[18] In addition, the Cuban confrontation had subsided more quickly than expected, and Moscow had begun to apply pressures against Peking. By November 20 China had achieved whatever could be gained from its military exploit. Peking wished only to discredit Nehru, not see him replaced. China, moreover, was in the position to show that she was magnanimous in victory and had no desire for territorial aggrandizement. This, it was hoped, would counterbalance some of the strong sympathy which had been building up in most parts of the world for India since the inception of the fighting. The decisiveness of the Chinese victory had undermined China's allegations of India's "aggression."

The war had ramifications for India's relations with Pakistan,

---

and therefore wanted to divert Indian resources from the economic to the military sphere. Granted that the Chinese economy was suffering from both natural and man-made calamities and that China resented the external assistance that India was receiving from abroad, but the attitude of the CCP toward the Congress party's performance was one of contempt, not jealousy.

18. On this point see Michael Edwardes, "Illusion and Reality in India's Foreign Policy," *International Affairs*, January, 1965, p. 52.

as well as for domestic politics. As a by-product of India's receipt of massive Western assistance, Pakistan became amenable to joining China (at least verbally) in common cause against a mutual enemy. Only several years earlier President Ayub had approached India to discuss joint defence arrangements for the subcontinent against China, but had been turned down.

The Indian military debacle generated severe discontent. Much criticism was directed at Krishna Menon, who had been a center of controversy since assuming the position of defence minister five years earlier. By interfering in the matter of promotion of senior officers, Menon provoked a good deal of intrigue in an armed forces which formerly had taken pride on being relatively free from politics.[19] Menon was also accused of having ignored advice by authorities in the fields of weaponry and strategic planning. Through the years Menon's abrasive personality had created many personal enemies. In the clamor for his dismissal many overlooked his significant steps in establishing indigenous facilities for arms production within India. He was a more efficient administrator than his predecessor, and he had inherited a difficult situation to begin with. Indian forces in NEFA were not well-trained for mountain fighting, were ill-equipped and ill-clothed, and were poorly led.[20] For all of this Menon certainly was not solely responsible.

The United States and Britain, which were providing India with military assistance, applied strong pressures for Menon's dismissal from the Cabinet. The decisive impetus to remove Menon, however, came from within the Congress party itself. Such senior party

19. For a summation of the civilian-military relationship in India and particularly the Menon–General Thimayya episode see Kavic, *India's Quest for Security*, pp. 141–68. An account of General Kaul's career is contained in Welles Hangen, *After Nehru, Who?* (London: Rupert Hart-Davis, 1963).

20. Kavic, *India's Quest for Security*, pp. 183–85, points out that "the performance of many of the senior officers charged with NEFA defences was marked by confusion, uncertainty, and lack of initiative . . . tactics were too conventional . . . and there was an overall shortage of equipment; much of what was in existence was obsolete."

members as the deputy leader, H. Mahatab, U. N. Dhebar, Mahavir Tyagi, and Raghunath Singh met together privately and called for Menon's dismissal.[21] Particularly influential was Raghunath Singh, secretary of the Congress Parliamentary party, and no friend of Menon's. He spoke for a substantial section of the Parliamentary party who disliked Menon both on personal and ideological grounds. Menon's haughtiness had prevented him from developing a real following in the party, despite the public acclaim for his role as India's spokesman on Kashmir and Goa, and the sympathy generated during his victorious campaign against American-supported J. B. Kripalani in the 1962 general elections in North Bombay. Those who supported him in the Parliamentary party did so for ideological reasons or because he was in Nehru's good graces. Krishna Menon had served the cause of Indian independence in London for many years. He had been Nehru's literary agent in Britain, and they had visited Spain together during the Civil War. Each had comforted the other in moments of personal despondancy during Nehru's European visit prior to World War II. Intellectually both had become committed to the principle of a "socialist pattern of society." It has been said, sometimes without justification, that in later years both men (particularly Menon) saw contemporary issues from a 1930s frame of reference. In the 1950s, as Nehru's representative in the United Nations, Menon worked diligently to promote India's case on Kashmir—an issue in which Nehru was involved emotionally as well as politically. Menon understood and presented Nehru's ideas well, although Menon's personality often undercut his effectiveness as a diplomat. Differences in their behavior and interests did not prevent a bond from developing between them. After the death of Maulana Azad and G. V. Pant, Menon became Nehru's closest political confident. In his last few years Nehru felt much more at home with Menon than he did with any of the Congress "Old Guard," and he in-

21. Articles in *Thought*, November 17, 1962, and *Hindu*, November 8 and 9, 1962.

directly shared the reins of power with Menon on certain critical issues.

Nehru knew that a good deal of the criticism directed at Menon was meant also for him. He defended Menon as long as it was politically feasible but finally accepted Menon's resignation first from the post of defence minister and then on November 7 from the newly-created post of minister of defence production. His own position would have become increasingly tenuous had Menon remained in the Government, and the continuing controversy greatly militated against the national solidarity needed to confront the crisis. Others retired from their positions as a result of the military setback were Lieutenant General B. M. Kaul and Lieutenant General P. N. Thapar, army chief of staff. There is no attempt here to weigh the relative responsibility of these men for the defeat, since many of the critical "facts" are either disputed or not a matter of public record. Perhaps, as General Kaul put it, whatever responsibility that is to be assigned has to be shared collectively by Nehru, Menon, Finance Minister Morarji Desai, and the senior army officers.

Nehru had been visibly shocked by the course of events. After playing down the military situation at first, he tended like others to exaggerate the scale of the Chinese offensive. Making a forthright public declaration of some of his miscalculations, he told the Lok Sabha on November 8 that India had been living in a world of illusions, illusions of its own creation. For a brief time there were some suggestions that Nehru himself resign. But Nehru symbolized India, and few would have wanted Nehru to step down while the country was undergoing its crisis.

The Soviet Reaction

What was the Soviet reaction to the outbreak of hostilities? From the beginning Moscow disclaimed any foreknowledge of the impending Chinese attack. As soon as Nehru learned that fighting had broken out, he instructed that his government's concern be conveyed directly to Khrushchev. A few hours later the Soviet ambassador in New Delhi, I. A. Benedictov, conveyed Khrushchev's return message. The Soviet premier reportedly expressed his sorrow over the fighting and called for a cease-fire to be followed by Sino-Indian negotiations.[22]

The *Times of India* correspondent, Ralph Parker, reported from Moscow that there was no official Soviet comment on the Chinese claim that India had provoked a Chinese counterattack by its aggressive actions. While maintaining an official silence, Soviet leaders privately were very disturbed with the situation.[23] Moscow appeared unable to deter the Chinese once the fighting had broken out.

On October 24 the Chinese proposed that the "line of actual control" on that date should serve as a cease-fire line, and that both sides should then withdraw their troops twelve and one half miles. The next day the Soviet press broke the official Soviet silence by publishing the Chinese statement and a front-page editorial urging India to accept the Chinese proposal for the demarcation of the Himalayan frontier:

The proposals made by the Chinese Government are constructive in our opinion. Without damaging the prestige of either side they are an acceptable basis for the beginning of talks and a peaceful settlement of the disputed question. A peaceful solution of the conflict requires more active efforts on the part of the progressive forces in India. One must take into account that in the present atmosphere of strained relations even some progressively-minded people can yield to nationalistic influence and adopt a chauvinistic position. . . . In questions involving war and peace and in solving controversial international problems, such a position serves no useful purpose. [What is needed is] not a kindling of hostilities and sharpening of the conflict, but settling it by peaceful methods and negotiations.[24]

For the most part the Indian press was surprised and concerned by the Soviet statement, while the government did not issue any

22. *New York Times*, October 25, 1962; *Times of India*, October 24, 1962.
23. *Times of India*, October 22, 1962.
24. *Pravda*, October 25, 1962.

official comment. There was good reason for this reaction. Ever since the border clashes of 1959, the Soviets had maintained "neutrality" on the issue, a neutrality that in some respects was pro-Indian. Moscow was not concerned with the merits of the territorial claims as such, but with the timing and intent of the Chinese action. In the three years, Sino-Soviet relations had seriously worsened while Indo-Soviet relations had continued along the plane of "peaceful coexistence" and "friendly cooperation." During this time the USSR had accelerated its economic aid program and in 1961 began deliveries of military and paramilitary equipment to India (thus giving substance to later Chinese charges that two-thirds of Russia's assistance to India had been sanctioned after September 1959). From the Indian standpoint it was to be expected that at least the USSR would remain silent in the event of recurring Sino-Indian hostilities. But the Soviets unexpectedly called upon India to accept the Chinese proposals for a cease-fire under preconditions that were unacceptable to the Nehru government.

The Soviet leaders surely knew that the acceptance of the Chinese proposal under duress was unthinkable, as it would cause the Nehru Government to have a complete loss of face. After several days the probable motivation for the *Pravda* editorial of October 25 became clearer. Khrushchev himself had suddenly become involved in an international imbroglio of critical proportions in Cuba.[25] The best explanation for his momentary support of the Chinese proposal was that he needed to have a united Communist front for bargaining purposes in the Caribbean. Russian preoccupation with Cuba is revealed by the following passage from the *Pravda* editorial:

[A Sino-Indian settlement would be] a new blow against the forces of imperialism and colonialism, against the intrigues of the aggressive circles of the USA who have just undertaken a most dangerous ad-

25. See *New York Times*, October 26, 1962.

venture aimed not only against Cuba and the Socialist states, but also against all peace-loving forces.

The Soviet construction of missile bases in Cuba and the Chinese attack in the NEFA did not appear to be coordinated acts by two allies but rather more the result of coincidence. The Chinese have since maintained that they consulted with the Soviets prior to their showdown with India; but even so, the Soviets did not anticipate the scale of the conflict which ensued. Nor did the Soviets take the Chinese into confidence during some of the most critical phases of their Cuban adventure.

On his part Nehru rejected Russia's call for a cease-fire and negotiations with the Chinese. Imposing preconditions of his own, he asserted that the Chinese forces must return to the pre-September 20, 1962 positions before any negotiations could take place.[26] In reply to a second letter by Khrushchev, in which the Soviet premier reportedly had expressed surprise over the Chinese action, Nehru on October 27 reiterated that he would negotiate only if China withdrew to the positions it held in September. Nehru undoubtedly was disturbed by the *Pravda* editorial of October 25, but withheld comment. His sentiments were conveyed to Khrushchev several days later by several Indian officials, including K. D. Malaviya, the minister for oil, who had a two hour meeting with the Soviet premier. The Indian officials stressed that the present situation might have consequences which could affect India's policy of nonalignment. They contrasted the USSR's speedy and effective intervention to halt the West's moves against Egypt and Cuba with the apparent reluctance of the Russians to use their influence to halt the Chinese attack on India.[27]

The Sino-Indian clash placed the USSR in a difficult position. On October 30 Valerian Zorin, the Soviet UN delegate, backed the Chinese proposal of October 24, declaring that "the frontier dispute between India and China should be settled by peaceful

26. Ibid., October 25, 26, 1962.
27. *Times of India*, October 29, 1962.

means through negotiations and the sooner the better." The Chinese proposal "could serve as the basis for the inception of negotiations," suggested Zorin, "without dealing any blows to the prestige of the parties concerned."[28] As late as November 3, Khrushchev in a personal letter urged the Indian prime minister to accept the Chinese cease-fire proposals.[29]

But China, like India, was not satisfied with the Soviet stand. The Russians, even during the height of the Cuban crisis, had not supported the charge of aggression made by Peking against New Delhi. The Chinese had given their fullest backing to Khrushchev, but according to an October 31 editorial in *Jenmin Jih Pao*, the Soviet leader had bowed to the "United States imperialist attempt to browbeat the people of Cuba" and had removed his missiles from Cuba. As a final exhortation to the Soviets, the Chinese published a statement, "More on Nehru's Philosophy in the Light of the Sino-Indian Boundary," which held that Moscow should renounce the "reactionary" Indian government and return to the fold of Marxism-Leninism.[30]

As if in reply to the blunt Chinese demands, Moscow gradually shifted its stance on the border dispute during the first week of November. At no time had the Soviets indicated that they would curtail their assistance to India. On the same day that the Chinese published "More on Nehru's Philosophy," a spokesman for the Indian Defense Ministry announced that arms "have been coming according to schedule" from the USSR.[31] At the conclusion of Malaviya's visit, the USSR reportedly promised to speed up its aid for India's coal, oil, and power industries.[32] In addition, the Soviets were not critical of Nehru's appeal to the United States and Great Britain for large quantities of military aid.

28. As quoted in the *Hindu Weekly Review*, November 5, 1962.

29. *Times* (London), November 5, 1962.

30. Reprinted in *Peking Review*, November 1962.

31. *Hindu Weekly Review*, November 5, 1962.

32. *Times of India*, November 3, 1962.

In an important editorial in *Pravda* on November 5 the USSR again called for a negotiated settlement between India and China. There was danger that the conflict might spread, and it was in both nations' interests that this should not happen. But in contrast to its October 25 editorial, *Pravda* did not term the supporters of India's national effort "chauvinistic," and in no way endorsed Peking's proposals over those of New Delhi. In a veiled criticism of China, *Pravda* pointed out that the nondemocratic forces in India were using the present crisis as an excuse to put pressure on the "progressive elements" to end the policy of nonalignment. The following day, Soviet Deputy Premier Alexei Kosygin called for a cease-fire on a reasonable basis and added that "there are no basic contradictions between India and China that could not be solved in round-table talks."[33] Several days later the position taken by the USSR in the November 5 editorial was endorsed by the Premiers of Bulgaria, Czechoslovakia, and later by the other Comecon nations.

Considering its prevailing alliance with China and its other Cold War commitments, the Soviet Union was not prepared to say openly anything stronger on the issue. It was acknowledged by New Delhi, however, that Moscow was basically sympathetic to India, and on November 9 Nehru expressed confidence that the USSR would fulfill its previous pledges of assistance, including the first consignment of MIGs scheduled for delivery in December. The Soviets undoubtedly wished to see Sino-Indian hostilities ended, but it is not known to what extent, if any, Moscow influenced the Chinese decision to declare a unilateral cease-fire on November 20. It might be added that the USSR encouraged the mediatory efforts of the six "nonaligned" Asian and African states which met in Ceylon in December 1962 and put forth the so-called Colombo Proposals to resolve the Sino-Indian dispute.[34]

33. *Times* (London), November 7, 1962.

34. Michael Brecher summarized the Colombo Proposals as follows: "In the Western Sector (Ladakh), (a) Chinese forces were to withdraw 20 kilometres from the actual line of control on 7 November 1959 (both India and China ac-

There were limitations upon Indian diplomacy in its attempt
to commit the Soviets more fully to India's position. An attempt
by the Indian External Affairs Ministry to elicit a stronger denunciation from the CPSU and Polish parties against the Chinese
attack annoyed the Communist leaders. The Russians had cut off
supplies of weapons, spare parts, and aircraft fuel to China, but
they were unwilling at that time to speak out publicly against the
Chinese.

Despite the military setbacks at the hands of the Chinese expedi-
tion, the Indian government weathered the shock of the one-month
conflict. India received large-scale military assistance from the
United States and Great Britain. This aid was given immediately
and virtually without condition (it was valued at an estimated
$100 million). And the Russians—after the Cuban crisis had
passed its peak—tried in their own way to bolster India's position.
At least momentarily the Indian nation was united—in the common
cause of opposing China.[35]

Departing from the narrative for a moment, we might mention
here some of the by-products of India's month-long clash with
China. The Chinese attack, of course, made the cleavage between
the two countries irreparable. It should be kept in mind, however,

---

cepted), and (b) pending final solution of the border dispute, the area of
Chinese withdrawal was to be a demilitarized zone, to be administered by civilian
posts of both sides, without prejudice to claims (India accepted but China insists
on Chinese posts only in the demilitarized zone) ; in the Eastern Sector (NEFA)
the line of actual control in areas recognized by both Governments was to serve
as a cease-fire line to their respective posts, the remaining areas to be settled
in the future discussions (India accepted, the Chinese insist that Indian troops
do not return to the MacMahon Line." (*The New States of Asia*, p. 172.)

Because the sponsoring nations had not condemned China's "aggression," New
Delhi was at first cool to the Colombo Proposals. It soon became apparent that
the Proposals were the best India could hope for, given the realities of the *de
facto* situation. Subsequently India has made diplomatic use of China's refusal
to accepted the Proposals without qualification.

35. One by-product, for example, is that the DMK party in Madras state
stopped threatening to secede from the Indian union. Its leader, C. N. Annadurai,
quickly affirmed his party's commitment to India and announced publicly that
the secessionist plank of the DMK platform would be speedily removed.

that the intractable positions previously adopted by both sides had already negated the possibility of a negotiated settlement of the border issue. For the Indian government the painful events of October 1962 served to resolve the issue of what to do about China. In previous years Indian policy had been marked by a great deal of equivocation and uncertainty—after 1958 New Delhi had indulged in a considerable amount of covert criticism of China's leaders while at the same time calling for a restoration of good relations. This indecision ended with the outbreak of hostilities in NEFA, and India's leaders, no longer feeling constraint, launched a full-scale denunciation of Peking. Only on the question of the seating of the CPR in the United Nations did India render any further diplomatic support to China. While withdrawing from her previous role as a sponsor of the annual resolutions calling for the seating of the Peking regime, India continued to vote affirmatively on the issue (although without enthusiasm and with a touch of cynicism).

It is doubtful whether the substantial American and British military aid during the crisis had much lasting impact on Indian policy. The rapid and apparently unconditional Western aid did strengthen the Swatantra party's critique of nonalignment, but the formalities of nonalignment between the West and the USSR were preserved, since India was not placed under any commitment to her beneficiaries. The USSR itself, while warning India of the dangers of dependence upon the West, tacitly accepted Nehru's request for and receipt of Anglo-American military aid.[36] One of the few loose strings attached to the aid was Nehru's agreement to discuss the Kashmir issue again with Pakistan. But when these discussions were held the following year, nothing was done to resolve the Kashmir dilemma.

36. The United States and Britain were divided on the degree to which they should impose conditions on India with respect to Kashmir in return for military aid. The British diplomat Duncan Sandys wanted to push harder on this point, but was opposed and eventually overruled by Averell Harriman and the American ambassador to India, John Galbraith.

Domestically, patriotic proclamations were issued and a Defence of India Fund was begun. But substantively there was little change in the life style and attitudes of the upper strata of Indian society. Public discontent was mollified in part by the dismissal of Krishna Menon, General B. M. Kaul, NEFA regional commander, and General Thapar, army chief of staff. While Nehru defended Menon and the generals, the availability of scapegoats took some of the pressure off his shoulders. By dismissing Menon and by the Kamaraj Plan of 1963 the impression was created that a substantial shakeup had occurred within the governing circles. On the whole, Nehru maintained his political equilibrium. But he emerged a disillusioned, weakened man and was unable to rekindle the spirit of the Congress party, which through the years had been sapped of its earlier vigor and idealism. This is not to suggest that the Congress party had not undergone and survived very serious crises in the past, but the accumulation of events had taken its toll. Particularly disheartening was the entire experience with China in which Nehru had staked so much politically and emotionally.

The emergency situation weakened the centrifugal forces within India and presented the opportunity for creating a greater national consciousness. But the dividing line between patriotism and narrow chauvinism is often tenuous. The treatment of the handful of people of Chinese origin in India evoked memories of the treatment of Japanese-Americans within the United States during the early years of World War II. Long-time Chinese residents in India were badly harrassed, and their properties damaged and often confiscated. The impassioned citizens often could not distinguish between Chinese and other orientals, and this lead to an assortment of indiscriminate incidents which greatly troubled Nehru and other thoughtful Indians.

The completely censored news dispatches on NEFA distorted the realities of the military situation. At first the press told of victories or strategic withdrawals by the Indian forces. When suddenly the Chinese were portrayed as poised on the upper banks of the Brahmaputra River, ready to strike at the plains below, panic began to break out in parts of northern India. The outside world also received the impression that India was suffering a great military setback. This impression had the salutary effect of hastening military assistance from the Western powers. Only after the Chinese declared their unilateral ceasefire and withdrew their forces was a sense of perspective somewhat restored. The great percentage of Indian forces, including the best equipped and trained units, had remained deployed in Kashmir and elsewhere along the Pakistan border. As it turned out the Indian armed forces were actually strengthened as a result of the conflict with China by the subsequent receipt of Anglo-American and Soviet military aid. Moreover, the publicity given to the ill-clad, poorly equipped jawans in NEFA had spurred much-needed reforms in the Indian military establishment.

In the following weeks, while trying to fathom the motivation of the Chinese action, New Delhi observed a worsening of the Sino-Soviet-fissure.

Speaking as an observer at the Italian Communist Party Congress early in December, Frol Kozlov termed China's Himalayan policy "adventurist." Khrushchev himself, increasingly exasperated by Chinese criticisms of his withdrawal of missiles from Cuba, his alleged "collusion with the imperialist leaders," and his "revisionist, anti-Leninist" policies, struck back verbally. Before the Supreme Soviet on December 12 Khrushchev gave his rebuttal, which stressed among other issues the Sino-Indian border strife.[37]

Khrushchev "welcomed the action of the Chinese comrades" in calling a cease-fire and beginning the withdrawal of their troops. Then he asked rhetorically,

How can you call this a reasonable step when it was taken after so many lives had been lost? . . . Would it not have been better if the sides did

37. N. S. Khrushchev, "The Present International Situation and Soviet Foreign Policy," reprinted in *Political Affairs*, 42 (January 1963) : 27–61.

not resort to hostilities altogether? Yes, of course it would have been better. We have said this constantly and repeat it again now.

Taunting the Chinese further he added:

There may, of course, be people who will say: the CPR is now withdrawing its troops actually to the line on which this conflict began. Would it not have been better not to move from the positions on which these troops stood at one time? These arguments are understandable, they show that people display concern and regret over what has happened.[38]

India's "policy of non-alignment with blocs . . . has won great moral and political weight in the world," declared Khrushchev. His implication was clear: Chinese action was driving India away from the path of nonalignment towards the "imperialist camp." Coming to the forefront in India were the "most brazen militarists and reactionaries" while the "progressive elements" were being weakened. There are no border disputes "that given mutual desire, cannot be settled without using arms." In effect, Khrushchev disapproved of the entire change in Chinese policy towards India.

A significant indicator of the direction of Soviet policy was the plan to build several factories to manufacture and assemble MIG fighters within India. Amid speculation that the project would be cancelled by the Soviets, several officials of the Indian Defence Ministry gave assurances that plans had not been altered. On December 7 the minister for Defence Production told the lower house that sites for the factories had been selected in Orissa and Maharashtra.[39] The next day Finance Minister Morarji Desai told the house that Russian aid was continuing according to schedule.[40]

In unofficial and official capacities Indians put forth their nation's case against Peking. New Delhi felt it necessary to deny that S. A. Dange, chairman of the CPI, was on a diplomatic mission

38. Ibid.
39. *Lok Sabha Debates*, vol. 11, no. 23 (December 7, 1962), cols. 4735–36.
40. Ibid., vol. 11, no. 24 (December 8, 1962), cols. 4917–18.

when he met with Soviet leaders in December.[41] R. K. Nehru, Secretary-General of the External Affairs Ministry, did not procure additional Soviet arms aid for India, but he was able to report after several weeks in Moscow in January 1963 that the USSR appreciated Indian nonalignment.[42]

The fact that the USSR had not supported China was used by the Indian government to justify the policy of nonalignment. "Our policy of nonalignment has stood the test of time and we should continue [it]," said M. C. Chagla, the high commissioner in London. He reasoned that the policy had not stood in the way of India receiving aid from the Western countries. If India were a member of the Western bloc, the USSR would have sided with China. India's nonalignment prevented the two Communist countries from coming together and bridging the ever-widening gulf between them. "Therefore in a . . . strange twist of history, we may succeed by our nonaligned policy in bringing the West and Russia closer together and isolating China."[43] Speaking at a public meeting in Lucknow on January 6, Prime Minister Nehru remarked: "We cannot give up our independence by discarding the nonalignment policy." Doing so would benefit only China. Some of the highlights in the Sino-Soviet polemical exchanges in 1963 dealt with India. From the Chinese standpoint the TASS statement of September 1959 was a "betrayal of proletarian internationalism [which] tipped off the enemy" that the socialist camp was not a monolithic whole. This act by the Soviet leaders "greatly encouraged the insolence of the Indian reactionaries in their campaign against China and [gave support to] the stubborn uncompromising stand which Nehru has always maintained on the Sino-Indian boundary question." Over the next three years the

41. A government spokesman emphasized that Dange had gone abroad to the USSR and Britain to attend conferences in his capacity as vice-president of the World Federation of Trade Unions. No foreign exchange was granted for his trip.

42. *Hindu*, January 30, 1963.

43. *Hindu*, January 14, 1963.

Russians, "in collusion with American imperialism," bolstered up Nehru "every time he needed support for his aggravation of the border dispute. The more frenzied the Nehru government became in its anti-China campaign, the greater were the large-scale increases which the Soviets made in their aid to India."[44] From 1955 to April 1963, the Soviet government agreed to give India five billion rupees in aid, "two-thirds of it after India provoked the Sino-Indian border conflict in 1959." Military equipment supplied by the USSR was used by India in its campaign against China in the autumn of 1962. Then the Soviet press had the audacity to complain that the Chinese position on the border conflict with India was one of "maintaining tension in the region and rejecting a speedy settlement of the territorial dispute by means of negotiation."[45] In signing the nuclear Test-ban Treaty in mid-1963, Khrushchev completed his betrayal by entering into a new "Holy Alliance" with Kennedy, Nehru, and Tito.[46]

On his part Khrushchev recalled that he had warned the Chinese that "the development of this dispute [with India] into a large armed conflict was undesirable and fraught with negative consequences not only for Chinese-Indian relations but also for the entire international situation." The conflict "had the most negative consequences for the cause of peace, inflicted great harm to the unity of the anti-imperialist front in Asia, and placed the progressive forces in India in an extremely difficult position."[47]

Apropos of the Soviet accusation that China had made the position of the "progressive forces" in India very difficult, it is relevant to note the plight of the Communist party of India after the Chinese

44. Editorial in the *Remnin Ribao*. Translated and reprinted in the *Peking Review*, 6 (August 30, 1963) : 7.

45. Ibid. Reference was made to *Pravda* editorials of August 13 and 16, 1963, which set forth these contentions.

46. "The New Holy Alliance Will End Up No Better Than The Old," *Peking Review*, vol. 6 (October 11, 1963).

47. "Statement of the Soviet Government," Sept. 21, 1963. Reprinted in *Current Soviet Documents*, Vol. I, no. 28 (Oct. 7, 1963), pp. 29–30.

attack. Without any directive from Moscow, the right-wing faction led by S. A. Dange had condemned the Chinese action almost from the beginning, and on November 1 the CPI National Council passed a resolution to this effect. The "right-wing" and "moderate" elements of the CPI used the crisis to oust the "leftists" from a number of key positions within the party.[48] A number of CPI members were arrested under the Emergency Act on November 7 and 21. The main targets of the arrests were those who had not come out unequivocally against the Chinese, but in many areas the detentions were made quite indiscriminately.

The Soviets themselves were unhappy about the cleavage within the CPI, and also they protested the jailing of such "moderates" as E.M.S. Namboodiripad by the Indian government.[49] In a circuitous way the Soviet press complained of an anti-Communist campaign in India, which was continuing well after the border fighting had ceased. On January 18, 1963, *Pravda* reported a wide movement among the progressive sections of India "to free the arrested Communists, including ten members of Parliament who . . . are deprived of the opportunity to take part in the opening session of Parliament on January 21."[50] Several weeks later *Pravda* quoted nearly in its entirety a long editorial from the *New Age's* special Republic Day issue. In quoting the *New Age* in this manner, *Pravda* implied its agreement with the CPI newspaper. The *New Age* observed:

from the time of the last anniversary of Republic day . . . the reactionaries have dealt several serious blows to the basic national policy. They lead the campaign for the repudiation of the non-align-

48. After the arrest of "pro-Peking" elements, the Chinese intensified their accusations against the "Dange clique" which allegedly was serving the interests of the Nehru government. When Dange consulted with Soviet and East European leaders during his December 1962 trip abroad, the Chinese requested that the CPI oppose further directives from Moscow (Gelman, *Communist Strategies in Asia*, p. 139).

49. *Pravda*, December 30, 1962.

50. *Pravda*, January 18, 1963.

ment policy . . . and organized the attack against the CPI—the most resolute and consistent champion of an independent foreign policy. . . . We would like to remind Prime Minister Nehru and his colleagues that in carrying out mass arrests in accordance with the accusations of the anti-Communist policy . . . the Government performs a service for the reactionary right-wing forces.[51]

Finally the *New Age* asked the government to end repressive measures against the CPI, "*if* the Government really wanted to defend the basic national policy against reactionary forces."[52]

Several articles in the *World Marxist Review* also conveyed the USSR's displeasure with the Indian government's policy towards the CPI.[53] By the summer of 1963, however, most of the Soviet-oriented Indian Communists had been released from prison. This fact, coupled with the increased volume and bitterness of Sino-Soviet polemics in mid-1963, brought a temporary end to these Soviet complaints.

The issue was reopened, however, with the jailing by the Shastri Government of an estimated 900 CPI leaders under the Defence of India rules on December 30–31, 1964. G. L. Nanda, who continued as home minister in the new cabinet formed after Nehru's death in May, defended the Government's action by citing alleged evidence of the "Left-Communists' plans to launch a violent revolutionary struggle" which would be synchronized with another Chinese attack on India's northern borders. Twenty-nine of the CPI detainees were from the 40 "left-Communists" elected to the Kerala State Assembly in February 1965.[54] The Soviets asked for the release of the Kerala legislators, even though they were members of the Peking-oriented group which formed a separate party after the CPI schism in mid-1964. Had the Russians not called for the

51. *New Age*, January 27, 1963.

52. *Pravda*, February 2, 1963.

53. See I. Sumar, "Arrest of Communists in India, and Who Stands to Gain," *World Marxist Review*, 6 (January, 1963) : 94.

54. *New York Times*, February 20, March 13, 1965.

freeing of all imprisoned Indian Communists, they would have been fair game for the Chinese accusation that Moscow had aligned itself with "reactionaries and counter-revolutionaries."

Soviet Support on Kashmir, 1962–64

By 1961 there were indications that Pakistan was becoming disenchanted with the West and might desire improved relations with the Communist nations.[55] Nonetheless, Moscow continued to give full support to India on the Kashmir question. In the UN Security Council on June 23, 1962, the Soviets were again called upon to cast a veto against a mildly-worded resolution sponsored by Ireland calling upon India and Pakistan to resume negotia- tions.[56] From New Delhi's standpoint the resolution represented unfair pressure being exerted by the United States and Great Britain against India on Pakistan's behalf.

Learning of the vetoed resolution shortly before the scheduled foreign affairs debate in the upper house of Parliament, Nehru indignantly told the assembly:

It is a matter for deep regret to me that repeatedly, when matters concerning subjects which concern us deeply, about which we feel rather passionate . . . it should be our misfortune that two great powers, the U.S. and the U.K. should almost invariably be against us. In a matter like Goa, . . . we delayed any action till it was almost thrust upon us by circumstances. Yet this was made an occasion for reading us homilies and lecturing to us as to why we should behave properly in international matters. In regard to Kashmir . . . India and Pakistan have been placed, notably by these two powers on the same level. . . . The [American] representative tells us what to do about Kashmir

55. An initial step by the USSR to encourage Pakistan's new flexibility was an offer to assist Pakistan's program of oil exploration. Negotiations began prior to the U-2 incident in 1960 and were continued despite Soviet displeasure over American use of the Peshawar airbase for overflights. On March 4, 1961, an agree- ment was signed calling for Soviet expertise and $33.2 million in credits to be utilized for oil exploration. (Levi, "Pakistan, the Soviet Union and China").

56. *UN Security Council Official Records*, 17th sess., 1015th mtg. (June 22, 1962).

not realizing that Kashmir is flesh of our flesh and bone of our bone and all that we know about the facts and about the law are in our favor.[57]

He then complained that the Western powers were indifferent to the security needs of India, thus making it necessary for India to turn to the USSR for MIG aircraft.

It was somewhat embarrassing for India to be so dependent upon the Russian veto. "New Delhi would much rather that things did not come to such a pass," commented an Indian journalist, "but when they do it cannot be particular where it gets its veto."[58]

Nehru's unwillingness to negotiate on Kashmir stemmed in large part from his assessment of conditions within the subcontinent. While recognizing the need for India and Pakistan to resolve their differences, he feared that the reopening of the Kashmir question would aggravate the volatile tensions between Hindu and Muslim. Having long worked for a secular solution to India's political problems, Nehru avoided the potentially explosive situation of a plebescite in Kashmir. Thus Nehru's irritation over the seeming lack of sympathy by the British and Americans for his dilemma, and his appreciation of the Russian's unhesitant support on a matter "vital to India's territorial integrity" and stability.

When the Indian government received American and British military assistance during the fighting with China in October-November, 1962, it was agreed that Indo-Pakistani bilateral talks would be held to discuss the Kashmir issues. These talks, as might have been expected, came to nothing. During Nehru's last year the decision was made to withdraw the special status given to Jammu and Kashmir and to integrate the area fully into the Indian Union. There was now absolutely nothing left to discuss on Kashmir so far as India was concerned. Nehru's concern that the Kashmir issue might precipitate communal violence was underscored by nine hectic days beginning December 27, 1963, with the dis-

57. *Rajya Sabha Debates*, vol. 39, no. 9 (June 23, 1962), cols. 1766–69.
58. "The Moment of Truth," by "Vidura" in *Times of India*, June 27, 1962.

appearance of a Muslim relic (a hair, purportedly from the prophet Mohammed) from the Hazratbal shrine outside Srinagar. Demonstrations soon took place in and around Srinagar, calling, among other things, for the release of the imprisoned former prime minister of Kashmir, Sheikh Abdullah. Violence broke out in Srinagar and shortly thereafter in East and West Bengal and Bihar. The Indian police had difficulty controlling the communal upheavals, particularly in Calcutta, but to its credit acted resolutely and impartially. Indians and Pakistanis each believed that the other nation was involved in the disappearance of the relic. On January 4, 1964, the hair suddenly reappeared at the shrine, just as mysteriously as it had disappeared.

When Kashmir again was debated in the Security Council in February 1964, India's representative, M. C. Chagla, was able to broaden India's case by pointing to the recent communal violence. So long as the Kashmir issue remained alive, it would continue to aggravate tensions; therefore it was necessary to end the matter once and for all.[59]

Before the debates began, the Soviets gave assurances that their support for India's position remained unaltered.[60] The USSR was not overly anxious to cast another veto, however, for an improvement in Soviet relations with Pakistan was now becoming possible. Pakistan's disenchantment with her Western allies was welcomed, but Moscow was concerned at the Rawalpindi-Peking agreement in common cause against India.

It was not necessary for the USSR to cast another veto on Kashmir in the Security Council, for the United States did not press strongly for a resolution. For the first time there were certain similarities in the Soviet and American approaches.[61] The USSR moved a little away from their oft-stated view that there were no

59. For text of the Council's proceedings on Kashmir see *UN Security Council Official Records*, 19th sess., meetings 1087–93, (February 3–17, 1964).

60. *Hindustan Times*, February 1, 1964.

61. An article in the *Times of India*, February 22, 1964, pointed to the "Similarities in the U.S.–Soviet Attitudes" on the need to resolve the Kashmir issue.

legitimate grounds for the Pakistani case, while the U.S. accepted the point that the situation in Kashmir had changed somewhat since the original resolution of 1948 which called for a plebescite. The Czech delegate to the Council (perhaps reflecting Russian views) did not rule out the possibility of outside mediation of the dispute if this procedure were acceptable to the two parties directly concerned. The Soviet delegate, N. Fedorenko, reiterated his support for India's position and asked that the long-standing dispute be resolved speedily. He cited Premier Khrushchev's 1964 New Year message to all heads of state calling for the "conclusion of an international agreement providing for the renunciation by states of the use of force for the settlement of territorial disputes or boundary questions."[62]

The Pakistani representatives, realizing that they could not get a resolution passed, called for adjournment of the debate. This writer recalls the triumphant return of M. Chagla from the United Nations to a standing ovation in the Indian Parliament. As Chagla spiritedly, spoke of his mission, V. K. Krishna Menon, who had in previous years been spotlighted in the Kashmir debates, got up from his seat among the Congress party backbenchers and strode almost unnoticed from the floor.

The influx of American and British military aid to India during and after the Sino-Indian conflict of 1962 had a jarring effect on Pakistani thinking. In the 1950's Pakistan had joined the American alliance system and had acquired considerable weaponry from the United States primarily with India, not Russia and China, in mind. There had been risks in being a Western ally; for example, the Soviet premier had made menacing threats after a U-2 spy plane which had taken off from Peshawar was shot down over Soviet Kazakhstan in May 1960. After October 1962 it appeared that India had acquired all the advantages of a military alignment

---

62. *UN Security Council Official Records*, 19th sess., 1091st mtg. (February 14, 1964), p. 6.

without the liabilities. As an enemy of Chinese Communism, India would have special advantages in obtaining arms from the United States. Also, with the growing American-Soviet rapprochement in 1963, Pakistan's future ability to get large quantities of American arms on a treaty basis seemed to be limited. The Indian military buildup along with the prospect of future arms aid from the West and the USSR seemed to point to a radical shift of military power on the Indian subcontinent.

With the emergence of American military support for India against China it also appeared likely that U.S. support for Pakistan's position on Kashmir would begin to weaken, an eventuality which soon began to occur in 1963-64. Pakistan protested to the United States on these matters but did not receive a satisfactory response. Rawalpindi then took steps to normalize relations with the USSR and draw closer to China.

The die had now been cast on Kashmir. In the months ahead, Nehru's successors would speed up the effort to fully integrate Kashmir with the rest of India. Pakistan's response was to force the issue before India achieved an overall military superiority; hence the tragic events of 1965.

7 Soviet Aid and Indo-Soviet Trade

Soviet Economic Aid to India

In a broad sense no aspect of Indo-Soviet relations can be termed nonpolitical. By its very nature the Soviet system precludes distinction between political and economic elements of its policy. For its part, India has sought to keep her dealings with the USSR on a government-to-government basis.

Prior to the establishment of the Technical Assistance Administration in 1949, the USSR maintained that financial assistance to underdeveloped areas should be channeled through the United Nations. However, "when confronted with tangible possibilities of implementing international economic aid through the UN, . . . the Soviet Government withheld its support."[1] From then on the USSR declared that aid administered by the UN was a ruse designed by the Western powers to retain influence in the newly-independent areas. The Soviets suggested they would assist those countries which remained outside the "imperialist camp," but nothing concrete was done along those lines until 1954. Then, as an integral part of the new Soviet leadership's policy of "peaceful coexistence" in the international sphere, a helping hand was extended to the

1. Alvin Rubinstein, "Soviet Policy Towards Underdeveloped Areas in the Economic and Social Council," *International Organization*, 9 (May, 1955), p. 236.

nonaligned nations. The motives underlying this shift in policy were complex. Joseph Berliner observed at the time that "perhaps the Soviet leaders are not much clearer in their minds about the precise results to be hoped for by the aid programs than the Western governments are. But this much is clear: before 1953 the policy of economic isolation had deprived the Russians of direct participation in the shaping of the economic development of the underdeveloped countries."[2]

The assistance programs were part of a more flexible approach to foreign relations and indirectly provided the Soviets with greater political leverage than they had been able to exert in the past. At the ECAFE conference in February 1954 the Russian delegate indicated that economic and technological assistance would be offered to those nations advancing "the cause of peace,"[3] that is, India, Afghanistan, Indonesia, Burma, and Egypt. Afghanistan became the first nation outside the Soviet bloc to negotiate an agreement with the Soviets for economic assistance, and India soon followed. Taking special note of the recipient nations' sensitivities, the USSR emphasized that there were no political strings attached to their aid.

A number of delegations were exchanged from 1954 on as Moscow and New Delhi explored the possibilities for expanded trade and the areas in which the USSR could assist India's economic development.[4] The prospect of Soviet aid was attractive to India primarily because the Soviets were willing to help the expansion of India's public sector, particularly in the field of heavy industry. Negotiations for Soviet assistance in building an Indian steel plant were begun in September 1954. A Russian survey team selected a site and signed the agreement for the Bhilai plant in Madhya Pradesh five months later. To finance the project the USSR authorized

2. Berliner, *Soviet Economic Aid*.

3. For an account of the Soviet proposal see *Hindu*, February 11, 1954.

4. A listing of the delegations in 1954–55 is given in Overstreet and Windmiller, *Communism in India*, pp. 463–65. *ISCUS*, the journal of the Indo-Soviet Cultural Society, also records such exchanges in its monthly issues.

credits worth about rupees 64.38 crores (or over $132 million), for use in India's Second Five Year Plan. The terms of the loan called for repayment in twelve annual installments at a yearly rate of two and one half percent interest.[5] It was projected that the Bhilai plant, with its million ton capacity, would help to raise India's annual output of steel to six million tons by the end of the Second Five Year Plan.

Bhilai was the first major project undertaken by the Soviets in a non-Communist nation, and much careful planning went into its preparation and construction. The favorable impression made by the Soviet technicians and their on-the-job training of their Indian counterparts has been contrasted with the West German and British efforts in constructing steel plants at Rourkela and Durgapur for the Indian public sector.[6] In conjunction with the Bhilai project, over 800 Indian engineers and skilled workers gained production experience in Soviet factories. The agreement on Bhilai—

clearly spelled out the division of responsibility between the Indian government and project authorities, on the one hand, and Soviet authorities on the other. India was to complete arrangements for raw

---

5. Repayment for each piece of equipment was scheduled to begin one year after delivery. Other aid authorized during the Second Five Year Plan (valued at rupees 76.6 crores) followed the same repayment schedule. "Agreements since 1959, however, have stipulated that repayment would not begin until one year after project completion." See G. Garnett and M. Crawford, "The Scope and Distribution of Soviet Economic Aid," in Joint Economic Committee, U.S. Congress, *Dimensions of Soviet Economic Power* (Washington, D. C., 1962), p. 468.

6. For example, John Lewis was impressed by the "extraordinarily high morale of the Indian participants in the project. . . . Sharing fully . . . in each step of the work, they had gained so much in-service training and experience during the project's planning and construction phases that they were thoroughly confident of their ability to move to an entirely Indian operation of the plant in very short order. . . . At all levels of the project . . . there was dual posting of Russian and Indian counterparts to most supervisory and technical positions." (*Quiet Crisis in India*, pp. 295–99.)

A Western economist with extensive service in India told this writer in 1964 that the Russians got along reasonably well with the local people and were not bothered by labor problems. The CPI influence in the unions was helpful

materials, transport, water supply, civil works, internal procurement of equipment, administration and financing. The USSR undertook the responsibility for supply of equipment at world competitive prices, supervision of construction, commissioning and operations, performance of individual items and the plant as a whole, provision of adequate Soviet personnel at USSR cost to supervise and advise, for up to three years after commission of the plant, training of Indian personnel for designing and operations in the USSR and at the site. . . .[7]

Work on the first blast furnace began in May 1957, and the mill began production in February 1959.

Plans for the construction of a second plant at Bhilai, enlarging the capacity to 2.5 million tons per year, were approved by the Indian government in December 1961 for implementation during the Third Five Year Plan. None of the subsequent Soviet projects, although some are quite substantial undertakings, have received nearly as much publicity. Whenever important Soviet officials visit India, Bhilai is very often on their itinerary.

Other Soviet assistance for India authorized during the Second Five Year Plan included credits for structural steel to be used in the construction of several large industrial plants. A Russian survey in February 1957 recommended that a plant be built in Ranchi to produce eventually about three-fourths of India's needs for new steel plant machinery.[8] The implementation of the

---

in this regard. The Soviets probably knew that the initial capacity of the plant would be closer to 1.3 million tons rather than the publicly announced goal of one million tons.

7. Friedmann, Kalmanoff, and Meagher, *International Financial Aid*, p. 343. The Soviets attached a great deal of importance to the successful completion of the project. For example, Soviet personnel assisted with the development of the Rajahara iron ore mine after November 1958, "when India found itself unable to develop the mine in time to feed the plant. Premier Khrushchev also took a personal interest; on one occasion he cabled Nehru directly when transportation bottlenecks threatened to delay delivery of Soviet equipment to the plant." (Ibid., p. 345.) See also V. A. Sergeyev, "Bhilai-2," *International Affairs* (Moscow), no. 3 (March 1962), p. 75.

8. An agreement based on the survey was signed in November 1957. It called for about $126 million worth of credits to be used over the next three years for

Soviet projects was slowed up considerably as the Second Five Year Plan ran into difficulty, and the projected target dates were set back. Apart from Bhilai, only rupees 4.32 crores of Russian assistance to the Second Five Year Plan were utilized by January 31, 1961; and the balance remaining, rupees 76.63 crores, was held over to the Third Five Year Plan period.[9]

Negotiations for the Soviet contribution to India's Third Five Year Plan began late in 1958. In May 1959 the Indian minister of steel, mines, and fuel headed an eighteen member delegation to the USSR. The group reviewed the progress of projects already undertaken in collaboration with the USSR and discussed potential projects for India's Third Five Year Plan.[10] In September 1959 the USSR announced that it would contribute credits worth rupees 180 crores for the Plan. The agreement in February 1960 called for:

1. expansion of the Bhilai Works capacity to 2.5 million tons of steel per year;

2. expansion of the Ranchi heavy machinery plant in Bihar to 80,000 tons output per year;

3. completion of the oil refinery at Barauni, Bihar—capacity planned for 2.6 million gallons of crude oil per year;

4. manufacture of heavy electrical equipment and precision instruments;

5. exploration, development, and production of oil and gas in Cambay and other areas;

---

the purchase of machinery and equipment for such projects as the thermal electric power station at Neyveli. See Wilfred Malenbaum, *East and West in India's Development: The Economics of Competitive Coexistence* (Washington, D. C.: National Planning Association, 1959), p. 39, and Government of India, *Foreign Affairs Record*, vol. 3, no. 1, p. 222, for terms of the agreement.

9. The remaining credits were specified for the purchase of industrial products (primarily steel), the oil refinery at Barauni, and pharmaceutical products. (From a table in the budget issue of the *Eastern Economist*, March 6, 1961, p. 675.)

10. See *Hindu*, May 31, 1959, and *Lok Sabha Debates*, vol. 32, no. 3 (Aug. 5, 1959), col. 555.

6. expansion of mining equipment plants;

7. expansion of the capacity of the Neyveli and Korba Power Plants.[11]

The USSR, on a much smaller scale, has also assisted firms and industries in the Indian private sector. Ironically, the first Soviet credits granted to India were to the Birla-owned Hindustan Gas Company. (Equipment was sold in the autumn of 1954 on a deferred payment basis.[12] Following the Soviet example, other East European nations entered into agreements with Indian private industry, and by the end of 1964, over seventy such agreements had been included.[13] Implicit in the Communist nations' willingness to cooperate with Indian private enterprise was their acceptance of the Indian status quo and the Congress Party's gradualist approach to socioeconomic change.

The Soviets have scrupulously attempted to avoid the charge that their assistance program to India interferes in any way with Indian domestic politics. For this reason the USSR on several occasions has refused aid to Communist-led coalition governments in the state of Kerala. The CPI chief minister of Kerala, E. M. S. Namboodiripad, hoped to get some aid from the Soviets during his trip to the USSR in January 1959—at a time when the anti-Communist opposition groups in Kerala had already launched their campaign to oust the CPI-led Government. Namboodiripad returned empty-handed, as the Soviets were unwilling to incur the wrath of the Congress party by assisting in the economic development of Kerala during a period of CPI rule. It might be noted, parenthetically, that New Delhi does not welcome negotiations by any State governments, CPI-led or not, with any of the aid-donor nations.

11. *Keesing Contemporary Archives*, March 19–26, 1960, p. 17322.

12. See Michael Kidron, *Foreign Investments in India* (Oxford University Press, 1965), p. 116.

13. East Germany by the end of 1964 had 38 collaboration agreements with privately owned Indian firms; Czechoslovakia and Poland, 14 each; Hungary, 9; and Rumania, 5 (Ibid., p. 116).

Significantly, the Soviets announced their contribution to India's Third Five Year Plan in September 1959, the very month when the world learned for the first time of the Sino-Indian dispute. In August 1960 New Delhi revealed that the USSR had offered an additional rupees 60 crores for use by the Third Five Year Plan. Coming shortly after the Bucharest Conference of June 1960, this additional Soviet aid to India had important political significance. Among other issues at Bucharest, Premier Krushchev and Marshal Peng had clashed sharply on the respective policies of the USSR and China towards India. The USSR answered the Chinese charge that their aid was being used to bolster up the "reactionary" Nehru government by further increasing its developmental aid to India. On February 20, 1961, the Soviet deputy premier, A. N. Kosygin, arrived in Delhi for talks with the Planning Commission on utilization of the aid, and the following day six projects, to be financed by the rupees 60 crore pledge, were announced. The projects included:

1. a hydroelectric plant on the bank of the Bhakra with a planned capacity of 480,000 Kilowatts;

2. an oil refinery in Gujerat;

3. a washery for coking coal at Kathara in Bihar—capacity three million tons per year;

4. a refractories plant near Bhilai to produce annually 125,000 tons of magnesite and fire clay;

5. oil exploration in Cambay;

6. production of pumps and compressors.[14]

The total Soviet commitment to the Third Five Year Plan was increased to rupees 240 crores (about $500 million U.S.) by the additional credits authorized in February 1961. In addition, several Eastern European allies of the USSR were encouraged to give

14. See Appendix A. Complete listings of aid pledged by foreign nations to India are included in the government of India's annual publication, *External Assistance*. For aid to the first three Five Year Plans see Columbia University School of Law, *Public International Development Financing in India*, Report no. 9, (New York, 1964).

assistance to the Plan (Czechoslovakia pledged rupees 23.10 crores and Poland 14.3 crores by January 1961). By comparison the Sino-Soviet Agreement of 1959 called for the dispersal of 5,000 million (pre-devaluation) rubles in credits for China's developmental projects, for use between 1960–68. The terms of the Sino-Soviet Agreement were in effect abrogated by the withdrawal of Soviet technicians from China and Chinese trainees from the USSR in the autumn of 1960.

According to government of India estimates, the needs for external assistance to the Third Five Year Plan approximated rupees 2600 crores (about $5.5 billion U.S.) exclusive of American Public Law 480 aid. The loans from the USSR alone constituted a little less than one-tenth of this requirement as of 1962. By contrast the United States pledged more than one billion dollars in credits and grants as its share of the Aid-to-India consortium "for the first two years of the Third FYP, and earlier it agreed to supply more than $1 billion worth of P.L. 480 foodgrains during the first four years of the Plan."[15] However, the political considerations in having the USSR as a donor nation and the nature of the Soviet projects enhanced the value of Soviet aid in the eyes of its recipients.

The USSR concentrated its aid on the types of projects which could best draw upon available Soviet resources and expertise, such as steel production, machine tools, and power plants. The Soviets also tried to select projects in fields in which the Indians received insufficient assistance from the West (or were dissatisfied with the assistance being rendered). This latter criterion most surely was a motivating factor in the decision of the USSR and the East European Communist nations to enter into projects in the exploration for and refining of oil. Work by Soviet specialists was begun in 1955–56 in the Punjab and Rajasthan. Indians began also to receive training in geophysics, geology, and related fields in the USSR. A Rumanian oil rig was set up in the Punjab in April 1957, and the Russians provided three rigs. A Soviet team

15. Lewis, *Quiet Crisis in India*, p. 249.

discovered oil in the Cambay area of Gujerat in November 1958. An impressive strike was made at Ankleshwar, Gujerat in 1960. Gas and oil were also discovered by Soviet specialists at several sites in Assam. To help refine India's increased oil needs, Rumania built a 500,000–750,000 ton capacity refinery at Gauhati, Assam, and the Russians a two million ton capacity refinery at Barauni.

Detailed plans for the Barauni project were discussed during the Kosygin visit to India in February 1961. (Several weeks later, in March, the USSR signed an agreement with Pakistan calling for Soviet specialists, equipment, and $30 million in credits to be advanced for oil exploration in Pakistan.) K. D. Malaviya, who in June 1960 had conducted talks with the Soviets on the import and refining of oil by the Indian government, returned to Moscow in October 1962. At the height of the Sino-Indian crisis he conveyed Nehru's views on the possible consequences that the military setback might have on India's policy of nonalignment. At that time the Russians promised to speed up aid to India's coal and oil industries.[16]

The Soviets themselves gave considerable publicity to the construction of the refinery at Barauni. An editorial in *Pravda* in January 1963, for example, stressed that "with assistance of the Soviet specialists, Indian technicians and engineers are mastering the most modern means of construction. Many of these methods are being adopted for the first time in India."[17] The plant was scheduled to begin production by the end of 1963, but a conference of Indian and Russian officials in February 1964 revealed that a substantial amount of the equipment to be utilized by the refinery had not yet arrived. V. A. Sergeev, Deputy Chairman of the Soviet State Committee for Economic Relations, informed Humayun Kabir, Indian Union minister for petroleum and chemicals, that the equipment would be delivered by the end of February and suggested

16. *Times of India*, October 29, 1962.

17. "Black Gold of India," *Pravda*, January 18, 1963. The only progress mentioned in the article was the earthenwork structure which raised the factory area two meters in order to safeguard it from flooding by the Ganges river.

that labor shortages at the project site had slowed down the plan of construction.[18] In late March Kabir announced that the first stage of the plant would be completed in April or May and that the capacity of the plant would be expanded from two million tons to three million tons. The refinery is now operative and is shipping oil to Kanpur via a pipeline completed in September 1966 with Italian assistance.[19]

Some of the Soviet projects for India's Third Five Year Plan were considerably behind schedule, but no more so than the projects sponsored by other foreign donors. On occasion the Soviets have been rather slow in their delivery of equipment, but generally they have not been responsible for whatever slowups have occurred.

The heavy machinery plant at Ranchi in Bihar was the most important public-sector industrial project of India's Third Five Year Plan. Opened formally by Prime Minister Nehru in November 1963, the plant was planned to produce 80,000 tons of steel-making equipment per year—the equivalent of 75 percent of the basic components for a two million ton capacity steel mill.[20] Initially the Ranchi plant was to manufacture the equipment required for the Russian-financed public sector steel plant at Bokaro (see page 185). The Soviets, however, have not hidden their dissatisfaction with the inefficient Indian management of the Ranchi project and its low output thus far, and their criticism contributed to the eventual selection of a new manager by the Indian government.

Significant for its political implications was the Soviet pledge to assist India's atomic energy research program. That the USSR might so collaborate with India was revealed publicly by Y. S. Yemelyanov, president of the Central Administration for Atomic Energy of the USSR, who was among the Khrushchev entourage

18. *Hindustan Times*, February 14, 1964.

19. *Times of India Yearbook and Directory, 1967*, p. 200.

20. The Ranchi plant was the first of four projects to be undertaken by the Indian Heavy Engineering Corporation with the aid of the USSR and Czechoslovakia. See *Statesman*, November 16, 1963.

that visited India in February 1960. An Indian delegation led by Dr. H. Bhabha paid a reciprocal visit in the summer of 1960 to discuss the terms of collaboration, and in February 1961 Bhabha announced that the Russians had agreed to build a reactor in India.[21] While India planned to use the reactor for peaceful purposes, it was not prepared to subscribe to the terms of the safeguard provisions that had been written into the statute of the International Atomic Energy Agency. The IAEA provisions infringed on India's sovereignty, said Bhabha. Unlike the Western sponsors of India's atomic energy program, the USSR was not a party to the IAEA provisions. The Soviets therefore readily hailed the opposition of India and other nonaligned Afro-Asian nations to IAEA controls over their nuclear development programs. To avoid such controls India has preferred to receive its reactors on the basis of bilateral arrangements.

The Indo-Soviet agreement of October 7, 1961, called for the following:

Cooperation in research connected with the development of atomic power reactors using natural and enriched uranium and development of the use of thorium-uranium-233. It provides for reciprocal exchange of scientific information and for visits of specialists in the various aspects of the peaceful uses of atomic energy. The USSR undertakes to supply small quantities of natural and enriched uranium U-233 and plutonium for scientific research.[22]

To assist in mining uranium ores, the USSR pledged to send advisers and specialists as well as equipment for prospecting and mining the ores. The supplies were to be paid for under the terms of the then current Indo-Soviet trade agreement. Unclassified information has not yet been made available on the extent to which this Soviet pledge has been implemented. In any event, the USSR contribution to India's nuclear program has been very in-

---

21. *Hindu*, February 3, 1961. Bhabha also estimated that the Soviet-built reactor possessed by the Chinese had only a fourth of the capacity of the reactor which Canada had assembled at Trombay for India.

22. *Statesman*, October 7, 1961.

significant in comparison to that of Canada and other Western
nations.

During the polemical exchanges of 1963, the Chinese asserted
that "from 1955 to April, 1963 the Soviet Government agreed to
give India 5,000 million rupees in aid, two-thirds of it after
India provoked the Sino-Indian border conflict in 1959."[23] The
Chinese estimate of five billion rupees is a little inflated. Taking
the conversion of rubles to rupees to dollars at the official exchange
rates, the USSR extended credits worth approximately $811.1
million to India during the aforementioned period. The Soviet aid
to India constituted almost a third of an estimated total of $3.56
billion in Soviet credits and grants extended to the less-developed
non-Communist countries between January 1, 1954, and June
30, 1962. During this period the bulk of the credits were given
in 1955 ($116 million) to cover the exchange costs of the Bhilai
plant; in 1956 ($126 million) for the purchase of steel products;
and in 1959 ($375 million) and in 1960 ($125 million) for those
projects listed in this chapter.[24] Almost all of the Soviet aid is in
the form of credits, repayable in goods at two and a half percent
interest over twelve years with a two-year grace period. The Indian
government has been repaying the Soviet bloc credits almost on
schedule.[25] With the exception of several small grants valued at
about $6 million (for the Suratgarh model farm in Northern

23. "No One Can Save the Indian Reactionaries from their Political Bank-
ruptcy," *Peking Review*, 6 (August 30, 1963) : 8.

24. From the inception of the Communist bloc aid program in India through
1963, it has been estimated that over 1,500 bloc technicians went to India in
connection with 75 projects, excluding doctors and scientists at work in hospitals and technical institutes.

25. Soviet aid to India and other developing economies often has a more
favorable rate of interest than Western aid, although this is not true in the case
of the United States AID and the International Development Association loans.
The repayment schedules of Western loans are generally more favorable to
India.

The complexities involved in assessing foreign exchange problems, tying
aid to purchases from donor countries, repayment schedules, and the relative
merits of grants and hard and soft loans are dealt with in Friedmann, Kalmanoff,
and Meagher, *International Financial Aid*, and elsewhere.

Rajasthan, equipment for the Bombay Institute of Technology, and personal airplanes for Nehru and Krishna Menon),[26] the Soviet assistance during Nehru's era was almost entirely in the form of repayable credits, in contrast to the substantial proportion of grants contained in America's contribution to Indian development.

Late in 1963 it was announced that the USSR's assistance for India's Fourth Five Year Plan would equal the $500 million pledged to the Third Five Year Plan. As before, the emphasis would be towards helping to strengthen the basic industries in the public sector. The major Soviet project during the Fourth Five Year Plan will be the Bokaro steel plant, which when completed will be India's fourth public-sector steel plant. Amid much publicity the Soviets agreed on May 1, 1964, to finance the construction at Bokaro, an undertaking which the United States had considered for some time but declined. The USSR then decided to subsidize the 1.5 million ton first stage of the plant, which would later be expanded to a four million ton annual capacity. On February 19, 1965, the minister of steel, Sanjiva Reddi, told the Lok Sabha that the Russians had thus far extended rupees 1,005 million ($211 million) for the first stage of the plant. He predicted that Bokaro would begin its production in 1970. The heavy engineering plant at Ranchi was expected to supply 40 percent of the needed machinery for Bokaro.

The following is mainly a paraphrase of Marshall Goldman's account of the Bokaro story.[27]

26. A grant of rupees 1.15 crores was given for the mechanized, irrigated experimental farm at Suratgarh in Rajasthan at the time of the Khrushchev visit in 1955. Despite the Russian effort put into the farm (the largest mechanized farm in Asia), the project, like other attempts at cooperative farming in India, has not been considered very successful.

Humayun Kabir, minister of scientific research and cultural affairs, announced the terms of the B.I.T. agreement: "The Soviet Government will supply in 1959–60 equipment costing three million rubles . . . , train 50 Indian specialists, make available the services of Soviet professors and teachers . . . , and arrange for translation into English of Soviet textbooks for higher educational purposes." See *Lok Sabha Debates*, vol. 30, no. 21 (April 21, 1959), cols. 12459–60.

27. Marshall Goldman, *Soviet Foreign Aid* (New York: Praeger, 1967), pp. 91–93.

India's request for American aid in building a fourth public-sector steel plant came at a time when the entire American foreign aid program was under attack in the United States Congress. The estimated costs for the first stage of production was $919 million, including $512 million in foreign exchange. (As it turned out, these figures were overestimated.) The Bokaro plant was expected to cost about double the capital expenditure per ton capacity of the other three foreign-built steel mills in India.

The political implications of the project were "equally if not more important." India's Ambassador to the UN, V. K. Krishna Menon, had embittered American thinking on India. "As in the case of Aswan there was doubt if the American public could tolerate open criticism over the period of time needed for the disbursal of the large sum required at Bokaro." Negotiations dragged on for several years. Ambassador Galbraith returned to the United States in order to testify at the congressional hearings on the matter. "But despite the pleas of Ambassador Galbraith and President Kennedy, an American steel mission recommended that the project not be supported. Rather than force an awkward vote on the issue in the American Congress, India decided to avoid any more embarrassment and withdrew its request for aid."[28]

Looking for an alternative source of aid, India approached several countries including the USSR. On April 30, 1964, the Soviets agreed to undertake the project and to lend India $211 million for the first stage of construction. India wanted to use its own resources as much as possible. The design work was divided among the Indian firm, Dastur and Company, and the Russians.[29]

---

28. One point of disagreement was "a demand by the American advisors that the project be built on a 'turn-key' basis; i.e., that the Americans construct and operate the plant for a ten-year period before turning it over to India. This was to avoid a repetition of the Rourkela experience. While most Indians agreed that some sort of stewardship might be wise, they were unable to understand the need for such a lengthy period of time." See Goldman, *Soviet Foreign Aid*, p. 92.

29. The Soviets are doing the bulk of the design work. According to one commentator, "Dasturs was 'allowed' to design only the outer structures and columns,

The plant's machinery will be supplied by the Heavy Engineering Corporation at Ranchi. There were some reservations on the part of India on the Soviet terms; but the arrangements were on the whole deemed satisfactory, and the agreement was formally concluded.

The first decade of Soviet aid to India ended in February 1965. During that period the USSR had authorized an estimated 4,842 million rupees ($1,017 million U. S.) in loans for various developmental projects in India.[30]

Table 1, based on a table compiled by Leo Tansky, lists Soviet economic aid extended to less-developed countries from 1954–65:[31]

---

apparently because foundations for the important plant are considered too difficult to be designed indigenously. Such drawings as are available are vetted by the Russians, then handed to Bokaro Steel Ltd. for 'approval,' then to Hindustan Steelworks Construction Ltd. for 'action' and then to the contractor. . . . Presumably, certification of the completed works will follow the same tortuous, four-phased path." "The Bokaro Colosseum," *Economic and Political Weekly*, March 2, 1968, pp. 379–80.) See also "Bokaro with Soviet Aid," *Economic Weekly* 16 (May 9, 1964) : 796–97; and "Bokaro Embroglio," *Economic Weekly* 15 (May 4, 1963) : 752–53.

30. *New York Times*, February 19, 1965.

31. Leo Tansky, "Soviet Foreign Aid to the Less Developed Countries," in *New Directions in the Soviet Economy*, prepared for the Joint Economic Committee, Congress of the United States, part 4 of *The World Outside* (Washington, D. C.: Government Printing Office, 1966), p. 974. Reviewing the Soviet aid program from 1954 to 1965, Tansky wrote: "During the past dozen years economic and military aid to the less developed countries has become a key instrument in Soviet efforts to project its presence into all areas of the developing world. From a small beginning in mid-1954 the program has grown dramatically, has widened in scope and content, and has attained a relatively high degree of sophistication. In 1954 about $6 million in foreign aid was extended by the Soviet Union. By the end of 1965 the cumulative total of Soviet economic assistance had grown to about $5 billion and its military aid program to about $4 billion. During these years about 13,500 academic students and nearly 25,000 military and technical trainees have trained in the USSR. In addition, an estimated 65,000 Soviet economic and military technicians have been employed in aid activities in recipient countries." [All figures in this paragraph exclude aid to Cuba.] (Ibid., pp. 949–50.)

TABLE 1

SOVIET AID TO LESS-DEVELOPED COUNTRIES

(In Millions of U.S. Dollars)

India	1,022	Greece	84
United Arab Republic	1,011	Guinea	70
Afghanistan	552	Somali Republic	57
Indonesia	372	Mali	55
Iran	330	Kenya	44
Algeria	230	Ceylon	30
Turkey	210	Tunisia	28
Iraq	184	Sudan	22
Syria	150	Cambodia	21
Argentina	115	Nepal	20
Ethiopia	102	Uganda	16
Pakistan	94	Burma	14
Yemen	92	Congo (Brazzaville)	9
Ghana	89	Senegal	7
		Total	5,030

The general scope of the Soviet aid program is clear enough, although attempts to account for the utilization of all the authorized funds are replete with difficulties.[32]

As portrayed by the Soviets, aid to the less-developed countries is given openheartedly

to promote natural economic progress and the rapid development of productive forces in those former colonies and dependent countries (India, Burma, Indonesia, the U.A.R. and others) . . . which have

32. Commenting on the hazards of dealing with data on Soviet aid programs, Charles McLane observed: "Things are not always what they seem in Soviet foreign aid. Unused credits are sometimes absorbed in new ones, with no announcement of the fact; projects begun may be abandoned, with no clear indication of how much was expended on the part completed; supplementary funds are often required for the completion of major programs, yet not always shown in the periodic credits and protocols which are announced; repayment schedules, tied to foreign trade, are rarely broken down after the initial announcement of a loan, so that it is the task of a wizard to calculate how much of a given credit has been repaid at a given juncture; arms deliveries, needless to say, are indicated —if at all—in the most meager detail and what portion of them is covered by credits, as distinct from direct purchase, is rarely shown." (Charles B. McLane, "Foreign Aid in Soviet Third World Policies," paper prepared for delivery at the 1968 Annual Meeting of the American Political Science Association, Washington, D. C. [September 2–7, 1968], pp. 2–3.)

broken away from the colonial system of imperialism. . . . The Soviet peoples, who themselves have experienced the yoke of exploitation by foreign capital, can fully sympathize with and understand the aspirations of the African, Asian and Latin American peoples for economic independence and a higher standard of living.[33]

This theme, while sometimes differently orchestrated, permeates nearly all official Soviet writing and speeches about its aid to the underdeveloped nations.

Generally speaking, during the years of rapprochment with India the Soviets gave almost unqualified praise to the achievements of the Indian government in the political, social, and economic spheres. Although their growing concern with China later brought the USSR and India even closer together in the international sphere, the USSR was not always reluctant in Nehru's last years to criticize aspects of India's domestic policies.

One such critique of the Indian scene appeared in a *New Times* article, written by three senior researchers at the Institute of the People of Asia.[34] Attention was given to the resolutions of the Congress party conclave held in Bhubaneswar, Orissa, early in January 1964. The concrete social and economic measures envisaged in the Congress resolutions were termed "very hazy" and formulated in "very nebulous terms." The *New Times* article observed that in reality little was said (or presumably will be done) about eliminating the "glaring social disparity" between the exploiters and the exploited, about nationalization of industries, or about eliminating the consequences of foreign capital investment. The advocates for following a capitalist path, the article concluded, had seemingly gained the upper hand at Bhubaneswar.

---

33. V. Rimalov, *Economic Cooperation*, p. 38. Also see V. Kondratyev, "The Role of India's Economic Collaboration with Countries of the Socialist Camp in the Development of India's Economy;" *Voprosi Ekonomiki*, 1:11; M. Nestrov and V. Sergeey, "Economic Cooperation between India and the USSR," *Foreign Affairs Record* (India) 8 (December, 1958): 142–52.

34. Kotovsky, Pavlov, and Redko, "Some Indian Economic and Political Problems."

Only the resolution on the international situation at Bhubaneswar was unreservedly praised.[35]

V. I. Pavlov's *India: Economic Freedom Versus Imperialism* provided a lengthy Soviet view on trends in the Indian economy. Pavlov explains that "state capitalism may be outliving its historic usefulness in the case of India." Like other Soviet writers,[36] he chides India for the slow development and implementation of land-reform programs.[37] The major concern, however, is with the over-dependence of India on Western capital. Using various "documentation" (but relying mainly on "bourgeois" Indian and American sources), Pavlov attempted to demonstrate how Western private investment, and even aid on an inter-governmental basis, is used to influence India's economic and political life. The notion that the United States has taken advantage of its economic aid program along with other diplomatic pressures in an attempt to prevent India from pursuing an independent foreign policy has been a recurrent theme in Soviet writings.[38]

Generally the Soviets have warned India of the imminent danger in becoming economically dependent upon Western capital and assistance. Yet the Soviet Union indirectly has cooperated with the United States in aiding India's development and thus in lending support to the political stability of India. Despite the embarrassment of being identified as collaborators with the Americans

35. A review of the article in the *Times of India*, February 20, 1964, noted that "hitherto the non-specialist Russian reader had been given a rough-and-ready image of the Congress as divided between 'reactionaries' and 'progressives.' Like a good wife the Indian political scene was not talked about. Perhaps it was the illness of Mr. Nehru that prompted Soviet observes to break their silence and look behind the figure which occupied most of the foreground in their view of India."

36. Pavlov, *India*.

37. Selections from Soviet writings on Indian land reform, the "composition and structure" of the Indian working class, etc., are included in Thorton, *The Third World in Soviet Perspective*.

38. See, for example, the section by G. Kolchalova, "Economic 'Aid' of the United States to India," in *Politika S. Sh. A. v. Stranax Yuzhnoi Azii* [Policy of the U.S.A. in countries of South Asia], ed. B. Gafurov (Moscow, 1961).

by their critics within the Communist world, the Soviet leaders found it expedient to increase their assistance to India during Nehru's last five years and the first years of the successor governments.

As the Soviets have not given India any large nonrepayable grants of aid, the Soviet program is not as generous as it is made out to be by their publicists. Their impressive statistics on Soviet projects in India often obscure the fact that the Soviets make a somewhat arbitrary distinction in their aid and trade programs. (The Soviets, incidentally, are not alone in this practice.) India repays the USSR in goods for a large proportion of the projects and commodities it receives, regardless of whether the Soviet items are listed as "aid" or "trade." On the other hand, detractors of Soviet aid to India and other developing nations often underplay or ignore a number of salient factors, which include the following: (1) Nehru and other Indian leaders have thought, with considerable justification, that it is in their nation's self-interest to receive assistance from the USSR. This aid has helped to strengthen the nation's political independence and its economic self-reliance. (2) The United States would have been unwilling to sponsor most of the types of public-sector projects undertaken by the USSR. (3) Although there are some exceptions (like tea), certain raw materials and other Indian commodities sent to the USSR might not have been absorbed at standard prices by the existing international markets.

Those Third World nations which receive more than half of their foreign assistance from the Communist countries have more often than not sided with the Soviet Union on Cold War issues. This point has been demonstrated by Jan Triska and David Finley in a statistical analysis of the correlation between Communist aid and trade with the "developing" nations and the voting patterns of these nations on "key votes" in the United Nations in 1961 and 1962. In this sample study those nations which received more economic aid from the Socialist bloc from 1954–62 than from the

West—Iraq, Guinea, Afghanistan, Yemen, Indonesia, Burma, Ghana, the U.A.R., Nepal, and Ethiopia—all voted more frequently with the Communist nations in 1961–62 on "key votes."[39] During that period, India voted with the West about as often as with the USSR. While the source of a developing nation's economic and technological assistance from abroad is a good indicator of the recipient's UN voting patterns, the extent of the cause and effect relationship between Communist aid and the voting behavior of the recipient nations is of course not fully ascertainable.[40]

39. Economic Aid from 1954–62 (Grants and Credits) (in millions of U.S. dollars):

	Aid from Party-States	Aid from the West
Iraq	218.0	18.0
Guinea	125.	13.4
Afghanistan	514.0	193.
Yemen	44.0	22.8
Indonesia	638.0	393.1
Burma	97.0	75.3
Ghana	196.0	156.0
U. A. R.	716.0	575.9
Nepal	54.0	47.6
Ethiopia	114.0	111.3
Ceylon	69.0	79.4
India	982.0	3533.3
Cambodia	65.0	250.7
Cyprus	1.0	16.9
Turkey	17.0	1251.3
Iran	6.0	657.3
Pakistan	33.0	1733.1

(Countries ranked in order of the total percentage of their foreign aid received from the USSR.)
(Figures extracted from table 7 in Triska and Finley, *Soviet Foreign Policy*, p. 276. Also see ibid., pp. 273–78.)

40. Some nonaligned nations would have voted alongside the USSR for a number of issues unrelated to Communist aid programs. Nonetheless in some instances the Soviet influence obviously was there.

India, although a recipient of 20 percent of the total Soviet foreign aid program, has received considerably more aid from the West than from the USSR. Despite the growing volume of Indo-Soviet trade, only 6–8 percent of New

India as a Recipient of Soviet Aid

The first Five Year Plan, initiated in 1950–51, achieved its rather limited objective of raising the average annual per capita income by 1.4 percent. Encouraged by this relative success, the Indian Planning Commission substantially increased the scope of the projected Second Five Year Plan. In January 1955 the annual session of the Congress party resolved that "planning should take place with a view to the establishment of a socialistic pattern of society, where the principal means of production are under social ownership or control."[41] This resolution was given substance by the greatly increased emphasis given to the government sector of the Second Five Year Plan. During the First Five Year Plan the expenditure for both the public and private sectors was about $4 billion each, whereas the proposed expenditure for the public sector in the Second Five Year Plan was approximately $10 billion as opposed to half that amount in the private sector.

In the formulation of the Second Five Year Plan, considerably more emphasis was given to the buildup of basic heavy industry in the public sector of the economy. To help underwrite the Second Five Year Plan, a considerable increase in foreign assistance was anticipated. The Planning Commission report in 1956 estimated that rupees 800 crores[42] would be received from external

---

Delhi's total foreign trade in the early 1960s was with the Socialist countries. India's UN voting record in selected key votes of the 1961–62 period numbered eight votes with the Communist nations, seven with the Western (USA, Britain, and France) nations, and five absentions.

41. Indian National Congress, Steering Committee, "Resolution on the 'Socialist Pattern of Society.'" Quoted in Malenbaum, *Prospects for Indian Development,* p. 48. Professor Malenbaum points out that the "broad objective of achieving a socialist pattern of society'" had remained unchanged since the Avadi Conference of 1955. The Congress session at Bhavnagar in 1961, for example, called upon the government to ensure the "good of the community as a whole."

42. One crore equals 10 million rupees; 1 rupee was the equivalent of about 21 U.S. cents until the devaluation of June 6, 1966. The present rate of exchange is 1 rupee for 13.33 U.S. cents.

assistance for credit in the public sector, "as against a total of Rs. 204 crores utilized in the first plan."[43]

As planning within the public sector was almost unprecedented in the Western democracies, it is only natural that the Indian planners took a closer look at the experiences of the Soviet Union and the Eastern European Communist nations. Professor Oscar Lange, the Polish economist, was one of the important foreign advisors to the Planning Commission. This is not to suggest that India used the Communist nations as an exclusive model for its Five Year Plan, but their experiences could hardly be ignored. The apparent liberalizing tendencies within the Communist world itself encouraged the Congress party leadership to view the "Socialist system" in a more favorable light than in years past.

It is difficult for the professional economist, let alone the student of politics, to measure the importance of the foreign aid component as a factor in Indian development. Yet it is obvious that foreign assistance has been of great importance to Indian planners.[44] Suffice it to say that the pattern of Indian development, particularly in the public sector, most probably would have been substantially different without such assistance. The implementation of most of the Five Year Plan projects would have been impossible without foreign aid, and it is unlikely that Indian leaders could thus far have avoided mobilizing the nation along more authoritarian lines.

While India during 1954–64 received more Soviet and American aid than any other nation, the aid received per capita was

43. Planning Commission, Government of India, *Second Five Year Plan* (New Delhi, 1956), p. 104.

44. Discussing the importance of foreign aid to India's Third Five Year Plan one study concludes: "The external aid has been of increasing significance in connection with India's attempts to achieve rates of economic growth in excess of its population growth. The large volume of assistance during the Third Five Year Plan was equal to the total of imports during this period for investment plus some for consumption; in other words, the external financial assistance has financed at least all imports in excess of those required for maintenance of the economy at current levels of activity." (Friedmann, Kalmanoff, and Meaghet, *International Financial Aid*, p. 219.)

considerably smaller than those countries on the periphery of the Communist world which had aligned themselves with the West.[45] Including P. L. 480 food, the total monetary value of American assistance to India during the Nehru years exceeded the Soviet contribution by roughly a 5–1 ratio. The total value of American aid might have been slightly greater had India been a member of the SEATO, but it is highly unlikely that the per capita aid for India's teeming millions would have approached anything near that received by Taiwan or South Korea. India could not have established rapport with the USSR in the 1950s if she had had formal ties with the Western alliance. The attendant political advantages of good political relations with the USSR therefore outweighed for India the possibility of additional American assistance. As it has turned out, India did not hurt herself economically by her close association with the Soviet Union. The Nehru government openly acknowledged the importance of the Soviet contribution, particularly in the construction of basic heavy industries in the public sector.[46] This Soviet aid has been tailored to the needs of India as conceived by the government and its Planning Commission. Aid from the Communist nations enabled India to become somewhat less dependent on the West. Also, American interest in and assistance to India increased considerably as a result of the Soviet "challenge."

As India's relations with China began to deteriorate seriously in 1958–59, Prime Minister Nehru attached prime importance to a Soviet-American detente. He hoped that India would become one of the "areas of agreement" between the global rivals. "It is

45. In a representative year, 1958–59, India received $1.60 per capita in foreign aid from all donor nations. By comparison, Pakistan received $3.80 per capita; Iran, $7.20; Taiwan, $17.60; South Korea, $28.60; Libya, $46.80; and Jordan, $68.10 (*United Nations Statistical Yearbook*, 1960).

46. See, for example, a series of articles on "Independent India's Cooperation with the Socialist World," in *Socialist Congressman*, vol. 2 (August 15, 1962). See also Sisir Gupta, "Aid from Soviet Union and its Allies," in Rajan, *India in World Affairs*, pp. 615–19.

a remarkable thing . . . ," he observed, "how these two tremendous protagonists of the Cold War can yet have this friendly feeling for India . . . [We are] equally grateful to the United States and the USSR for help."[47] In time, it was hoped that American and Soviet aid to India would become mutually complementary, and that both countries would become increasingly committed to India's developmental progress.

There remained, however, a suspicion among many politically conscious Indians that the USSR had become too involved in India's economic and developmental planning. Nehru was not insensitive to expressions of concern. Whenever possible his Government played down the fact that Communist nations were participating in Indian development. For example, a proposal was put forth by Rumania and Czechoslovakia early in 1961 which called for East European countries to give aid to India on a multilateral rather than a bilateral basis. In effect this would have created a Comecon consortium similar to the Western Aid-India Club. India objected to the proposal on the grounds that multilateral aid would be too difficult to coordinate. More important, however, commented the *Hindu*, was the concern over the "political by-products" of projects being labeled "Communist projects rather than Russian, Czech, Polish or Rumanian."[48]

Indo-Soviet Trade Relations

Commerce between British India and the Soviet Union had been very limited. In 1938 India exported goods valued at $1.3 million to the USSR and imported $.7 million worth of Soviet products. This trade constituted about .2 percent of the total exports of both India and the USSR in the year prior to the outbreak

47. *Rajya Sabha Official Reports*, vol. 30, no. 8 (August 18, 1960), col. 1353.

48. *Hindu*, January 30, 1961. An editorial in the same paper on February 2, 1961, noted that the USSR contributed about 90 percent of the aid to India by Communist nations, and Czechoslovakia, Rumania, and Poland, the other 10 percent.

of World War II.[49] A goodly percentage of India's trade was with the "mother country," whereas most of the prewar commerce of the USSR was with its European neighbors.

After the war there was an increase in Indo-Soviet commerce, although the volume was still very little. Then with the hardening of Cold War lines in 1948, trade dwindled to a trickle. Between 1948 and 1953 the value of Soviet trade with underdeveloped, non-Communist areas decreased by approximately two-thirds. In the case of India specifically, the value of Soviet imports (from India) fell from $16.2 million in 1948 to $.7 million in 1953, and exports (to India) during that five year period fell from $9.8 million to $.9 million. (See Appendix B for table of Indo-Soviet trade statistics).

As part of their policy of improving relations with the non-aligned countries, Stalin's successors put forth attractive offers to enter negotiations for trade expansion. On December 2, 1953, the USSR and India signed a five year agreement, calling for a substantial increase in the volume of their trade over the 1954–58 period.[50] Some of the commodities specified for exchange on a barter basis included jute goods, coffee, tea, tobacco, spices, and vegetable oils from India; and food-grains, crude petroleum products, iron and steel manufactures, industrial equipment, and tractors from the USSR.

In December 1955, during the Khrushchev-Bulganin state tour of India, it was announced that the projected level of Indo-Soviet trade envisaged by the 1953 agreement would be surpassed. The new terms called for a substantial increase in Soviet purchases from

49. The UN publication, *Direction of International Trade*, provides annual listings of Indian imports and exports and Soviet totals for years when the figures are released by the USSR. Also see UN, *Yearbook of International Trade Statistics* and Government of India, *Annual Statement of Foreign Trade of India*. Trade percentages listed in this section were calculated by the author.

50. Czechoslovakia began trade talks with India shortly before the USSR and an Indo-Czech Agreement was concluded on November 17, 1953. This and subsequent trade pacts between India and other Commuist nations are detailed in the monthly Indian governmental publication, *Foreign Affairs Record*.

India and for the USSR to supply India with one million tons of steel and steel products during a three-year period beginning in 1956. As in the previous agreement, it was determined that the total value of India's purchases would equal the value of India's exports to the USSR and that each party would give the other "most-favored nation" treatment.

Indo-Soviet trade continued to increase in volume, and the 1955 agreement had to be replaced by another five-year pact in November 1958.[51] The greatest increases were in 1955–56, when Indian imports rose from $5.2 million to $26.2 million and exports increased from $6.4 million to $31.3 million over the one-year span. In 1958 India's imports from the USSR, valued at $45.6 million, constituted approximately 1.8 percent of its total imports. Exports to the USSR in 1958 totaled about $49 million, or 4.2 percent of India's overall exports. The percentage increase in Indo-Soviet trade from 1953–59 was very impressive. Russian statisticians almost always pointed to these percentages—representing a "fifteen fold increase" from 1951–59—rather than to the actual total volume of the trade. In fact only slightly more than one percent of the USSR's total world trade in 1959 was conducted with India, but this did not negate the political advantages which accrued from the trade. Combined with the program of economic and technological assistance, changing trade patterns provide an effective indicator of the direction of Soviet policy.[52] Increased commerce helped to normalize and later to solidify a cooperative relationship with India.

Interestingly enough, political developments within the Sino-Soviet-Indian triangle from 1957–59 were paralleled closely by changes in the volume of steel products exported by the USSR to India and China. The initial decrease of Soviet exports of steel products to China in 1957 can be explained in part by the Chinese

---

51. *Foreign Affairs Record*, no. 11, November 1958.

52. For a study of Soviet trade patterns see F. L. Pryor, *The Communist Foreign Trade System* (London, 1963).

attempt to increase their own self-sufficiency in steel. But the level of Soviet shipments of steel in China did not return to the 1956 level despite the failure of the Chinese "Great Leap Forward."[53]

In the 1960s India became the USSR's most important trading partner among the developing nations.[54] While India's main trading partners in the early 1960s were still the United Kingdom, the United States, and Japan, the percentage of India's trade with the Soviet Union and the Eastern European Communist countries continued to increase. By 1963–64 the USSR ranked fourth behind these nations in total trade with India, and in 1965–66 the Soviets displaced Japan as the third-ranked.[55] An Indo-Soviet

53. Soviet steel products exports to India, China, and to the Far-East as a whole were as follows:

To all of Far East (including India and China)		To India	To China
1956	739.2	247.5	429.7
1957	516	251.4	217.9
1958	536.6	256.7	259.8
1959	477	237.6	185.9

See UN, Statistics in World Trade in Steel (New York, 1960).

54. A few comparative statistics should help to provide some perspective of the Soviet and East European trade with India. The level of commerce between the European Communist nations and the developing nations of Asia, Latin America, and Africa increased by about 300 percent during the decade of rapidly expanding trade from 1955 to 1964. The overall rate of growth over that ten-year period was 13 percent, although it slowed down to 11 percent annually after 1960. By 1964 Asian countries accounted for about 40 percent of Communist trade with the developing countries (India, Indonesia, and Malaysia together accounted for 70 percent of this Asian trade). Altogether Soviet and East European trade with India represented 15 percent of their total trade with the developing nations. In 1964 Soviet exports to India were valued at an estimated $231.8 million, while East European (including Yugoslav) exports to India that year were $132.8 million. Soviet imports from India during 1964 were totalled $155.9 million, while East European imports from India were valued at $139.9 million. In 1964, 29.8 percent of Soviet exports to developing countries went to India while 23.5 percent of its imports came from India. (All the statistics in this note are from Sawyer, *Communist Trade with Developing Countries*, pp. 7, 12, 13, 100–103.)

55. India's leading trade partners, fiscal year April 1965–March 1966 (in pre-devaluation rupees; figures rounded off at nearest 10,000) :

agreement, signed in Moscow on June 10, 1963, had called for an average annual increase during 1964–68 double that of the 1962 volume of trade.

In 1966 the estimated total trade between the two countries was rupees 198 crores ($416.8 million), and in 1967, rupees 280 crores ($373.3 million after devaluation at the new exchange rate of $1. = 7.5 Indian rupees).[56] The projected total trade for 1968 was rupees 300 crores ($400 million).

Indian imports in 1968 included capital goods, components, and spares for the maintenance of production in forty-odd Soviet projects in India. A second category of products included fertilizers, zinc and tin plates, chemicals for the manufacture of drugs, dyestuffs, laboratory chemicals, wood pulp, kerosene, and other oil products. Exports of traditional Indian items like tea, spices, mica, and oil cake extract remained at the 1967 levels. Among the Indian exports that were increased were leather shoes, textiles, ready-made garments, woolen knitwear, rolled steel products, automobile tires, and light electrical products.[57]

The most important Indian exports have been jute and tea, which together accounted for 35 percent of India's total exports in 1964–65 and for 27.5 percent of India's exports to the Communist nations. During the same year, coffee, cashews, tobacco, and iron

	Exports to	Imports from
USA	1,469,990,000	5,253,420,000
United Kingdom	1,454,960,000	1,491,086,000
USSR	928,730,000	825,260,000
Japan	569,180,000	791,890,000

(From *Times of India Directory and Yearbook 1967*, p. 109.)

56. *Times of India*, December 27, 1967. These 1966–67 figures show the hazard of measuring the value of Indo-Soviet trade in U.S. dollar equivalents. In actuality the volume of Indo-Soviet trade increased during the year after the devaluation of the Indian rupee, for the pricing system of the goods exchanged is not contingent on the official exchange rates of the rupee and ruble. Both currencies are nonconvertible.

57. Ibid.

ore each accounted for from 5 to 6 percent of Indian exports. On the other hand, machinery (excluding electric) comprised fifty-four percent of the value of Indian imports from the Communist nations in 1964–65, followed by base metals (15.2 percent) and electrical machinery and appliances (8.5 percent). These and previous Soviet goods were important in providing an infrastructure for public-sector industrial development in India's Second and Third Five Year Plans.[58]

During the 1950s India's percentage of the world's total trade decreased, as she was hard pressed even to maintain her 1948 level of exports.[59] The Indian government was seriously concerned over the yearly decline in its sterling balance.[60] Thus India welcomed the trade agreements with the USSR and Eastern Europe which called for a parity in the value of the products exported and imported. Trade with the USSR and other Communist nations was expected to help ease the strain on New Delhi's balance of payments difficulties and to help create long-term stability and growth for exports.

But even with this seemingly equitable arrangement, a number of problems have arisen on both sides. For example, the Government of India through the State Trading Corporation handles all arrangements for the import of Soviet products. The decision on which products will be available for export, however, is largely in the hands of private businessmen and manufacturers. While the government can induce production of some items by offering various incentives, there is on the whole a lack of coordination between New Delhi and private capital which makes long-range

58. Figures in this paragraph are from *Problems Arising in Trade Relations between Countries Having Different Economic and Social Systems: Case Study Prepared by the UNCTAD Secretariat on Trade and Economic Relations between India and the Socialist Countries of Eastern Europe* (Geneva, July 1967), pp. 43.

59. For a discussion of the problems involved in expanding India's exports, in the context of the condition of the Indian economy as a whole, see Rosen, *Democracy and Economic Change in India*, pp. 211–42.

60. The sterling balance decreased from rupees 735.18 crores in 1955 to rupees 147.67 in January 1961. See *Eastern Economist*, March 6, 1961, p. 672.

planning difficult. Perhaps this is inevitable in an essentially private-enterprise society like India. During trade talks in December 1967 Soviet delegates sought to deal with private Indian exporters directly, but they were reminded by New Delhi that the Indian State Trading Corporation had been set up specifically to handle all dealings between the Communist countries and India. During the same 1967 talks, incidentally, the Soviets rejected the Indian suggestion that India cooperate with the USSR by supplying capital goods and other equipment for certain Soviet projects in Africa.

There is, in addition, the complex problem of deciding the value of the commodities which are to be traded. This involves a wide range of questions dealing with monetary standards and pricing systems. There have been unofficial[61] Indian complaints that the Soviets and East Europeans have sometimes undervalued Indian products. Arguments have been advanced that India could have done better in the mid-1960s by selling on the open market the jute, cashews, and tea sent to the communist countries. Between 1961–62 and 1965–66, for example, Indian exports of tea to the communist countries increased considerably while exports of Indian tea to the rest of the world market declined. Almost the entire crop of Darjeeling tea was absorbed by the USSR and Eastern Europe. During that period world prices for tea rose considerably. India could have sold much more tea on the open market during this period, as did producers in Ceylon and East Africa.[62] The Soviet comeback to this argument is that commodity prices are renegotiated each year and reflect considerations such as world market supply and demand. Also the Communist coun-

61. Officially, "The Indian Ministry of International Trade has stated that trade with the Communist nations has not hurt Indian exports to other markets." ("Rupee Payment Agreements: A Balance Sheet," *Economic Weekly*, October 28, 1961, p. 1959.)

62. Rosario makes this argument forcefully in his article "India's Trade with the Socialist Bloc."

tries "have purchased large quantities of agricultural surpluses that could have been sold outside the communist area only by lowering the price."[63] There seems little doubt in this instance, however, that India would have done better by selling its tea on the competitive international market.

There are also unofficial Indian inferences that the USSR overvalues its exports to India. This may of course sometimes happen. Another charge made is that the USSR has engaged in the practice of reselling on the West European market some of the primary products imported from the "developing" countries. There was no available evidence to this writer that the USSR has done this, although several communist countries in East Europe have done so on occasion.[64] Everything considered, it seems to this writer that the Indo-Soviet trade relationship has been mutually beneficial for both countries.

From 1968 onward the USSR for the first time will be purchasing large quantities of Indian steel and steel products. A contract was signed in February 1968 for 600,000 tons of Indian steel produced at the Bhilai plants to be delivered over a three-year period.[65] This brought the total of Indian steel (excluding pig iron) to be imported by the USSR from 1968 to 1970 to one million tons. After Premier Kosygin's visit to India in January 1968, Soviet negotiators surprised their Indian counterparts by requesting a large number of Indian built railway wagons. Beginning with 4,000 railway cars in 1969, the projected quantity would reach 10,000 a year by 1972. A large Soviet delegation headed by the deputy chairman of the Soviet State Planning Committee (GOSPLAN) visited India for over three weeks begin-

---

63. "Included among these purchases have been cocoa from Ghana, coffee from Colombia, cashew nuts from India, jute from Pakistan, fish from Iceland, wheat from Argentina, rubber from Malaysia, and so forth." (Quoted from Sawyer, *Communist Trade with Developing Countries*, p. 45.)

64. See *Economist* (London), January 14, 1967.

65. *New York Times*, March 9, 1968.

ning March 26, 1968, to discuss Indo-Soviet trade, the Soviet assisted projects in India, and possible Indo-Soviet joint manufacturing ventures.

A perceptive article in the *Economic and Political Weekly* pointed to a new "problem" which has arisen in India's economic dealings with the USSR.[66] India is confronted with the question of what new products to take from the USSR, while the Soviets are concerned, for the first time, with finding sufficient rupees with which to pay for Indian imports. While Indian imports from the USSR "rose from Rs 57 crores in 1962 to Rs 95 crores [in 1967] exports during the same period increased from Rs 36 crores to Rs 135 crores (in pre-devaluation terms)." During that period India used the export surplus to help repay the short and medium term credits extended to her by the USSR as well as interest on the loans. While the Soviets are willing to import more products from India, they would like India in turn to increase her intake of Soviet manufactures, particularly machinery and components.

At the time of writing (December 1968) attention has been focused on the problems which have arisen in Indo-Soviet economic relations. A high-level Soviet delegation headed by Mr. Skachkov, chairman of the USSR State Committee for Economic Relations with Foreign Countries, came to India in early December to study the functioning of Soviet projects in India. During the visit an article appeared in *Mainstream* which is worth summarizing here at some length.[67]

The article called attention to the end of "the heady days of rapid and uninterrupted quantiative growth of Indo-Soviet economic cooperation and trade," initiated during India's Second Five Year Plan. The Soviet effort had made it possible for India "to make a significant breakthrough in several crucial sectors in

66. *Economic and Political Weekly* (Bombay), May 4, 1968, p. 698.

67. B. M., "Indo-Soviet Co-operation: New Phase," *Mainstream* 8 (December 14, 1968): 11–12, 30.

the industrial structure and establish important productive assets."
But the specific forms of past Indo-Soviet economic cooperation
have now nearly been exhausted. It will be necessary to search for
new and more complex forms if the relationship "is to regain its
vitality and further growth potential."

The Indian Fourth Five Year Plan (now rescheduled for 1969–
74) was delayed for three years, and most plans for new public
sector projects were put aside. The Soviet pledges for project aid
for the Fourth Five Year plan were therefore not drawn upon as
of the end of 1968. The Soviets have been concerned that the
projects set up during the first phase of industrial planning are
being underutilized and are not contributing sufficiently to India's
economic growth. One reason for the underutilization is the lack
of orders for some of the commodities being produced.

In any event India, with Soviet help, now has "a fairly sizeable
and diversified industrial structure"—especially in the metallurgical sector. Further development in that sector requires little or no
assistance from abroad. There is therefore less scope for Soviet
assistance in the industrial field. India desires to export manufactures from her new industries, and it is not known how much of
these the USSR can absorb on a long-term basis. Also India is
interested in importing more raw materials and component parts
from the USSR, and it "is still not clear how far these items can
be spared by the Soviet Union from its rather stretched resources
committed to many claimants." The *Mainstream* article closed by
urging each side to carefully assess the other's needs and capabilities in the search for new modes of cooperation.

Soviet Military Assistance to India

In 1955 military attachés were first exchanged by India and
the USSR and assigned to their respective embassies in New
Delhi and Moscow. As early as May 1957 Nehru mentioned (most
probably only a trial balloon) that "there is nothing to prevent
India from purchasing Soviet aircraft or any other type of ma-

chine" from the USSR if it desired to do so. He denied that the
Soviets as yet had made an offer to supply aircraft or that India
had requested to purchase aircraft from the USSR.

What has happened and what normally happens is that our Defense
Ministry keeps in touch with developments in various countries;
whether it is the USA, Great Britain, the USSR or any other country.
. . . It is true that apart from defense . . . the Soviet leaders . . . (have)
said, generally speaking, that they would like to cooperate with us
and help us wherever they could.[68]

After both India's and the USSR's relations with China worsened,
the Soviets offered to supply certain kinds of aircraft to the Indian
Defense Ministry. An Indian delegation went to Moscow in October 1960 to negotiate the purchase of Russian transport planes,
helicopters, and heavy roadmaking equipment.

In March 1961 it was announced that India had purchased from
the USSR eight AN-12 transports for use in the Ladakh area.[69]
Forty Russian pilots, navigators, and mechanics came to India
to instruct Indians in the operation and maintenance of the aircraft. Some concern was evinced by opposition members in Parliament that the Soviet airmen were permitted to go into strategic
areas on their training missions. In answer to a question put to
him by Dr. Kunzru in the Rajya Sabha on March 31, Nehru replied
that "adequate precaution has been taken to see that no secret
information could leak out." In 1964 it was estimated that thirty
AN-12 transport planes had thus far been purchased from the
USSR and that an unknown number of MI-14 helicopters had also
been purchased, more than twenty of which had been delivered by
May of that year.[70]

68. *Lok Sabha Debates*, vol. 2, no. 16 (May 30, 1957), cols. 2938–39.

69. *Hindu*, April 10, 1961. The Indian government emphasized the comparative
cost advantage of the Soviet craft which sold for nearly rupees 1 crore. A comparable American plane for use in mountainous areas cost rupees 1.25 crores.

70. From Thomas Brady, "Soviet Military Aid to India," *New York Times*,
May 13, 1964.

The Indian procurement of Soviet MIGs has been a controversial and rumor-fraught issue. From 1959 on, the Defence Ministry, headed by Krishna Menon, sought to increase the strength of the Indian armed forces and to move in the direction of military self-sufficiency. One key priority was the obtaining of aircraft equal in capability to the F-104s supplied by the United States to Pakistan. In 1962 negotiations were carried on with both Britain and the USSR for the purchase of supersonic aircraft and for help in building aircraft factories in India.[71] Irritated by the proceedings on Kashmir at the UN, Nehru on June 23 told the Lok Sabha that the United States was attempting to block India from getting the MIGs. Several weeks later the Indian government signed an agreement under which the Russians would assist India in manufacturing a modified MIG engine for the Indian built HF-24. In October it was announced (before the outbreak of fighting with China) that the Soviets would supply two squadrons of MIG-21s to match Pakistan's F-104s and would later build several factories in India for the manufacture of MIGs and ancillary equipment. The Soviet decision to supply the aircraft to India became another of the numerous grievances the Chinese were accumulating against India and the USSR. After prolonged speculation on whether or not the MIGs would be delivered, a consignment of four fighters arrived in Bombay in February 1963. In all, perhaps another eight partially equipped MIGs were received by India in the year that followed. Factory sites were selected by April in Maharashtra and Orissa for the manufacture of the MIG airframes and engines. Six months later, plans were revealed for a factory in Hyderabad which would produce air-to-air missiles and radar equipment for the aircraft.

For some time it was unclear whether the Soviets actually were going ahead with the MIG factories as scheduled. In an article in the *Washington Post* on December 17, 1963, Selig Harrison

71. For a detailed account of the MIG negotiations see Ian Graham, "The Indo-Soviet MIG Deal and its International Repercussions," *Asian Survey*, Vol. IV: 5 (May, 1964), pp. 823–832.

noted that one reason for the USSR's vacillation was that the cost estimates for the project rose from the original "$143 million at its inception in August, 1962, to a current working figure of $336 million." He also indicated that there were important differences of opinion in Indian official circles over the MIG question. American supersonic planes would have been preferred—at least in 1962–63—by the Indian air force and Finance Ministry. The air force in particular was concerned that a long-term commitment to the MIG program might enable the USSR to wield undue influence over its activities. Concern was expressed lest the Soviets supply only the blueprints for the factories, rather than assume total responsibility until the plants are completed. Early in February 1964, the Indian Defence Minister, Y. B. Chavan, declared with certainty that the projects were going according to schedule. Addressing pressmen at Nagpur, Chavan said that it was only "wishful rumor" by some who did not want the project to materialize that was causing all the speculation. Then he announced that the first group of Soviet experts would arrive shortly to commence work.[72] In answer to questions in the Lok Sabha on February 18, the Minister for Defence Production, K. Raghuramiah, said that he was not aware of any avoidable delays at the Nasik site. He added that such modifications as were needed in the design of the aircraft to prevent obsolescence would be incorporated as production began. Moscow, however, continued to show indifference to the Indian urgency on the aircraft.

For the Soviets, the long-term political implications of the MIG plants were extremely complex. The project gave Peking an additional grievance. It is uncertain whether the Soviet leaders wanted to get into a position where they would be called upon to supply a considerable portion of India's defence needs over a long period of time. While the Soviets had accrued advantages from their courtship of India over the previous decade, the prospect of moving even closer to India in the coming years had potential dis-

72. *Hindu*, February 3, 1964.

advantages that could restrict Soviet maneuverability, particularly vis-à-vis China. Yet the USSR had made a public commitment to build the MIG factories, and it would have been extremely difficult to back down. This latter point was well understood in New Delhi. As one journalist noted, "it would not be easy for the Russians to quit the deal after all the fanfare about it to the extent of its becoming a prickly issue with Peking."[73] During the summer of 1964 the Soviets put aside their inhibitions regarding the MIGs. Shortly before India's President Radhakrishnan began his state visit to the USSR in September 1964, an agreement was reached under which the USSR would provide thirty-eight additional MIG aircraft and would step up the schedule for the MIG factories in India. (Manufacture of component parts began in 1967 at the Nasik and Hyderabad plants, and production at Koraput was scheduled to begin in 1968.)

In August 1963 an Indian military mission was sent to Moscow to procure equipment, including missiles, to be used for India's defenses against China.[74] In May 1964 it was reported that a missile program for India, estimated to cost "slightly more than $40 million," had been worked out and that fifty ground-to-air missiles had already been delivered. The cost included radar equipment and fixed and mobile installations. By mid-1964 India had also received from the USSR air-to-air missiles, samples of infantry support weapons, and army engineering equipment.[75]

An authority on the Indian defense program characterized India's post-1962 military planning as based upon four major assumptions: "the People's Republic of China posed the major threat to Indian security; a Pakistani threat could materialize at any time; Sino-Pakistan collusion against India was conceivable;

73. *Hindustan Times*, February 16, 1964.

74. *New York Times*, August 31, 1963.

75. *New York Times*, May 13, 1964. The account set the total value of "Soviet military aid delivered or firmly committed to India" since the autumn of 1962 at about $130 million. Presumably this figure included the projected expenditures for the MIG factories, the final disposition of which is not yet clear.

and India required a credible military sanction for her diplomacy."[76] In this context Soviet military aid assumed great importance to India after the suspension of shipments of American and
British military equipment to India and Pakistan during the fighting in September 1965. The United States continued its ban on
weapons sales to India or Pakistan, although since March 1966 it
has permitted the supply of some spare parts and "nonlethal" military aid to both countries. Since 1945 the flow of Soviet military
wares to India has increased considerably.[77] It was reported in
May 1968 that the USSR was in the process of sending India about
one hundred SU-7 fighter bombers. The aircraft are designed for
close air support and will complement the MIG high-altitude
fighters. During his January 1968 visit to New Delhi, Premier
Kosygin attended India's Republic Day celebration and witnessed
a flyover of Soviet-supplied MIGs and transports and the first
Russian-built surface-to-air missiles shown publicly in India. SAMs
have been deployed at least since 1965 for the defense of a number of major Indian cities.[78]

Like the United States, the USSR has become a global military
power.[79] In recent years it has developed a rapidly increasing

76. Kavic, *India's Quest for Security*, p. 207.

77. This account of Indian acquisitions of Soviet weaponry is based upon
information which has appeared in the public media and other published sources.
The figures are sometimes inexact and probably incomplete, but they give an
idea of the extent to which the Indian military sector has become increasingly
involved with the USSR.

78. Ernest Weatherall in the *Christian Science Monitor*, March 5, 1968.

79. Since concluding its first arms deal with the United Arab Republic in
1955, the USSR has provided between $4 and $5 billion in military weaponry
to Third World developing nations as of 1968. By 1965 Soviet arms exports were
running about $400 million annually, and it is believed that this figure has since
been increased to $500 million per year. Nigeria was the twenty-second and latest
recipient of Soviet arms. "American arms exports to the underdeveloped nations
have also increased in recent years, and sales alone totaled $534 million for the
fiscal year that ended June 30, 1968." (*New York Times*, September 5, 1968.)

Between 1955 and 1965 the USSR gave an estimated $3 to $4 billion worth of
military aid to the nonaligned nations. The United Arab Republic and Indonesia

naval presence in the Indian Ocean. As a result, the Soviet navy has shown considerable interest in using Indian ports for refueling and repairs and as ports of call. Early in 1968 the Soviet navy chief, Admiral Sergei Gorshkov, made a trip to India for discussions with Indian officials on these matters.

The first of several Soviet submarines ordered by India, the "Kavari," was scheduled to arrive in India during the spring of 1968 to join a growing navy which includes several Soviet-supplied destroyer escorts.[80] Anticipating the withdrawal of British naval strength in the Indian Ocean, India has been increasing its naval forces and has begun a new base on the Andaman Islands.

---

received about one-half of this total, while Algeria, Afghanistan, India, and Syria together received approximately one-third. See Stephen P. Gilbert, "Wars of Liberation and Soviet Military Policy," *Orbis*, 10 (Fall, 1966) : 840.

80. *Christian Science Monitor*, March 5, 1968.

8 Other Aspects of the Relationship

In the wake of improved Indo-Soviet relations came a substantial increase in various kinds of contacts between the two nations. This chapter is intended to provide an idea of the nature and scope of these contacts over the decade 1954–64, dealing with the exchange of delegations, Indian travel to and study in the USSR, Soviet interest in Indian culture, Indian opinion on the USSR, academic study of the USSR in India, and the various Soviet efforts to influence Indian opinion. Some information, where relevant and available, is also included for the period beyond 1964. The data presented, while not all-inclusive gives additional breadth to any appraisal of the relationship.

Exchange of Delegations

Due mainly to foreign exchange shortages, foreign travel abroad by Indian nationals has generally been limited to those who are on some public or private business encouraged by the government and those receiving educational and technological training. This is particularly true with regard to Indian visitors to the USSR and other Communist nations.[1]

1. Discussing the travel restrictions, one writer in 1962 noted that, aside from those granted special consideration, Indian nationals were not permitted to take more than rupees 50 (about $10) out of the country. For several

As relations became more cordial from late in 1953 onward, delegations representing agricultural, industrial, commercial, cultural, and other sectors of Indian and Soviet society were exchanged. The frequency of these contacts rose considerably in August–September 1954 and remained high thereafter.[2]

Groups of Soviet scholars and scientists periodically visit India. For example, a large delegation led by B. Gafurov and V. Balabushevich arrived in New Delhi in January 1964 to attend the twenty-sixth International Conference of Orientalists. Seventeen papers were originally scheduled to be delivered by Soviet scholars at the conference, and about ten additional addresses were added to this list shortly before the conference began. Four of the Soviet Indologists arrived early to attend the annual meeting of the Indian History Congress held in Poona late in December.

years prior to 1959, when Indian citizens were permitted to take out rupees 250, Intourist set up a special tour within this amount for Indian visitors. Since January 1959 there have been no Indian "tourists" as such to the USSR. See G. Khanna, "Exchange of Visitors," *ISCUS*, 9 (June, 1962): p. 33.

2. The exchanges during the above-mentioned period (as reported in various Indian and Soviet publications) were as follows:

July 31	Indian delegation to Moscow (for 10 days) to attend a Soviet agricultural exhibition.
August 1	Group of Indian scientists visited USSR.
August 3	New Delhi announced that military attachés (to the respective embassies in Moscow and New Delhi) would be exchanged for the *first* time.
August 22	Indian farm mission attended Russian agricultural exhibition in Moscow.
August 24	Indian cultural delegation (artists and performers) to USSR for six weeks, then to Poland.
September 1	Delegation of Indian teachers and students visited Moscow University for a month. (Twenty-six members from Madras, Calcutta, Lucknow, Agra, Delhi, and Benares universities.)
September 4	Fourteen-member Indian delegation to study industrial and agricultural developments for one month in Russia, two weeks in Poland.
September 24–9	Five Indian films shown in nineteen Soviet cities. (One million people saw the films in Moscow.)
September 16	Three Soviet mining and engineering experts sent to assist Indian diamond mining industry.

At the same time a group of eminent Soviet scientists attended the Pugwash Conference in Udaipur, Rajasthan. These occasions and their aftermath provided the scholars with an opportunity to address segments of the Indian public. On February 4, 1964, for instance, the scientist N. Filchenkov lectured in New Delhi on the achievements of Soviet science while V. Khvostov spoke at Sapru House on the foundation of his country's foreign policy.[3]

Those Russians who visit India for short periods of time clearly enjoy the sightseeing aspects of their stay. As elsewhere, they invariably travel in groups and not individually. Their exposure to Indian parliamentary institutions is kept to a minimum, however. I recall speaking with several members of one Soviet delegation during a session of the Indian Parliament in February 1964. The group, which numbered about twenty-five in all (mainly from Central Asia), arrived shortly after a series of questions dealing with "corruption" had been posed to government ministers by members of the opposition parties. A heated discussion took place on the floor of the House, but the Soviet visitors had no way of knowing what was happening. Fifteen minutes later the group arose and filed out. An Uzbek sitting next to me explained that the group was now going to see other sights before heading to Madras for a conference. Thus ended his group's brief exposure to the give and take of Indian parliamentary debate.

In a representative year, 1960, the visiting delegations could be roughly grouped according to their function as follows:

Indian Delegations to the USSR—Total 35

9 youth groups	14 scientific, technical,
3 women's groups	and professional
3 trade union	6 CPI and Front groups

Soviet Delegations to India—Total 15

1 youth group	8 scientific, technical,
2 trade union	and professional
2 sports groups	1 cultural
	1 party (CPSU)

3. See *Statesman*, December 9, 1963; *Hindustan Times*, December 27, 1963; and *Times of India*, January 4 and February 5, 1964.

During 1967 there were 25 Indian delegations of various kinds sent to the USSR, and conversely 25 Soviet delegations came to India. Indicative of the improving Soviet-Pakistani relationship in the post-Khrushchev year was the substantial increase in the exchange of delegations between the two countries. In 1967, 15 Soviet delegations went to Pakistan, and an equal number of Pakistani groups visited the USSR.[4]

Indian Travel to and Study in the USSR

Virtually all of the Indian delegations to the USSR have been organized by governmental agencies or by groups approved and encouraged by the government. One major reason that the Indian government discourages unofficial delegations to the USSR is that such groups would most often be sponsored by the CPI. For instance, the CPI was prepared to send as many as a thousand delegates to the Moscow Youth Festival in 1957, but passports were issued to only about 80 youths. Since 1959, exceptions to the general rule have been made to such CPI leaders as the late Ajoy Ghosh and S. A. Dange who are known to follow the Soviet line in international affairs. From 1959 on it has been extremely difficult for any person to obtain a passport if suspected by the C.I.B. (India's security agency) to be among the "Chinese-orientated" wing of the CPI.

On the other hand Indian delegates during the early 1960s were permitted to attend such Communist-inspired conclaves as those sponsored by the World Peace Council. At such conferences the Indian delegates served the purpose of countering Chinese charges against India. For example, after the World Peace Council sessions in December 1964 had ended, the head of the Indian delegation, Arjun Arora, M. P., reported that the Chinese had been isolated "all along the line." He continued: "From India's point of view, the achievement of the Warsaw session of the World Peace Council

4. The Soviet, Indian, and Pakistani delegations exchanged in 1967 represented governmental, trade, public organizations, public media, educational, scientific, and cultural groups.

is that its main report supported the Colombo proposals as the basis for a peaceful settlement of the Sino-Indian border conflict."[5]

Students who wish to study abroad are carefully screened, as are applicants for Indian governmental services, particularly the foreign service.[6] An applicant for study abroad or for government service who has been marked as a participant in Communist sponsored activities, generally has less chance to achieve his objective. The contention is widely held that the C.I.B. and the Indian police in most locales were in practice considerably more anti-Communist than the official government position during the Nehru years.

Before 1960 those Indians studying in the USSR were trainees in factories and technical institutes. They received practical instruction for work on Soviet projects in India. In addition, at the end of 1960, some 82 Indian students were enrolled in Soviet universities. Forty places were given to Indian students beginning in December 1960 at the newly-created Friendship University in Moscow. In reply to questions in the Lok Sabha, Prime Minister Nehru and Mrs. Lakshmi Menon disclosed that the Indian students at Friendship University would not have to take any politically or ideologically oriented courses. They would be enrolled only in engineering and science curricula.[7] From 1956 to 1962, 300 Indian students went to the USSR for study, mainly on the postgraduate level.[8] By January 1964 an estimated 325 Indian students had gone

5. *Hindu,* December 8, 1963.

6. Several instances were related to this writer where qualified men in such sensitive locales as Calcutta were prevented from joining government service because they had participated in leftist student activities during their university days.

7. *Times of India,* November 18, 1960.

8. Those other nations which sent more than 100 students for higher education to the Soviet Union during the 1956–62 period were Iraq, 2755; Indonesia, 830; the UAR, 775; Guinea, 580; Syria, 555; Somali Republic, 450; Ghana, 420; Yemen, 400; Sudan, 290; Mali, 280; Morocco, 150; Nepal, 110. (The figures for Ghana, Mali, and Yemen include secondary students.) See Maurice D. Simon "Communist System Interaction with the Developing State, 1954–1962: A Preliminary Analysis," Stanford Studies of the Communist System, Research Paper no. 10, (Stanford, 1966), pp. 93–94.

to the USSR and other Communist countries for academic study, while an additional 800 had received technical training in such countries over a shorter period.[9]

If Indian students have had cause for discontent with their studies in the USSR, it has not been expressed publicly.[10]

On the other hand this writer has gathered the opinion that most Indian students, if given the choice, would prefer to do post-graduate study in a Western university rather than in the USSR. One obvious reason for this preference is climatic—the Russian winter is very difficult for the South Asian. There are of course other reasons, academic and personal.

In the 1950s the increased contact between India and USSR led to the need for establishment of a regular air service. An agreement was concluded on July 2, 1958, between the Indian international airline, Air India, and the Soviet counterpart, Aeroflot, calling for several weekly flights between Moscow and New Delhi.[11] The two

9. Correspondence with S. Costikyan, U.S.I.A., May, 1964.

10. On the occasion of demonstrations by African students in Moscow after the unexplained death of a Ghanaian medical student, the *Times of India* correspondent, Ralph Parker, gave his impression of the incident. He concluded: "From the fact that the large Indian body of students are on the whole a contented lot and that what complaints they have to make are rather of an academic than a social character, one cannot help thinking that the African body should *cleanse itself* before taking action of so sensational a character." (Italics added.) (*Times of India*, January 19, 1964.)

It might be added parenthetically that Indian students do not encounter as many problems, particularly in interracial dating, as do African students in the USSR. African students encounter considerable race prejudice in India as well as in such "white" societies as the United States and the USSR.

11. With the inherent difficulty of intercommunication between land and sea, important shipments of Soviet machinery are often airfreighted directly. There is little passenger travel aside from members of Indian or bloc delegations going to the other country for political, techological, cultural, or other purposes.

Originally the flight from New Delhi via Amritsar and Tashkent to Moscow took about 13 hours, but the acquisition of new jetliners by Air-India now permits a direct flight in one-third the 1958 time. At the beginning of 1964 there were two regularly scheduled flights per week in each direction between New Delhi and Moscow.

airlines pool their monthly income from this service and divide it on the basis of scheduled and nonscheduled one-way flights operated by each airline. Inasmuch as overland travel across the Himalayan regions is virtually nonexistent and the oceanic route involves a long passage, air travel between India and the USSR is extremely important.

The volume of sea freight between India and the USSR has increased with the expansion of bilateral trade. The major ports which handle Indo-Soviet commerce are Bombay and Odessa. The closing of the Suez Canal after the 1967 Arab-Israel conflict has necessitated, for the time being, the rerouting of shipping between India and USSR around the tip of southern Africa.

Soviet Interest in Indian Culture and Society

Many Soviet citizens show considerable interest, not only in present-day India, but in the fantasy-like portrayals of India's past. Classical Indian dance and Indian movies provide the same kind of diversion from the workaday world as do the romantic music and opera of pre-Soviet Russia. There is considerable interest in things Indian in the larger cities of Soviet Central Asia. While visiting in the Uzbek, Kazakh, and Tadjik Republics in 1960, this writer was impressed by the local interest in Indian films and art.

An unofficial listing of books by Indian authors translated into the languages of the Soviet peoples and published between 1918 and 1958 showed the authors listed in table 2 to be most frequently published.[12]

Most of these writers urged social reforms, even if they do not fully meet Soviet ideological specifications. Those "who depict the life of their people during the years of colonial dependence show us the background of misery," remarked one Soviet critic. "Their books move us, they evoke feelings of protest against

12. From a chart in the reading room of the branch of the Soviet embassy on Curzon Road, New Delhi, in 1963. Included were only those authors who have had more than 100,000 copies published in the USSR as of 1958. Altogether 283 titles were published with 11.3 million copies in 28 languages of the USSR.

TABLE 2

TRANSLATIONS OF INDIAN AUTHORS INTO
SOVIET LANGUAGES, 1918–58

Authors	No. of Titles	Thousands of Copies	Languages
R. Tagore	84	2631	18
Mulk Raj Anand	13	1003	5
C. Krishen	17	740	9
Prem Chand	11	613	4
V. Chattopadhyaya	5	198	1
D. K. Mukherjee	10	194	6
B. Bhattacharya	5	164	4
A. Vafa	15	117	3

colonialism and instill faith in the inevitable downfall of the shameful colonial system."[13] (The works of Tagore have been published extensively even though they are outside the pale of "socialist realism.")

More recent figures indicate that over 16 million copies of books by Indian authors had been published in the USSR by October 1961. This means that over the three-year period 1958–61, 5.5 million copies were turned out. In 1961 the new editions published included R. Tagore's *Choturongo*, the *Panchatantra*, Prem Chand's *Godan*, R. K. Narayan's *The Guide*, selected short stories of Padameipittam, poems of S. Tripathi, I. Joshi's *Nirila*, short stories of K. Abbas, and a selection of Tagore's lyrical poems.

The tradition in Sanskirt studies at Moscow University dates back to the mid-nineteenth century. But it was not until the 1950s that Indian studies began to receive substantial attention in the USSR. The Moscow State University currently has departments for the study of Hindi, Bengali, and Urdu. At the Leningrad Institute of Living Indian Languages, Hindi, Bengali, Marathi, and several other languages are taught. In Tashkent there is extensive study of Indian and other Asian languages at the univer-

13. Chelyshev, "Soviet Translations of Indian Authors," *ISCUS*, 9 (March 1962) : 50.

sity level. Since 1957 Hindi has been introduced even into a few secondary schools in Moscow, Leningrad, and Tashkent.

Aside from general cultural interests, the intensive study of Indian languages serves important practical purposes. Many Russian academic texts (particularly in the fields of science and technology), works of literature, and Soviet political materials are translated into indigenous Indian languages for use in India. Secondly, Russians who are going to India in some working capacity, especially those technicians or teachers who work with Indian counterparts, are often given language training.

The Institute Narody Azii (Institute of the Peoples of Asia) in Moscow has a section for the study of South Asian politics and international relations. Through the 1950s there was no scope for objective research on Indian politics, as virtually all work during this period was subordinate to political directives. One prolific writer on Indian politics during this period certainly capable of better scholarly work was A. M. Diakov. The calibre of the Institute's work has improved somewhat as the political controls have loosened. Now, at least in certain areas, there is scope for independent judgment, and there is even disagreement among Soviet scholars in their interpretation of some aspects of South Asian society. Since Soviet-Pakistani relations began to improve in the early 1960s, Soviet writings on Pakistan do not use the polemical style previously employed. The present need for serious work on Pakistan has cut into the limited number of capable individuals who have been specializing on India.

Indian Opinion on the USSR

Almost every politically important Indian who has visited the USSR since 1954 has written an article or two about his experiences and impressions while visiting the USSR and/or has been interviewed upon his return to India by newsmen. Generally speaking, the accounts of Indian visitors are non-provocative. But on at least one or two occasions government officials were rebuked by the Indian public for overly favorable remarks about the worth of certain Soviet institutions. For example, M. C. Setalvad, India's attorney-general, visited the USSR in 1961. Shortly thereafter, in an address to the Indo-Soviet Cultural Society in Bombay, he is reported to have said that two features of the Soviet legal system, the procurator-general and the greater association of people with the administration of justice at the lower court level, could with some modifications be accepted in India. Letters to the editor and editorials appeared in a number of prominent Indian newspapers criticizing the attorney-general's talk, prompting him to clarify his remarks in a talk before the Indian Bar Association several weeks later.[14]

Critical assessments of the USSR are infrequent. One brief but interesting book contrasts the theory and reality of life in the USSR. Its author expressed dissatisfaction with the Soviet bureaucratic system. Synthesizing Marx and Manu, he wrote of a classless society that could be established in India, incorporating the better features of communism and capitalism.[15]

Meaningful assessment of public opinion is a difficult task in the newly independent nations. Of the substantial majority of India's population that live in villages, few have opinions on foreign policy matters outside the subcontinent and even fewer have adequate substantive knowledge on which to base their opinions. Urban dwellers are more prone to venture opinion and generally speaking have more access to the public information media.

Several polls taken by the Indian Institute of Public Opinion provide some idea of what the Indian public has thought about the USSR. The Institute's work in its first years was handicapped by limited resources. Its survey data were also limited by the sampling techniques employed; sampling was generally skewed toward urban and educated opinion. The results of the polls are nonetheless of interest. One such survey conducted during 1957–

14. *Hindustan Times*, July 14, 27, 1961.
15. M. Patwardham, *Mirage of the Classless Society*, (Bombay, 1959).

58 made samplings in Delhi, Calcutta, Madras, Bombay, Kanpur, and Lucknow and obtained responses to their queries as shown below:[16]

1. "Which country will be strongest ten years from now?" (Either the USSR, the USA, or India)

USSR	USA	USSR and USA equally	India	No Opinion
39.5%	9%	8%	4.9%	33.8%

Of the men, 49.5 percent thought the USSR would be the strongest nation in a decade. Of the formally educated, 65.7 percent of the matriculates and 51.9 percent of the graduates attested to the future "strength" of the USSR.

2. "How likely will it be that relations will become even better between India and China, the USSR, and the United States?"

	Between India and—		
	(a) *China*	(b) *USSR*	(c) *USA*
Very likely to improve	46%	29%	3%
Likely to improve	36%	47%	41%
Not so likely	3%	6%	12%
Not at all	1%	2%	1%
No answer	14%	14%	13%

It should be noted that the above poll was taken during 1957–58 at a time when the Indian public was not as yet aware of the growing Sino-Indian antagonism. Moreover, in 1957 the Indian press emphasized that the USSR had come to India's support with a veto in the United Nations against the Western sponsored resolution on Kashmir.

In a survey in 1959 by International Research Associates, the following question was asked 200 respondents in each of the four

16. Indian Institute of Public Opinion, *Monthly Public Opinion Surveys*.

largest cities: "Please tell me your feelings about various countries—do you have a very good opinion, good, fair, bad or very bad opinion . . . about Russia?" The results in Calcutta, the city of greatest CPI electoral strength, were 55 percent very good or good opinion, 30 percent fair, 20 percent bad, and 13 percent "don't know." The city of Bombay, with 30 percent designating very good or good opinion, 19 percent fair, 11 percent bad or very bad, and 40 percent "don't know", gave the lowest opinion rating to the USSR. Another question asked in the same poll was "At the present time, do you personally think that India should be on the side of the Communist powers, on the side of the anti-Communist powers or on neither side." Ten percent of the respondents replied, "side with Communist powers," 13 percent "side with anti-Communist powers," 62 percent "neither side," and 15 percent "don't know."[17]

An Indian monthly public opinion survey early in 1962 asked which of the following statements applied to the Soviet Union and the United States: "friendly to Asian countries, generous in aid to India, war-loving or peace loving," etc. While the United States fared slightly better than the Soviets in this comparison, the results were not significantly different.[18] In another 1962 poll taken in eleven Indian states, the question asked was, "Should [world] war come, do you think it is more likely to be started by the United States, Russia, or some other way?" Of the 895 respondents, 6.1 percent designated the USA, 7.6 percent the USSR, 5.3 percent China and 31.4 percent both Russia and China, the remainder replying "other ways" or "don't know."[19]

An "International Popularity Scale" was conducted in April 1959 to gauge the feelings of Indians toward six foreign countries and their leaders—the USA, USSR, Egypt, China, Yugoslavia,

17. International Research Associates, *Public Opinion in India: A Research Report*, vol. 2 (February, 1959).

18. *Monthly Public Opinion Surveys*, # 77–78, vol. VII: 5, 6 (February–March, 1962), pp. 41–42.

19. Ibid., #82, vol. VII:10 (July, 1962), pp. 7–13.

and Germany.[20] The ratings of President Eisenhower and Premier
Khrushchev were practically identical. Among the urban citizens
who were polled, Eisenhower received 24.2 percent in the "very
good" and "good" categories, while Khrushchev received 23.1
percent. Only 4.5 percent rated Eisenhower bad or very bad compared with 3.4 percent for Khrushchev; 61.4 percent gave a "don't
know" or "no opinion" for Eisenhower and 61.6 percent answered
the same for the Soviet leader. In the rural areas both leaders did
equally well, although the "don't know" category rose to over
75 percent.

An extensive survey of Indian attitudes on various subjects was
carried out in the summer of 1962 under the guidance of Dr. Had-
ley Cantril.[21] Another set of interviews repeating the same questions were conducted after the Sino-Indian border conflict of 1962
to determine what effect the fighting had on Indian opinion. The
survey clearly indicated that the Chinese action lowered the stature
of the USSR in Indian eyes. One representative question asked,
"In your opinion, with which countries should India cooperate
very closely under present conditions?" In the first poll 49 percent
of the respondents favored very close cooperation with the USA,
26 percent with the United Kingdom, and 43 percent with the
USSR. After the Sino-Indian fighting, 58 percent favored very
close relations with the USA, and 36 percent with the UK, while
the percentage of those favoring close ties with the USSR fell to
16 percent.[22]

After the above polls were taken, the Soviet image was gradually restored to its pre–October 1962 level. The Indian government and most important media for public information in 1963–64

20. "The Structure of Indian Opinion on International Personalities and
Countries," *Monthly Public Opinion Surveys,* #45, 46, 47, 48. (June–September,
1959), pp. 78–120.

21. "The Impact of the Sino-Indian Border Clash," *Monthly Public Opinion
Surveys,* #97, vol. IX:1 (Oct., 1963). The second phase of the study was directed
by Albert H. Cantril.

22. Ibid., p. 9.

made a clear-cut distinction between China and the USSR, portraying the Soviets as friends and the Chinese as the betrayers of India. In a 1965 poll of Indian literates, 80 percent of the respondents termed the Soviet image at the time "very good" or "good," 11 percent described it as "neither good nor bad," and 11 percent replied "don't know."[23] Continued Indo-Soviet cooperation in the post-Nehru period further implanted a favorable impression of the USSR in the Indian "public consciousness." A poll taken in January–February 1966, after the Tashkent Conference, showed widespread Indian approval of the USSR's mediatory role after the 1965 Indo-Pakistani conflict.[24]

Academic Study of the USSR in India

During the British period there was practically no way for the interested Indian student to study about the USSR. The arts curricula had a heavy British orientation in literature, language, politics, philosophy, etc., and there was little chance for an Indian to study other countries, or his own for that matter. The few privileged Indians who studied in Britain had a much better opportunity to learn something about the USSR. Students at even the leading institutions could get no better than a dilettante's knowledge of Russian history, philosophy, or politics. Jawaharlal Nehru on at least one occasion called for introduction of more courses on USSR into the university curricula, but the British authorities were of course not interested. Not until several years after Indian independence did any Indian university offer a course in Russian language.

Today, more than two decades after independence, there are still few trained Indian scholars in the field of Soviet studies. Most universities have a general course or so on Russian government or

23. "The Changing Structure of Indian International Images, A Decade Trend: 1955–65," *Monthly Public Opinion Surveys*, #116, 117, vol. X:9–10, pp. 14–17.

24. *Monthly Public Opinion Surveys* #116, 117, Vol. 10: 9–10 (March–April, 1966).

history, but these are taught with the main stress on the Soviet constitution and institutions and have little to say on the dynamics of Soviet society. About the only academic center where research is being done on Soviet politics is the Indian School of International Studies (ISIS) in New Delhi.

Established in 1955, the School's purpose is to provide research facilities for the study of other nations. Each of its graduate students selects a single country or region for specialized study. The greatest emphasis has been placed on contemporary political developments and international relations. The Ph.D.-level students often receive the opportunity to go abroad to complete their research projects.[25] The Indian School of International Studies has good potential, but thus far (as of 1968) its work has been handicapped by intramural political problems and by the tendency to be too much influenced by contemporary trends in Indian foreign policy. The ISIS has shared the same building, Sapru House, with the Indian Council on World Affairs, whose specific function is to research and elucidate the goals and role of Indian foreign policy. Perhaps its planned move into a separate new building may help the ISIS develop a more distinct identity of its own.

In August 1963 the ISIS set up a division for Soviet studies. Its head (and sole member as of 1968), Dr. R. Vaidyanath, was the first Indian scholar to do extensive work (from 1960 to 1964) in the USSR on a subject dealing with Soviet political history. There are currently several students at the doctoral level at the ISIS doing work on Soviet topics. The Sapru House library possesses the largest collection of Soviet materials in India, and its fine collection of contemporary Russian-language publications on subjects relating to politics, economics, and international relations is certainly among the most complete in Asia. The major gap in the holdings is in Soviet publications of earlier periods.

---

25. Much of the commentary in this and the preceding two paragraphs is extracted from the article by Vaidyanath, "Izuchenie SSSR v Indii i Ego Perspektivy."

Over the past decade the study of the Russian language has become increasingly widespread. With the exception of English (which of course is an officially recognized language in India), there were possibly more students in 1967–68 studying Russian than any other foreign language. An estimated twenty-two universities are now offering language instruction in Russian. The Soviets are encouraging this language study and have sent a number of teachers and texts for this purpose.[26] Also, the Soviet consulates in major Indian cities and the Indo-Soviet Friendship Society sponsor well-planned courses in Russian language and culture for interested Indians. A reader, the *Russian Language Monthly*, published in English and several indigenous languages, is widely circulated.[27]

To fulfill the growing need for personnel with Russian language training, the Institute of Russian Studies was opened in New Delhi in November 1965. The Institute is sponsored jointly by the governments of India and the USSR, but it is financed by India. The Russians help to provide teachers and texts. At the end of 1967 there were an estimated 150 students doing full-time work (about thirty hours a week) studying language and literature. The Institute (which is scheduled eventually to become part of the planned Nehru University) does not offer any courses in the social sciences pertaining to the USSR, although students may eventually do work elsewhere in New Delhi as facilities become available.

Prior to the crisis in Sino-Indian relations, the only Indian institution with a tradition of Chinese study was Viswa-Bharati in West Bengal where classical Chinese culture and the arts were emphasized. Since 1962, however, a crash program has been under-

26. Information on Russian language instruction in India was provided the author by an instructor at the Institute of Russian Studies in New Delhi.

27. A great many science and technology students, particularly at the M. Tech. and Ph. D. levels, study Russian. For a description of the Russian program at the Indian Institute of Technology, Bombay, see A. M. Gaziev, *Russian Language Monthly* (A Soviet Land Publication, New Delhi), 2 (December 1967): pp. 20–23.)

taken to develop a course and research on contemporary China. This in large part is the result of the same sort of catalyst which stimulated American interest in the USSR and China in the post–World War II years. A Chinese studies program, emphasizing Chinese Communist institutions and politics as well as providing language training, was established with American foundation assistance at Delhi University. There are obviously no reservations in India about engaging in critical studies of China.

Such is not the case, however, in regard to Indian studies of the USSR. The Soviet government is not enthusiastic about Indians doing the sort of critical evaluation of the Soviet system which is not permitted within the USSR itself. Such evaluations would do little to improve the Indian image of the USSR. Since the Government of India does not want to do anything to unduly antagonize the USSR, it has been very cautious about encouraging programs of Soviet studies in India.

Soviet Broadcasts to India

In recent years there has been a substantial increase in Soviet broadcasts directed at South Asian audiences. In the years 1961 through 1964, and in 1967, for example, programs were beamed from transmitters in the USSR in the languages shown in table 3.[28] As a point of comparison, Soviet broadcast hours in 1963 more than doubled Chinese hours to the region. In 1964 Soviet total hours to South Asia more than tripled the Chinese efforts.

Soviet programs consist of news, documentaries, features, music, and entertainment. Until 1964 more hours were devoted to broadcasts in Urdu than in any other language of the subcontinent. Thereafter, programs in Hindi were given equal prominence. Programs in Malayalam, the major language of Kerala, were belatedly introduced only in 1964, but the number of hours of broadcast to that center of CPI strength increased substantially by 1967. One

28. U.S.I.A., Research and Reference Service, *Developments in International Broadcasting by Communist Countries in 1964* (Washington, 1965), p. 21; and *Communist Propaganda Activities in the Near East and South Asia, 1967* (Washington, 1968), p. 19.

TABLE 3

Soviet Foreign Language Broadcasts
Beamed to South Asia

	1961	1962	1963	1964	1967
Bengali	17:30 hrs.	17:30 hrs.	17:30 hrs.	17:30 hrs.	17:30 hrs.
Hindi	15:45	19:15	22:45	24:30	45:30
Malayalam	——	——	——	7:	24:30
Nepalese	——	——	1:45	3:	3:30
Sinhalese	——	——	7:	7:	7:
Tamil	3:30	3:30	7:	7:	14:
Urdu	24:30	24:30	24:30	24:30	24:30
English	22:45	7:	7:	21:	28:
Punjab	——	——	——	——	7:
Marathi	——	——	——	——	7:
Telegu	——	——	——	——	7:
	84:00	71:45	87:30	111:30	185:30

can only speculate on the reasons why English language broadcasts decreased markedly in 1962–63. The Soviet decision was probably influenced by the consideration that many among the rising political elites in the Indian states are more fluent in their indigenous tongues than in English; also that English was soon scheduled to be dropped as a second national language along with Hindi. This decision undoubtedly was well noted in Moscow.

With the exception of the popular Radio Ceylon, no foreign radio station has a widespread audience in India. According to a 1964 survey among urban Indian radio listeners, 76 percent never listen to Radio Moscow, 3 percent "occasionally," while 21 percent responded that they did not listen to any foreign radio stations. In rural India only 1 percent of the respondents "occasionally" listened to Radio Moscow.[29] Those who do listen to Radio Moscow are often the same people who sometimes pick up the BBC, Radio Pakistan, the Voice of America, and other foreign stations.

Soviet Publications for Indian Consumption

The question how to deal with publications printed in the USSR and sold or distributed in India had to be re-evaluated by the Indian

---

29. *Monthly Public Opinion Surveys,* #108, Vol. IX: 12 (Sept., 1964) p. 36.

government after Indo-Soviet relations improved in 1954–55. Prior to that time undesirable pamphlets dealing with such subjects as revolution could be seized and destroyed without second thought. The government's position was summarized in a remark by Mr. Alagesan, then deputy minister of railways, to the Lok Sabha in August 1955. With reference to the sale of inexpensive Soviet literature at railway stations, he explained:

There is no general ban on the sale of Soviet literature as such at Railway bookstalls. Books, however, of a tendentious or undesirable nature are not permitted to be sold. . . . We have no objection to books like those of Tolstoi, Marx or Engels, which have now become classics, being sold at railway bookstalls.[30]

As the years passed, fewer Soviet books were termed "tendentious or undesirable" by Indian censors. Since 1955 there has been an annual increase in Soviet publications distributed in India.

According to unofficial figures the USSR in 1964 published books and pamphlets in Indian languages as shown in table 4.[31]

TABLE 4

INDIAN LANGUAGE BOOKS PUBLISHED IN
USSR IN 1964

Language	Less than 50 pages		More than 50 pages	
	Titles	Copies	Titles	Copies
Hindi	23	239,155	7	84,000
Bengali	15	78,000	4	23,100
Telugu	6	23,100	3	22,000
Marathi	4	23,500	1	3 000

An additional 76,400 copies of works in Tamil were also printed. (Using the Soviet *Knizhnaya Letopis* (Book Herald) as a guide, the USIA lists titles in Indian languages under the headings of "works by the founders of Marxism-Leninism; international affairs–foreign policy; general education, philology, linguistics;

30. *Lok Sabha Debates*, pt. 1, vol. 4, no. 14 (August 12, 1955), cols. 3583–84.

31. U.S.I.A., *Soviet Book Publishing for Export, 1964* (Washington, 1965), pp. 5–14.

belletristic literature; and children's literature.") There is no way of determining the precise number of books in English sent to India. In recent years the USSR has printed a substantial number of texts on scientific and technological subjects for Indian schools and colleges. An Indian brochure in 1964 listed about 50 of these texts, all but one of which are in the English language.[32] Substantial work has been done in the translation of Soviet literature and children's stories into indigenous Indian languages. Children's stories and literature rank first and second among the categories of Soviet books sold in India.

In addition, the Soviets publish periodicals in English and the vernacular Indian languages for distribution in India. Foremost of these is the pictorial magazine *Soviet Land,* which was first published in India in 1951. Estimated circulation of *Soviet Land* in 1963 came to about 350,000 copies per issue in 13 Indian languages including English. Other Soviet periodicals circulated in India include *News and Views from Soviet Literature, Moscow News, International Affairs,* the *Soviet Union* and *Soviet Women.*

A wide variety of publications from other Communist countries are also circulated in India. (Circulation of such mainland Chinese magazines as *China Pictorial* and *China Reconstructs* were discontinued following the Sino-Indian border war.) Such Communist publications are well produced and appealingly illustrated, and they attract a large number of readers. These publications, and those of the Indian Communist party, are sold inexpensively, sometimes at prices less than the actual cost of publication.

The Soviet Propaganda Effort

Over the years the USSR like the USA has put considerable effort into its propaganda programs abroad.[33] In 1954 an information department attached to the Soviet embassy in New Delhi was set up

32. Ibid., p. 5.

33. See Frederick C. Barghoorn, *Soviet Foreign Propaganda* (Princeton: Princeton University Press, 1964) ; and I. A. Zeleznev, *Voina i ideologicheskaia borba.*

to handle some of the functions previously handled by TASS, the official news bureau of the Soviet government.[34] By the end of 1965 the information department alone employed 20 Russians and 165 Indians in its various activities.

In an attempt to improve the Soviet image abroad, Khrushchev in 1961 set up the Novosti agency. Novosti, with a well-staffed headquarters in Moscow and over one thousand Soviet foreign correspondents, has concentrated on public relations, as opposed to TASS's more conventional news gathering activities. Among its most important activities in India, Novosti has since its inception distributed articles on Soviet political, economic, and cultural subjects to Indian publications. Some Indian publications have availed themselves of this service more than others. In a list reportedly compiled in 1964 by the Soviet embassy's information department, such newspapers and periodicals as *Patriot*, *Link*, *Century*, *Mainstream*, and *Blitz* published special articles on request, used Soviet copy regularly, and took a friendly editorial attitude towards the USSR.[35]

Most Communist publications in New Delhi are available in Hindi, Urdu, and English; "other languages in which Communist publications are available are, in a descending order of priority, Punjabi, Bengali, Tamil, Telegu, Malayalam, and Kannada." Seventy-eight percent of those book shops in New Delhi which sold Communist publications in 1960 had materials available in Hindi and Urdu, 65 percent had English-language materials, 29 percent Punjabi, and 5 percent Bengali. In Calcutta, a non-Hindi speaking area, 74 percent of those shops selling Communist publi-

---

34. The information in this and the following paragraph comes from Sager, *Moscow's Hand in India*, which dwells solely on the Soviet propaganda effort in India. According to Sager, the Soviet Committee for State Security (KGB) and the Central Administration for Intelligence Services (GRU)—the Soviet espionage and counter-espionage agencies respectively—were well represented in the 1950s in New Delhi. For example, the head of the TASS from 1954 to 1959, and cultural attache with the Soviet embassy in 1960, Mr. Efimov, was a GRU colonel (ibid., pp. 33–35).

35. Ibid., pp. 102–3.

cations stocked materials in Bengali, 70 percent stocked English-language materials, and only 17 percent had Hindi periodicals available.[36] Discounts ranging from 33⅓ percent to 40 percent were given to those Indian retailers handling Soviet publications. Sales of Soviet publications in India help to finance such CPI publications as the weekly *New Age* (formerly Crossroads). According to official figures in 1965, there were 22 CPI newspapers and magazines in India—seven in Hindi, four in Malayalam, two each in English, Punjabi, and Kannada, two bilingual periodicals, and one each in Marathi, Oriya, and Manipuri.[37] The circulation figures for these publications are small; but like other vernacular papers, they are often passed on from reader to reader.

The USSR has obviously put forth a considerable effort toward influencing Indian opinion. It is, of course, difficult to gauge the impact of this effort on Indian policymakers and opinion makers. Nonetheless we can make some impressionistic attempt to differentiate its impact on various levels of Indian society.

The influence of Soviet radio broadcasts is for the most part negligible. Only 3 percent of India's urban radio listeners told pollsters in 1964 that they had ever listened to Radio Moscow. More than in any other Indian city, Radio Moscow has a listening audience in Calcutta, but Bengali intellectuals after the Sino-Soviet fallout listen more frequently to Radio Peking. The Russian programs themselves are not overly propagandistic, except for news broadcasts; they present a variety of features ranging from Indian music to English language lessons.

In 1967 a new "unofficial" Soviet radio station, Radio Peace and Progress, began occasional broadcasting to India and other

36. U.S.I.S., "Book Stall Surveys in New Delhi and Calcutta" (September, 1960; unpublished).

37. *Press in India*, part 1, Ninth Annual Report of the Registrar of Newspapers for India (New Delhi, 1965), p. 48. Sager claimed to have come across 53 official organs of the Communist party of India during the same period (*Moscow's Hand in India*, p. 167).

developing countries. Some of its programs present points of view
on the socio-political systems of the Asian countries which differ
from the usual Communist party statements. Radio Peace and
Progress represents a franker version of contemporary Soviet
thinking than do the other media. For example, it termed some of
the Congress candidates running in India's 1967 elections "reactionary," whereas Radio Moscow and the Soviet press had little
or nothing to say on the matter. The Government of India, prodded
by Swatantra, Jan Sangh, the P.S.P. and some elements within
the Congress party, had protested, saying in effect that there is no
such thing as unofficial Soviet opinion. It is obviously true that
Radio Peace and Progress functions with official Soviet approval.
The Soviets have taken the position, however, that Radio Peace
and Progress is an independent organization, noting that the official radio stations and newspapers "made no references to which
the Government of India could take exception."

As mentioned previously, the USSR produces and/or subsidizes
a wide range of publications dealing with life in the Soviet Union.
The most notable of these is *Soviet Land,* which is published in
thirteen major Indian languages and English and circulates more
widely than any other magazine in India. The Soviet embassy,
consulates, and reading rooms also distribute free "newsletters,"
like *News and Views from the Soviet Union,* and other publications. Such publications cannot help but give their generally un-
sophisticated readers a more favorable impression than they might
otherwise have had about life in the USSR and about Soviet
policies.

It is doubtful whether the above-mentioned materials influence
the relatively small group of individuals who have been involved
with and influential in Indian foreign policy matters. A more
subtle influence on this group has been the "good press" that the
USSR generally receives in the respected English language newspapers.[38] The Soviet economic assistance program in India, for

38. In 1965 the most widely read English-language daily newspapers with
circulations of over 100,000 were—

instance, gets excellent coverage. A quantitative content analysis of the Indian press over the past dozen years would undoubtedly confirm this writer's observation that the USSR's aid programs receive at least as much coverage as those of the United States. Considerably more of the commentary on American assistance is of a negative nature, as the USSR does not go through the annual throes of a Congressional foreign aid debate.

News from the USSR is generally obtained by the PTI (Press Trust of India), which in turn relies heavily on Reuters news service coverage. Surprisingly, from 1966 to mid–1968 only the *Indian Express* maintained a permanent correspondent in the USSR.[39]

The information department of the Soviet embassy distributes materials to the Indian newspapers and journals for possible use in their publications. On October 1, 1967, an agreement became operative by which Novosti (the Soviet News and feature agency) and PIB (the Indian Press Information Bureau) supply each other with feature articles and background material. The Novosti material would be available in PIB libraries, like materials from

Newspaper	Daily Circulation (1965 average)
Indian Express (Delhi, Bombay, Madras, Vijayawada, and Bangalore)	352,106
Times of India (Delhi and Bombay)	195,354
Statesman (Calcutta and Delhi)	151,341
Hindu (Madras)	141,327
Hindustan Times (Delhi)	115,632
Amrita Bazar Patrika (Calcutta)	111,783

(*Times of India, Yearbook and Directory, 1967*, p. 285)

Hugh Tinker, in his *India and Pakistan*, p. 165, had this to say about several of these newspapers: "Among the other big English language papers, the *Hindustan Times* is the voice of right-wing Congress opinion. The *Statesman* and the *Times of India* contrive to appear somewhat detached although generally supporting Nehru. The Madras *Hindu* wears its Congress colours with a liberal, sometimes internationalist air. . . . All these eminently respectable and responsible journals are owned, however, by powerful business interests, Marwari and Parsi."

39. The knowledgeable *Indian Express* correspondent, Dev Murarka, had been based in Moscow for three years as of early 1968.

other foreign information agencies. The Novosti agreement created a furor in the Indian Parliament and was attacked on a number of occasions in December 1967 by the non-Communist opposition parties in both houses.[40] In reality, however, the debates over the Novosti agreement had a certain irrelevancy—Indian newspapers for years had received materials directly from the Soviet embassy.

The major English language newspapers generally give a balanced picture of Indian thinking on the USSR's international behavior. The USSR receives praise in the Indian press when it acts on India's behalf or, in the eyes of the editors, acts commendably in other matters. Conversely, the press expresses disapprobation of Soviet policies when it believes such a position is called for. In this respect the journalists do not very often reflect the inhibitions exercised by the Government of India. During the Nehru period the most complete coverage of Soviet affairs was contained in *The Hindu*. By 1966–67 the *Times of India* had become the leading Indian newspaper in this respect.

Among the Indian-owned weekly publications in English, *Blitz* has by far the widest circulation.[41] This journal champions the USSR and sometimes prints unverifiable articles about American

40. When the minister for information, Mr. K. K. Shah, told the Lok Sabha that he saw nothing wrong with the Novosti-PIB agreement, only the Congress and Communist benches remained silent.

"There were cries of 'shame' from both Opposition and Congress benches when the Swatantra member, Mr. Patodia, said that Radio Peace and Progress from Moscow had carried on a tirade against the Indian leaders. He asked why should the Government enter into an agreement under which it became an agent or party and was obliged to distribute Russian material and that too of an agency which was indulging in anti-Indian propaganda.

"Earlier Mr. Hem Barua (PSP) said the Novosti agency was a Soviet counterpart of the Central Intelligence Agency. He questioned the Government's 'wisdom' in entering into an agreement particularly after the great storm raised following the Voice of America deal." (*Hindu Weekly Review*, December 11, 1967.)

41. The average weekly circulation of *Blitz News Magazine* in 1965 was 199,384. No other weekly purporting to be concerned with public affairs has a circulation approaching 100,000.

policies and motives. Misinformation from *Blitz* or misleading stories in the weekly magazine *Link* or the daily newspaper *Patriot* are more valuable to the Soviet cause than its own identifiable propaganda or that put out by the Communist party of India publications. The *Patriot*, a New Delhi paper which began publication in January 1963, reflects the Soviet line on international affairs. Outside financial support enabled the *Patriot* to sell its papers for eight naya paisa (less than 2¢ U.S.).

The detractors of the United States rely most heavily on the activities—both real and imagined—of the CIA. Even the most legitimate Western (particularly American) scholars have been smeared with the CIA label, and research on political, economic, or sociological studies has become increasingly difficult to carry out. One of the most widely circulated pamphlets in India in 1968 was John Smith's *I Was A C.I.A. Agent in India*. Smith was with the American embassy in New Delhi for a few years in the mid-1950s as a "coding clerk" and apparently was employed by the CIA. He later went to the USSR and has since written his "memoirs" about his stint in India in a series of four articles published in the Soviet journal *Literaturnaya Gazeta* in 1967. The articles were subsequently translated and are being sold as a pamphlet by the Communist party of India.[42] Smith accuses a large number of pro-Western Indian editors, writers, industrialists, and politicians of receiving CIA backing and/or acting in devious ways as "American agents." While there is probably an element of truth in a few of his revelations the work as a whole was crudely done. One canard which Smith revives was that the CIA was responsible for sabotaging the Air-India aircraft, the *Princess of Kashmir*, that crashed in the spring of 1955 after it had left Peking with a planeload of delegates to the Bandung Conference.

---

42. John D. Smith, *I Was a CIA Agent in India* (New Delhi, 1967), pp. 36. (I mention the Smith accusations at some length here, not only as an important example of anti-American, anti–Right Wing Congress, propaganda, but also for the contribution such "documents" make toward the creating of a xenophobic nationalism within India.)

The Smith papers were embarrassing to the Government of India. The home minister, Y. B. Chavan, denied emphatically that generals Thimayya and Bannerjee "were big agents of C.I.A. in Indian Army Headquarters," and other allegations. The Government of India, through its Central Intelligence Bureau, made inquiries about illicit foreign interference in Indian politics. Home Minister Chavan told the Parliament in December 1967 that the government had evidence of both Soviet and American agencies spending funds in Indian elections in attempts to elect or defeat specific candidates.[43] The Indian government did not make the CIB report public, nor has it wished to openly embarrass its American and Soviet benefactors. It was necessary, however, to reveal that the study had been made, in order to counteract the charges being levied by pro-Soviet anti-American and pro-American anti-Soviet journals in India about the extensiveness of the two superpowers' involvements in Indian politics. Also, the Government of India, in alluding to its findings, let it be known that it would not countenance such future activities by foreign agencies.

Compared with its operations elsewhere, the known espionage activity of the USSR in India since the 1950s has been slight. After a minor but embarrassing scandal involving several minor officials in the Soviet embassy in New Delhi in 1961, Khrushchev warned the Soviet KGB to tone down its activities in India.[44] It might be said, though, that the flow of information to Moscow has not been hindered by the cutback in Soviet clandestine activities.

There are levels of Soviet attempts to influence Indians other than the crasser forms mentioned above. One of these is support for the widespread study of Russian at India's advanced educational institutions, particularly for students in the sciences. Also,

43. Mr. Chavan's disclosure was made in answer to a question put by a member of the Swatantra party. He ruled out a judicial inquiry into the matter as unfeasible, but said he would later share the broad conclusions of the CIB report with the House. See *Hindustan Times*, December 21, 1967.

44. See *Hindu*, February 24, March 1, 3, 1962.

there are courses in Russian available to interested adults through the Indo-Soviet Friendship Societies and the Soviet consulates in a growing number of Indian cities. Study of languages, culture, and literature is much more palatable to the mind in quest of knowledge than is political propaganda.

After 1953 the Soviets tried to cultivate good personal relations with those who have made and implemented Indian foreign policy. This effort was, of course, helped to a large extent by the range of commonly held interests of the leaders of the two countries. V. K. Krishna Menon, for example, has always thought well of the USSR. Interestingly, however, Menon was one of the few prominent government ministers of his day never to visit the USSR. This is particularly surprising because during his days as defence minister he had had a number of direct dealings with the Soviets on purchases of military equipment and related matters. It appears that Menon, a man who in his own way was very concerned about his public image, did not want to give anyone the impression that he was being used by the Soviets. While Menon was a popular figure and received a very good press in the USSR for his stance on international issues and for his anti-American outbursts, he was personally an enigma for the Soviet leaders. Perhaps Menon preferred to view the USSR from a distance. He liked the Soviet Union in large part because it had been misunderstood and persecuted so long by other nations and because, of the Great Powers involved in the Cold War, "it had shown the most restraint."[45]

Jawaharlal Nehru and his daughter Indira enjoyed good personal relations with the Soviet leaders when Nehru was prime minister. Their Russian visits struck a responsive chord in both of them. They found the Russians warm, friendly people who, after 1954, had a good appreciation of India's policies and aspirations. Lal Bahadur Shastri, who had little occasion to give much thought to the USSR before becoming prime minister, died not long after-

45. Views in this paragraph are derived from discussions with Krishna Menon in February 1964 and January 1968 in New Delhi and with several people who knew Mr. Menon well.

wards while at the Tashkent Conference. His successor, Indira Gandhi, has made several trips to the USSR since 1966, the most recent being at the time of the fiftieth anniversary of the October Revolution in November 1967. She was the only non-Communist head of state to come to Moscow for the occasion. The following January, Premier Kosygin repaid the courtesy by flanking Mrs. Gandhi, with President Tito, at India's Republic Day procession.

Everything considered, the USSR during Nehru's last decade was rather successful in cultivating those members of the External Affairs Ministry and the academic and journalistic communities who identified closely with the left-wing of the Congress party. One can not make a blanket statement as to why individual members of the elite of policy implementors and opinion makers shared Nehru's views on the USSR. Some undoubtedly did so in solid agreement with Nehru's reasoning; others because it was politically expedient. Even though the strength of the Congress "left" has been weakened considerably since 1964, this group continues to dominate the foreign-policy making process, especially toward countries outside the subcontinent.

The electoral position of the Communist party of India is not of much relevance as an indicator of whether or not the Soviet image in India has improved over the years. There is, for example, no evidence to support the contention that the CPI does better electorally in areas where the USSR has aid projects.[46] India's Communists have not improved their position much since 1952. In fact there is a remarkable consistency in Communist electoral strength in all the first four general elections. Communist candidates have done very well in Kerala, West Bengal, in parts of

46. It has been noted that of "the 17 areas where the Soviet Union supported projects, the Communist Party contested three of the constituencies for the Lok Sabha in 1957 and won all three. In 1962 it won the same three again with a higher percentage, and lost significantly the three new constituencies it contested." [Complete figures on the 1967 elections are not yet available.] See Warren Ilchman, "A Political Economy of Foreign Aid: The Case of India," *Asian Survey*, (October, 1967) : 687.

Andhra Pradesh, and in sections of some metropolitan areas, but they have not picked up additional strength elsewhere. Neither internal issues (such as the formal split of the Communist party from 1964 onward or India's domestic problems) nor external issues (the Sino-Indian conflict of 1962) seem to change the voting patterns. As in France and Italy, those who vote Communist in India—for whatever reasons—do so consistently, but the party (parties) pick up few new supporters. T. B. Bottomore has written:

Although the Communist Party (in India) constitutes the principal opposition to the ruling Congress Party, the intellectual influence of Marxism or of any revolutionary ideas, is slight. In India few of those who can be described as intellectuals in the modern, secular sense are in any consistent, radical or effective way critics of their society or creators of new social doctrines which can inspire popular action, and for the most part the influence of the intellectuals is assimilated to that of the new middle classes as a whole, whose style of life brings about small and gradual changes in taste and manners.[47]

While one can quibble about a few points in this statement, it sums up well one of the reasons why Indian Communists have not extended their base much beyond Kerala and Bengal, and why even in those states they have had difficulty in putting forth a sustained program for change. The Indian intelligentsia, from which leaders of revolutionary movements emerge, has for the most part not been radicalized and, except in limited areas, has not inspired popular support.

Soviet Personnel in India

Many technicians from bloc countries, mainly Soviet, have worked in India in conjunction with specific projects. Additional scientific and medical personnel are attached to technical institutes, universities, and hospitals. Members of Soviet cultural, technical, professional, trade union, and other groups come to India to meet

47. Bottomore, *Elites and Society*, p. 95.

with their Indian counterparts, conduct surveys, negotiate agreements, and so forth.

Practically every high ranking official of the CPSU visited India during Nehru's last decade—Khrushchev, Brezhnev, Koslov, Voroshilov, Suslov, Kosygin, Gromyko, Mikoyan, and others. The 1955 visit of Krushchev and Bulganin marked the first venture by either outside the Soviet bloc. It was no accident that the celebrated cosmonauts, Tereshkova and Nikolaev, came to India for their honeymoon.

Soviet visitors generally conduct themselves in a discreet manner. For example, an Indian official told this writer that he accompanied several Soviet diplomats on a visit to Kerala when that state was under a CPI government. The visitors were rather uneasy, lest the Keralan Communists give them a special reception. They wished to be identified only as backers of Nehru's policies. Premier Khrushchev did not have any special meetings with members of the CPI during his two Indian tours, although he naturally met some CPI leaders at official receptions. Even in Moscow, Khrushchev did not openly consort with Indian Communists. The following story is told by a prominent Indian diplomat who once introduced Khrushchev to E. M. S. Namboodiripad, then secretary-general of the CPI, at a reception in the Indian embassy at Moscow. The two men were silent, not quite knowing what to say to one another. After Namboodiripad walked away, Khrushchev pondered for a moment and then remarked to his host: "Dark isn't he, even for an Indian?" The anecdote is not meant to convey any racial overtones, but does indicate Khrushchev's estrangement in meeting the prominent CPI leader.

In New Delhi there is not much intermingling between the Soviet diplomatic community and the diplomats of other nations. The Russian diplomats remain more aloof than their comrades from Eastern Europe. Contacts between Russians and Indians in New Delhi, Bombay, and other cities are arranged mainly by such organizations as the Indo-Soviet Cultural Society and the All-India Peace Council.

The conduct of Russian technicians working in India is generally characterized as "correct." They give good on-the-job instruction to their Indian co-workers, live unostentatiously, and in this sense give a good impression in the communities in which they are working. There is probably more contact between Russians and Indians on a personal level in those rural areas where Soviet-sponsored projects have been undertaken than in urban areas.

9 Nehru's Last Decade
An Overview

THE pattern of Indo-Soviet relations established during the 1954–56 formative period prevailed during the remander of the Nehru-Khrushchev years. The shift in Soviet orientation toward India brought about a number of significant changes. For India, the most important by-products of this shift included Soviet support for India's position on Kashmir, Soviet economic and technological assistance programs, a relative degree of Soviet non-interference in Indian domestic politics, and strong Soviet backing for India's bid to play a more prominent role in world affairs. Thereafter, the most basic factor in shaping the relationship was the falling-out with China by both India and the USSR beginning in 1958–59. Toward the end of the Nehru years, the USSR also became a supplier of military equipment to India. Public opinion in India never quite kept pace with the intensity of the government's ties with the USSR, but the apparent success of the relationship blunted criticisms that India was too close to the Soviet Union.

At the risk of being repetitious, it might be useful to summarize chronologically some of the milestones of New Delhi–Moscow relations during the 1953–64 period. Following that, we will turn to a more thematic evaluation of the relationship.

The historic moment of Indian independence coincided with

242

the hardening of Cold War lines in Europe. With problems enough of its own, the Nehru government had little interest in taking sides in the Great Powers' dispute. But as most of India's political and commercial ties continued to be with Great Britain and other Western nations, the USSR did not accept India's professed non-alignment at face value. In 1948–49 the CPSU gave tacit approval to the militant course pursued by the CPI and portrayed the Congress party as a reactionary party which was deluding the Indian masses.

Despite this turn, Nehru continued to leave the door open for improved relations with the USSR. During the Korean War the Indian government gave visible demonstration of an increasingly independent attitude toward the East-West conflict. Nonetheless the tensions between Moscow and New Delhi did not lessen substantially until the dark night of Stalin's rule ended.

Even while jockeying for position in the leadership struggle, Stalin's successors agreed on the need to refurbish Soviet diplomatic tactics. In this context a re-evaluation of policy toward the newly independent nations of Asia took place. India, the most populous and influential of these nations, received the most attention in the subsequent Soviet drive to diminish Western influence in South and Southeast Asia. In August 1953 Premier Malenkov hailed India's "significant contribution to the efforts of the peace-loving countries toward ending the Korean War" and expressed the hope that "in the future, relations between India and the USSR will grow stronger and develop in a spirit of friendly cooperation." After Chou En-lai's visit to India in 1954, the Soviets echoed support for Asian solidarity based on the Five Principles of Peaceful Coexistence. Assistance was promised for developmental projects in the public sector of the Indian economy, and an agreement was concluded early in 1955 for the Soviets to build a steel mill at Bhilai. From 1954 on the Soviet press gave almost unqualified praise to Nehru's policies. Communist diplomats also began to argue that India should have a substantially larger role in important international conferences and councils. In the years that followed, the Soviets sought to reinforce rather than to alter the general direction of Indian policy. The fact that overt pressure was rarely exerted to obtain Indian support for its Cold War policies contributed to the success of the Soviet diplomatic effort. Of fundamental importance also was Nehru's conception of India's national interests which led to policies that often overlapped those pursued by the USSR.

Proceeding with some caution at first, the Indian government soon welcomed the changed Soviet attitude. The Soviet overtures opportunely coincided with the beginning of American military aid to Pakistan and the formation of the SEATO. Rankled that the United States had not heeded his pleas, Nehru was gratified by the new respect accorded his views by the USSR and China and met the Communist powers halfway in developing a modus vivendi. Such an understanding, he believed, would enable India to assume the role of a bridge between East and West and would enhance India's bid for an equitable share of Asia's future leadership.

Nehru regarded the Soviet acceptance of a compromise settlement on Indochina at the Geneva Conference of mid-1954 as evidence of a genuine change in Soviet policy. He was also impressed by the Soviet gestures of reconciliation toward Yugoslavia. By early 1955 he began to speak of liberalizing trends within the Communist world. In the decades prior to Indian independence he had believed that the USSR would have behaved differently had it been treated as a member of the international community instead of as a pariah. Now he saw a new opportunity for India and other nations to encourage the thaw within the USSR by accepting the Soviet bid to coexist peacefully.

The improvement in Indo-Soviet relations was marked in 1955 by the exchange of delegations and by reciprocal state visits. Nehru's trip to the USSR in June gave him a chance to exchange views with the Soviet leaders. Significantly, he was the first non-Communist leader permitted to speak directly to Russian audiences. He balanced his praise for the steps that the USSR had taken to lessen world tension with the reminder that the USSR and India, because of their differing historical experiences, had to respect the path chosen by the other to achieve its national objectives. The Khrushchev-Bulganin visits to India, Afghanistan, and Burma marked the first such peacetime venture by Soviet leaders outside the Communist camp. Whatever embarrassment Khrushchev's occasional anti-Western remarks may have caused his Indian hosts was more than offset by unqualified Soviet support for India on the Kashmir and Goa issues. Despite their nations' differing political and socioeconomic milieux, a good working relationship developed between Indian and Soviet leaders. Over the next decade almost every prominent Indian and Soviet political figure visited the other's country.

The proceedings of the CPSU Twentieth Congress seemingly confirmed Nehru's assessment of the "trend toward normalcy" within the USSR. Speaking before Parliament in March 1956 he observed: "There can be no doubt that the CPSU Congress has developed a new line and a new policy. This new line, both in political thinking and on practical policy appears to be based on a more realistic appreciation of the world situation and represents a significant process of adaptation and adjustment." The dissolution of the Cominform a month later was interpreted by Nehru as another indicator of Soviet good intentions.

The processes of de-Stalinization unleashed long pent-up forces in Eastern Europe. When the Hungarian crisis broke out, Nehru's primary concern was that the conflict should remain localized. Ten days after the revolt was crushed, Nehru requested that the USSR remove its troops and permit self-determination by the Hungarian people. Yet he did not support the application of any pressures by the UN to achieve these ends. Pleased by Nehru's initial response to the Hungarian situation, the Soviets became somewhat annoyed by later Indian criticisms. In return they pointedly reminded New Delhi of India's own domestic problems.

When Nehru expressed concern in 1958 over worsening Soviet-Yugoslav relations, Khrushchev asked that India live up to the Five Principles agreement and not interfere in the affairs of other nations. Nehru was also called to task for his article "The Basic Approach," in which he pointed to "the growing contradictions within the rigid framework of communism," and "its unfortunate association with violence."

But from March 1959 onward, developments in Tibet and along India's Himalayan borders brought an end to Nehru's criticisms of the USSR. Relations with China, deteriorating steadily since 1957, had reached a critical juncture. The goodwill generated during the "Hindi-Chini bhai-bhai" period was quickly dissipated. Secret negotiations held to discuss the unmarked boundary in Ladakh had ended inconclusively. More was involved than a border dispute. A conflict between two rivals—each offering a distinct approach to the socio-political problems confronting Asia—was about to assume major proportions.

Nehru had hoped that the USSR would act as a restraining influence on China. Unfortunately for India, all was not well in the Sino-Soviet alliance, and the Soviets could not guarantee amicable Chinese conduct toward India. Among the Chinese grievances against the USSR was the preferential treatment given to the "reactionary" Indian government. For example, even after the Chinese had complained about the quantity of Soviet aid to India, the USSR in September 1959 pledged $378 million for projects to assist India's Third Five Year Plan.

The first Soviet commentary on the Sino-Indian border dispute merely called on the two governments to resolve their problems. But the Chinese understood the meaning of the seemingly innocuous statement. For the first time the USSR had not supported a fraternal party in a dispute involving a Communist and a non-Communist nation. Khrushchev's trip to Peking in October did nothing to heal the growing Sino-Soviet rift.

Nehru made a clear distinction between the Soviet and Chinese brands of communism during the months following the 1959 border clashes. He stated that Russia was "eager and anxious" for an East-West understanding but that the same anxiety for peace did not exist in Peking. The USSR had reached a state of normalcy and was a territorially satisfied power; China by contrast had not gotten over the "first flush of its revolutionary mentality." On another occasion he said that "there is not any country in the world which cares more for peace than the USSR and none that cares less than China."

Soviet ties to India were further solidified by Khrushchev's state visit in February 1960, an additional Soviet loan of $126 million in February 1961 for Indian projects, and India's purchase in April 1961 of Soviet transport planes to be used in Ladakh. Concurrently, during 1960–62, Sino-Soviet relations were marked by the withdrawal of Soviet technicians from China, a decrease in trade, and the harsh tone of polemical exchanges.

Yet when the Chinese attacked India's northeast frontier region in October 1962, the USSR did not speak out immediately on India's behalf. Involved in a major crisis of his own, Khrushchev sought to present the image of a united Communist front for bar· gaining purposes with the United States. The Cuban situation was apparently the reason for the *Pravda* editorial of October 25 endorsing Peking's cease-fire proposal as the basis for the beginning of Sino-Indian talks. But while this stand was unacceptable to Nehru, it did not placate Peking.

In effect China demanded that Khrushchev make a full denunciation of Indian policy. Such a step would have undermined nine years of Soviet diplomatic courting of India and would have represented a major concession by Khrushchev to his rivals for leadership of the Communist world. With the passing of the Cuban crisis, Soviet leaders were less constrained to withhold criticism of the Chinese. In December Khrushchev openly rebutted Chinese charges of his "collusion" with the Americans in the withdrawal of missiles from Cuba. With reference to India he reminded the Chinese that the Himalayan conflict benefited only the "imperialists." The conflict was strengthening the "reactionary" elements and weakening the "progressive" forces within India, and could adversely affect India's policy of nonalignment. These themes were elaborated by the Soviets in the polemical exchanges with the Chinese in 1963.

The Indian government welcomed Khrushchev's strong remarks. Yet it recognized that the USSR had been unable to restrain China; indeed the Chinese possibly had acted in October without Soviet foreknowledge. At the height of the crisis India had been the recipient of substantial American and British military assistance, while the Soviets were reluctant for several weeks to provide even verbal support. From mid-November, 1962, however, the USSR openly criticised the Chinese action and called for a peaceful end to the border dispute by negotiations.

Despite Chinese disapproval, the USSR further increased its already sizable commitments to India. Late in 1963 Moscow announced that Soviet assistance for India's Fourth Five Year Plan would equal the $500 million it had pledged to the Third Five Year Plan projects. Then in May 1964 the Soviets formally agreed to undertake the construction of a public-sector steel plant at Bokaro. Also in 1964 India purchased MI-4 helicopters, transport planes, and other military equipment; and delivery reportedly began on Soviet ground-to-air missiles with fixed launching installations. A dozen or so MIG-21 aircraft were received by India in 1963–64. Speculation for some time centered on whether the Soviets would fulfill their pledge made in 1962 to build three factories in India for the manufacture of MIG airframes, engines, electronic equipment, and missiles; but after some initial delay the project has almost been completed.

The mutual concern over China did not prevent disagreement between New Delhi and Moscow from arising over some matters. At the turbulent session of the United Nations in September 1960, Nehru opposed Khrushchev's plans to revise the Secretariat. In addition, the two nations were at variance on the Congo issue. Unlike the Soviets, India held that all aid to the Congo—financial, technical, and military—should be channeled through the United Nations. The Soviets were displeased by India's substantive military contribution to the UN peace-keeping force in the Congo. When the USSR broke its unofficial moratorium on the testing of nuclear weapons on the eve of the Belgrade Conference of non-aligned nations in September 1961, Nehru registered a protest in Moscow.

Nonetheless, on matters directly affecting the Indian subcontinent, India received almost unreserved support from the USSR. For example, the UN Security Council draft resolution condemning India's military takeover of Goa was vetoed by the USSR. Leonid Brezhnev, on a state visit to India at the time, assured his hosts that "the Soviet people regarded with full understanding and sympathy the desire of the Indian people to liberate" Goa.

It was also politically expedient for the USSR to side unreservedly with India on the Kashmir dispute from 1955 onward. In 1957 and in 1962 the USSR cast vetoes backing India against a Western-sponsored resolution which proposed a plebiscite in Kashmir, but Moscow was not displeased when the United States did not press for a similar resolution in 1964. Encouraged by Pakistan's disenchantment with her Western allies in the 1960s, and concerned about Pakistan's subsequent inclination to find common cause with China against India, the USSR gradually modified its hostile attitude toward the Ayub regime. While maintaining its support for the Indian position on Kashmir, Moscow attempted to improve its standing with Pakistan.

Both India and the USSR, usually in an unobtrusive manner, sought to influence the other's international policies.[1] On the whole, Moscow was probably satisfied with Indian policy on Cold War matters after the midway point of the Korean War. The Soviets overtures of 1954–55 can therefore be interpreted as intended not to alter the direction of Indian policy, but to reinforce and perpetuate the Indian tendency toward nonalignment and increased independence from the West. Only after a measure of

---

1. For a good theoretical article on the reciprocal effects of two nations attempting to influence the other's international policies, see Singer, "Inter-Nation Influence."

rapport had been established in later years did the Soviets overtly try to enlist Nehru's support more on a quid pro quo basis; but so far as it is possible to know, the Soviets rarely employed coercive tactics. We can surmise that the Soviets came to understand the psychology of Nehru and V. K. Krishna Menon reasonably well and were not heavy-handed in their dealings with the Indian leaders. A coincidence of interests in certain areas made it possible for cooperative Indian-Soviet relationship to develop.

An interesting question arises as to whether the nonaligned nations, particularly India, were able to influence the course of Soviet policy towards themselves. It can be argued, of course, that the Soviet cooperation with the "bourgeois" leadership of India is only a temporary phase and that Moscow would be well disposed to an eventual coming to power of a Communist movement. Nonetheless, long-range preferences or goals do not constitute a workable policy. Soviet leaders, like those of other countries, are called upon to make short-term decisions and are limited in their freedom of action by the cumulative effect of those decisions. Despite his previous ideological orientation, Khrushchev showed a capacity for pragmatic adaptation in his relations with the new states.

The very process of attempting to influence the political elites of India had some impact on Soviet behavior over a period of time. Moscow could not cultivate friendly relations with foreign governments and, at the same time, attempt to undermine their political systems. The very success in the Soviet relationship with India and some of the other nonaligned states undoubtedly encouraged the Soviets to continue the line adopted during 1954–56.

Nehru welcomed the changes in international politics brought about by the increased Soviet interest in the nonaligned countries. Challenged by the Communist nations, the Western powers now had to devote more attention to the problems of the "developing" nations. The very existence of an increasing number of new nations contributed to the breakdown of the European-centered bipolar system.

On his part Nehru sought to make "peaceful coexistence" attractive to the Soviets. His cordiality with the Soviet leaders and his contention that significant change was occurring in the USSR helped to lend respectability abroad to the Khrushchev regime in its first years. Other Afro-Asian nations, influenced by the Indian example, adopted nonaligned foreign policies, thus helping to render ineffective the cordon sanitaire around the Communist bloc. India served briefly as an intercessor for the Communist powers in the mid-1950s. Later, when the USSR had established more direct channels of communication with the West, India's support was valued on other grounds, for example, as endorsing Soviet disarmament proposals and Soviet calls for Summit meetings. Over the years India has voted more often with the USSR than with the United States in the UN General Assembly,[2] although careful evaluation has to be made of votes on individual issues for the overall statistics to have much qualitative meaning. From 1959 onward the widening Sino-Soviet rift provided further incentive for the USSR to develop even closer ties with India, as both were interested in preventing the extension of Chinese influence in Asia and among the "developing" nations. In general Nehru's policies were useful to the USSR in its bid to equal the United States as an influential world power.

From the standpoint of his basic policy objectives, Nehru's

2. The following compilations are indicative of this trend in India's UN voting pattern during the Nehru years. On roll-call votes in plenary sessions of the General Assembly from 1946 to 1957 the correspondence of India's vote with the USSR was 49.3 percent and with the United States, 37.3 percent. See Gertrude Boland, "India and the United Nations: India's Role in the General Assembly, 1946–57" (Ph.D. diss., Claremont College, 1961), p. 21.

In 80 important roll-call votes at the fifteenth and sixteenth sessions of the General Assembly in 1960–61, India's position coincided with that of the USSR 41.2 percent and with the USA 10 percent of the time on issues where there was disagreement between the two superpowers. See Francis Wilcox, "The Non-Aligned States and the United Nations," *Neutralism and Non-Alignment: The New States in World Affairs*, ed. Laurence W. Martin (New York, 1962), pp. 121–51.

dealings with the USSR in his last decade turned out well. Nehru regretted the harsh Soviet suppression of the Hungarian revolt, the resumption of nuclear testing on the eve of the Belgrade Conference, and the unwillingness to condemn immediately the Chinese military move against India in October 1962. He opposed Khrushchev's threat to send "volunteers" into the Middle East and the Congo in times of crises and the plan to revise the UN Secretariat. From time to time he was dismayed by Soviet intransigence on resolving Cold War issues and with Khrushchev's occasional tendency to identify India too closely with his own policy. Nevertheless, there were far more significant advantages than drawbacks for India in the relationship. Soviet backing for India on Kashmir and on the Himalayan dispute with China were and remain of critical importance to the Congress government's policies. In addition, the USSR provided substantial assistance for Indian developmental programs, called for Indian participation in most important international conferences and for the eventual inclusion of India on a revised UN Security Council, and supported India's contention that its nuclear reactors should not be subjected to IAEA controls. And this is not an all-inclusive list.

Nehru made a clear distinction between his dealings with the USSR and with the CPI. At election times he was extremely critical of the Indian Communists, accusing them of having foreign loyalties and for a number of years recalling vividly their disruptive tactics of 1948–50. His government's triennial Preventive Detention Act, and later the Defence of India Act (initiated in late 1962), while directed against all extremist elements, enabled the government to take extra-constitutional measures against the CPI. Indians with any record of Communist activity almost invariably have been kept out of the governmental and public services. The Soviet leaders rarely objected to the Indian government's treatment of the CPI. While applauding the coming to power of the CPI in Kerala in April 1957, they did not speak out when the central government, on the basis of its constitutional authority, imposed presidential rule and removed the Communist-led coalition from office in 1959. They had little public contact with their Indian comrades, preferring to be identified with the left-wing of the Congress party. Yet the CPI benefited indirectly from the improved Indo-Soviet relationship, as the party increased its membership and electoral strength somewhat from 1954 until the Sino-Indian conflict of 1962.

By the late 1950s the CPI had become the most consistent supporter among the Indian opposition parties of Nehru's foreign policy. Then the growing Sino-Soviet rift caused a process of polarization within the faction-riven CPI. The rightist, Moscow-oriented wing of the CPI praised the "progressive elements" of the Congress party represented by Nehru and Krishna Menon. After 1959 the Indian government did not discourage CPI contacts with the USSR nearly so much as those with China. During his visit to Moscow in December 1962, S. A. Dange, Secretary-General of the CPI, may even have served as an unofficial liason between Nehru and Khrushchev. After the conflict with China in 1962, Nehru yielded to public pressures calling for the imprisonment of leftist CPI leaders. But he was receptive in later months to Soviet appeals that all CPI leaders must be released. The early 1960s found the local Communist parties banned in practically every country of North Africa and the Middle East and repressed in many sub-Saharan nations. At the same time many of these very countries enjoyed close state relations with the USSR, received Soviet aid, and espoused anti-imperialist foreign policies. The one-party revolutionary regimes in such nations as Egypt, Syria, and Algeria resented the fact that indigenous Communists (even though generally cooperative with the party in power) maintained their own organizational identity and sometimes advocated their own programs. To meet this critical situation, the USSR in 1963 pragmatically began to describe as "national revolutionary" those single-party regimes which were firmly committed to anti-

Western imperialism and non-capitalist paths of development. The local Communists in Egypt, Guinea, Mali, Ghana, Algeria, and Burma were subsequently advised by the USSR to support the "revolutionary-nationalist" leaders and not to put forth an independent policy line.[3]

India, by contrast, has a multi-party system in which the CPI has never been banned. Acts of limited repression have been carried out, however, under the Preventive Detention Acts and the Defence of India Act. Despite the patriotic sentiments expressed by many Communist leaders after the Chinese attack in 1962, the CPI understandably was subjected to heavy pressures within India. The denunciations of the Chinese by party chairman S. A. Dange contributed to the growing cleavage in CPI ranks which culminated in the formal break between the "right" and the "left" factions in mid-1964.[4] The Right-CPI, which identifies closely with the USSR on foreign policy matters, sought to dispel all doubts of the party's loyalty to India. When the Chinese delivered their "ultimatum" to India during the Indo-Pakistan conflict of 1965, a Right-CPI spokesman, Z. A. Ahmed, denounced the Chinese as "crooks, opportunists, imperialists and saboteurs."[5] By contrast, the leader of the Left-CPI termed the incident unfortunate and called for a negotiated Sino-Indian settlement on the basis of formalizing the status quo both in Ladakh and along the MacMahon Line. In 1964 the Right-CPI, with Moscow's blessing, formally revised their 1951 party program which had called for the establishment of a "people's democracy" under the exclusive leadership of the working class. The new conception of a "national democracy" was one in which "leadership of the alliance of the

3. Richard Lowenthal, "Russia, the One-Party System, and the Third World," *Survey*, no. 58 (January 1966), pp. 43–58.

4. Ralph Retzlaff, "Revisionism and Dogmatism in the Communist Party of India," in *The Communist Revolution in Asia*, ed. Robert Scalapino (Englewood Cliffs, N. J., 1965); and John Wood, "Observations on the Indian Communist Party Split," *Pacific Affairs*, Spring, 1965, pp. 47–63.

5. *Patriot* (New Delhi), September 19, 1965.

patriotic classes is shared between the national bourgeoisie and the working class."[6] This doctrinal change gave official sanction to the CPI's cooperation with the Congress party. On its part the Left-CPI declared that any move away from the concept of people's democracy is a deviation from the correct path to socialism.

On matters not immediately involving the Indian subcontinent, Nehru developed his nation's foreign policy by taking into consideration as much or as little advice from confidants as he deemed desirable. While he occasionally met with opposition leaders to explain his policies, these leaders had little tangible influence on his thinking. Only after 1962 did the parties of the Indian "right" have a major foreign policy issue on which to criticise the Congress party. Within the Congress party itself Nehru's word on foreign affairs remained unchallenged until 1962; thereafter the Working Committee on External Affairs ceased to be a mere rubber stamp for his policies.

While Nehru exercised control over Indian policy toward the Great Powers, he did not often use his prominent position to initiate new approaches on issues involving India's relations with Pakistan and China. Here the influential opinions of India's elites, the voices of opposition parties, and the emotional undercurrents of the larger polity limited the range of Nehru's alternatives. Compromise on Kashmir at any time or on Ladakh after 1959 would have hurt Nehru and the Congress party politically; yet Nehru's personal prestige was so great that, at least until October 1962, he probably could have weathered the repercussions of an unpopular compromise settlement with Pakistan or with China. This is not meant to suggest that substantive compromises compatible with Indian interests were readily available or that Pakistani and Chinese leaders were models of reasonableness in their demands on Nehru.

6. "Draft Program of Communist Party of India," *World Marxist Review Information Bulletin*, no. 18 (July 9, 1964), pp. 23–24.

India was assured an eminent role among the nonaligned nations, for Nasser, Tito, and other advocates of a "third world" recognized that they could exert little international leverage without India and her prestigious leader. Even so, Indian influence almost inevitably declined with the emergence of several dozen independent African states, many of which viewed Indian policy as overly conservative. New Delhi was reproached by a number of African states for having lost some of its earlier anti-imperialist vigor. For example, India had remained aloof during the struggle for Algerian independence rather than alienate the French government. And when Guinea flouted Charles de Gaulle by severing ties with Paris, New Delhi did not offer any assistance to the Sekou Touré regime. By contrast China had openly backed the FLN and Guinea with political support and token economic assistance when these were most needed. China's diplomatic initiative over India in Afro-Asia turned out to be short-lived, however, in the light of events from 1965 to 1968.

Whatever influence India had previously exerted in Asia also waned in the early 1960s. The leadership role which Nehru had sought to develop for India failed to materialize. Practically no attempt was made to establish meaningful contacts with the nations militarily aligned with the United States. And with the partial exception of Malaya, the Government of India did little to cultivate close ties with the other Asian nations which, like India, were committed to the institutions of parliamentary democracy. Only after the Sino-Indian conflict of 1962 did India become significantly aware of Japan's potential role in Asia; and despite Israel's repeated offers to assist in India's developmental programs, New Delhi has kept that West Asian nation at arms length for fear of antagonizing the Arab nations.

The major thrust of India's Asian diplomacy (aside from that involving China) was toward her geographic neighbors and the nonaligned nations of Southeast Asia. But this effort also was, in varying degrees, not very successful. The process of developing good relations is a two-way street, and India was less responsible than some other nations for the implementation of the Bandung pledges calling for cooperative solidarity. Still, India was generally neglectful of her neighbors in Southeast Asia. The undermanned Indian Foreign Office devoted much of its energies and limited resources to the arena of Great Power politics. From New Delhi there emanated a running commentary on international affairs which often appeared unrelated to the immediate concerns of a regional Asian power. Some of India's potential friends resented what they termed a rather patronizing attitude on India's part. India's academic institutions and public information media did little to stimulate interest in other Asian societies. Plans for regional economic cooperation scarcely left the drawing boards. In short, India did not exert much regional leadership, nor was she fully successful in allaying the fears of Indian hegemony held by some of the smaller nations on her borders.

Because of his great stature among the Congress party leaders and the Indian people at large, Nehru's policies were unhealthily free from criticism by responsible, politically conscious elements of the Indian community. Only in 1959 did informed opinion begin to clamor that some of India's pressing problems were not being dealt with resolutely. The conflict with China served to shake the lethargy within the ruling Congress party, but the situation could not be altered overnight.

At the time of Nehru's death in May, 1964, India still faced the ever-plexing Kashmir situation and a plentitude of socioeconomic problems. Much of the idealism and drive which had characterized the Congress movement during the struggle for independence had ebbed away. Yet Nehru left behind a land which had not succumbed to the divisive forces which beset it. The stress on India's many unsolved problems should not obscure Nehru's important achievements—for example, restraining the passions of communalism, laying the foundation for a modest rate of industrial growth, and nurturing the practices of representative government.

More than most of his contemporaries, Nehru had a sense of the urgent need to resolve the pressing international issues of his day. Yet, like those of all national leaders, his policies stemmed from and were a projection of his nation's domestic situation. His thoughts on the USSR and communism were inextricably tied to his appraisal of conditions within India, as were his hopes to remove India from the Cold War arena.

Nehru's Panchsheel diplomacy of the mid-1950s was conceived both as a statement of principle and as a means to commit the Communist powers to responsibilities from which they could not easily withdraw. In retrospect his policy has been vindicated with regard to Russia, but it did not succeed in the case of China. As the years passed, Nehru learned, sometimes in a painful way, of the limitations on his power to influence international events. It should be said, however, that those who criticize Nehru's China policy while accepting or even applauding his diplomacy toward the USSR do not take into account that the rationale and underlying premises of both policies were essentially the same.

After it became apparent by 1959 that Peking would not accept his concept of an Asia in which India and China would coexist as equals, Nehru placed an even greater premium on more cooperative relations with the USSR and the West. His diplomacy in this area proved successful, for both superpowers were interested, albeit for different reasons, in Indian political stability and economic development. Each provided India with material assistance without pressing for a change in her basic international orientation. The working relationship with the United States and the Soviet Union formed an important part of Nehru's legacy to his successors.

10 Epilogue
The Post-Nehru Period

MORE than four years have gone by since the mantle of governmental leadership in India passed from Nehru's shoulders.[1] In the context of India's domestic and international situation since

1. The writing of contemporary history is, at best, a hazardous task. It would nonetheless be remiss not to mention some of the more important developments in Indo-Soviet relations which have occurred since the period covered in this study. Certain of these already have been discussed in chapters 7 and 8.

During the four years since Nehru's death, India has experienced a marked increase in the amount of civil unrest, a brief war with Pakistan, rebellions on the part of dissident Nagas and Mizos, several poor harvests in 1965–66, a continuing language crisis, political instability in a number of states, widespread strikes, and a general increase in regional demands—all of which have placed a serious strain on the political structure.

Still, there are encouraging signs as well. Despite dire predictions, orderly transitions of political power took place after the deaths of Nehru and Lal Bahadur Shastri. Indian journalists have begun to address themselves to the socio-economic condition of the nation's downtrodden. In some cities a sense of civic consciousness is stirring. There is also an increasing awareness of the need to make better use of India's intellectual resources and to tackle the problem of population control. Higher priority during the Fourth Five Year Plan is to be given the long-neglected but critical agricultural sector. In short, many problems which had been shunted aside during the Nehru years have now come into the open and will have to be dealt with. Whether or not the central government will be able to deal with the increased demands from various sectors of society and the centrifugal forces discussed in Selig Harrison's, *India: The Most Dangerous Decades*, remains an open question.

259

Nehru's death, it is understandable that both Lal Bahadur Shastri and Indira Gandhi attempted to maintain the nonalignment concept as a cornerstone of the foreign policy of their respective governments. But the concept, born of the Cold War, has lost much of its relevance in the 1960s with the polycentrism and discord within the Communist world and, to a lesser extent, within the Western alliance. Today India has the equivalent of an alliance against China in the sense that the United States and most probably the USSR would render support to India in the unlikely event of a major Sino-Indian military clash. India receives considerable economic and technological aid from the Western powers and from the USSR and the other Communist nations of Eastern Europe without the constraints of a formal alliance—a situation which has irked Pakistan. Continued emphasis on the nonalignment theme helps to counter the growing criticism among the Indian "left" that Nehru's foreign policy is being subtly undermined by his successors. It also serves to placate the Soviet Union which, like India itself, has in the past reaped diplomatic advantages from the existence of the group of nonaligned nations.

In the post-Nehru, post-Khrushchev period, the leaders of India and the Soviet Union continue to minimize the differences and emphasize the similarities in their respective positions on international political issues. The ways in which the two governments have approached the Vietnam conflict provides a good example of this tendency. New Delhi's failure to follow Moscow in demanding an immediate withdrawal of American forces from Vietnam was ignored in the public statements of both governments. Instead, stress was placed upon their joint opposition to escalation of the conflict and to the bombing of North Vietnam. During his visit to Moscow in May 1965, Prime Minister Shastri stood alongside Premier Kosygin while the latter denounced imperialism and called upon the nonaligned nations to help end the American aggressions in the Congo, the Dominican Republic, and Vietnam. A joint communiqué after the visit included a call for a halt to American bombings of North Vietnam and a plea that the Vietnam conflict be settled on the basis of the 1954 Geneva Agreement.[2] When Mrs. Gandhi visited the USSR in July 1966, she also called for a cessation of the bombing of North Vietnam. Interestingly, a few days earlier, in Cairo, Mrs. Gandhi had linked the ending of the bombing of the North with a cease-fire in the South. One might infer that in the interim Moscow had exerted pressure on New Delhi to drop the latter condition. (As of January 1969, however, the USSR had not been able to elicit a condemnatory statement on America's overall Vietnam policy from Mrs. Gandhi, nor did it appear likely that one would be forthcoming.)

As chairman of the International Control Commission on Indochina since 1954, India has experienced the frustration of helplessly watching the increased violations of the Geneva accords.[3] Mrs. Gandhi's government in 1966 called upon the USSR and Britain to reconvene the Geneva Conference but received a negative response from the Soviets. New Delhi has indicated that it would play a mediatory role in ending the fighting, but the likelihood of India's being called upon in such a capacity is very limited. As during the Korean conflict, the efficacy of India's pleas that the fighting be terminated is negligible. But if the belligerents and their major supporters reach a negotiated agreement, as commission chairman, India conceivably could play a useful role in the agreement's implementation. Lacking a Soviet go-ahead, India has not sought to emphasize the role of the International Control Commission. For example, the United States more than once requested that the commission take an active part in guaranteeing Cambodia's borders, but India would not make such a move without Soviet approval.

China

New Delhi's views on Vietnam are of course related to its appraisals of China's intentions. One point rarely mentioned pub-

2. See "Sovmestnoe Sovetskoe Indiiskoe Kommiunike," in *Pravda*, May 20, 1965; see also *New York Times*, May 13, 20, 1965.

3. For a study of Indian attitudes and policy on the Vietnamese question see Sar Desai, *India's Foreign Policy in Cambodia, Laos and Vietnam, 1947–64*.

licly by Indian officials is that the escalation of the war in Vietnam may have contributed to the relative quiet on China's Himalayan borders with India. After the fighting in 1962 China withdrew her forces entirely from the NEFA, but she continues to occupy the Aksai Chin region of Ladakh with its Sinkiang-Tibet roadway. An uneasy truce prevails with neither side willing to make the sort of concessions requisite to a negotiated settlement. On several occasions limited skirmishes have occurred. During the Indo-Pakistani conflict of 1965 Chinese troops menacingly appeared on the Sikkim border, but fortunately, the potential crisis soon subsided. Some skirmishes took place at the Nathula Pass on the Sikkim border in the fall of 1967, but the incidents did not escalate into serious hostilities. India's current leaders continue to strengthen defenses and communications in the border regions, for they no longer hold the disproven belief that Soviet counsel can restrain China vis-à-vis India.

Peking's opinion of Indian foreign and domestic policies has not changed; neither has its resentment of Soviet coddling of India. As a result, Peking's criticisms of India since 1964 often have been couched within the framework of its denouncements of the Soviet leaders.[4]

During the early 1960s India lost ground to China in the contest for influence among the Asian and African nations. But by the close of 1965 India's diplomatic position had improved considerably. This was due in large part to the combination of gaucheries and mishaps which brought the Chinese a series of foreign policy setbacks—in Indonesia, at the abortive Afro-Asian Conference in Algiers, and elsewhere. Moreover, such friends of China as Nkrumah, Sukarno, and Ben Bella fell from power. Peking's domestic policies, culminating in the disruptive Cultural Revolution of 1966–67, diminished the attraction of China for countries of the *tiers-monde*. This has not resulted in a corresponding rise

4. See "Arming India Against Its Neighbors," in *Peking Review*, 9 (June 3, 1966), and "Washington–Moscow–New Delhi: Anti-China Rumour Combine," *Peking Review*, 10 (February 10, 1967).

of Indian influence abroad, and it is unlikely that India will regain the eminent role which it enjoyed among the newly-emerging nations in the 1950s. The Chinese campaign to isolate India from the Afro-Asian countries collapsed, however, and New Delhi once again found itself on good terms with several nonaligned states with whom relations had deteriorated badly in the 1963–65 period. It should be noted that the decline and subsequent improvement of Indian relations with nations such as Indonesia and Ghana were largely the result of forces and events independent of Indian policy.

Pakistan

Although the Indo-Pakistani conflict of 1965 was far more embarrassing to the United States and Britain than to the USSR, the Soviets wanted a quick end to the fighting. In September Premier Kosygin made four separate appeals to New Delhi and Rawalpindi calling for a cease-fire. A major reason for the Soviet desire for a speedy end to the conflict was the fear that the Chinese might intervene on the side of Pakistan. Moscow warned against outside forces which were trying to further aggravate the military conflict.[5] A Chinese ultimatum calling for immediate dismantling of Indian posts allegedly violating the China border particularly angered the Soviets.

The USSR cooperated with the other major Security Council powers in drawing up several cease-fire resolutions. The belligerents heeded them after some major battles in which large quantities of American, British, and to a much lesser extent, Soviet weapons were destroyed. Unlike the Americans and British, the Soviets did not discontinue their military aid to India during and after the conflict. Nonetheless the Soviets had no interest in being a supplier of weaponry to India in an extended conflict with Pakistan and possibly China.

Using its good offices, the Soviet government provided the city of Tashkent for the Ayub-Shastri meetings in January 1966. As

5. *Pravda*, September 14, 23, 1965.

host, Premier Kosygin was helpful in bringing about the restoration of Indo-Pakistani relations, although nothing was done to
permanently resolve the Kashmir situation. It was the first time that
the USSR had ever mediated a dispute between two non-Communist nations.[6]

To what extent was the Soviet peacemaking effort welcomed
within India? According to a public opinion poll shortly after the
Tashkent Conference, there was widespread approval of the Soviet
role.[7] Yet had Shastri lived, he would have faced considerable
criticism from the rightist opposition parties upon returning to
India. The Indian prime minister had gone back on his pledge not
to yield Haji Pir and Kargil—strategic points for Pakistani infiltration into Kashmir. It was believed that Kosygin was somehow
responsible in pressuring Shastri into yielding to the *status quo
ante bellum.*

Almost inevitably the concern grew in New Delhi that the Soviets
might be moving in the direction of an impartial attitude toward
India and Pakistan. To allay this concern the Soviets reaffirmed
that they continued, as before, to stand behind India on Kashmir.
The USSR currently (1968) favors the formal recognition of the
status quo in Kashmir (a position to which New Delhi has in-
formally given its approval). While seeking opportunities to improve its standing with Pakistan, the USSR will not risk its more
important relationship with India. If and when the Kashmir issue
becomes less volatile, a major impediment between Moscow and
Rawalpindi will be diminished.

Pakistan was angered by the United States' arms embargo imposed during the 1965 Indo-Pakistani War. The conflict, although
brief, resulted in the loss of hundreds of tanks and other armored

6. Two articles by a Pakistani and an Indian scholar present views on Soviet
policy toward their respective countries: Chaudhri, "Pakistan's Relations with
the Soviet Union," and Vaidyanath, "Some Recent Trends in Soviet Policies
Towards India and Pakistan."

7. See "International Images After Tashkent; January–February, 1966; The
Results of a 'Literate' Metropolitan Survey," *Monthly Public Opinion Surveys,*
11 (March–April, 1966) : 3 ff.

vehicles by both combatants. Pakistan, which was far more dependent than India on American-manufactured weaponry, was then forced to find alternate sources. Rawalpindi was able to replenish its spare parts for previously-supplied American weapons through purchases from West European surplus-arms dealers. Turning to China in 1966, Pakistan reportedly signed an agreement for arms valued at $120 million. The deal, which was to be completed in 1968, involved the purchase of 100 T-59 tanks, 80 MIG-19s and 10 IL-28 aircraft.[8] The United States did not welcome Pakistan's becoming too dependent upon China and resumed shipment of some "nonlethal" equipment to its SEATO partner. Also, America authorized Italy to sell surplus M-47 tanks and Iran to supply surplus transport aircraft to Pakistan.

The Soviets were also concerned about the growing Sino-Pakistani ties and sought to mollify Pakistani criticism that the USSR's stepped-up military aid violated the Tashkent Agreement. In April 1968 Premier Kosygin paid a five-day visit to Pakistan, the first state tour ever made by a Soviet leader to that nation. On the eve of Kosygin's arrival, it was announced that the USSR would help to build a steel mill to utilize iron-ore deposits from the Kalabagh Hills, a region about a thousand miles northeast of Karachi in West Pakistan. It was also revealed that the USSR would support the development of a 140 megawatt power station at Roopur in East Pakistan and that the volume of Soviet-Pakistani trade would be increased considerably.[9] A month later Pakistan informed the United States that the Americans would have to close their strategic communications base in Peshawar, West Pakistan, when the ten-year lease expired on July 1, 1969.[10] Then in July 1968 it was

8. Institute for Strategic Studies, *Military Balance, 1967–68* (London, 1967).

9. As reported by Q. Aziz in the *Christian Science Monitor*, May 3, 1968.

10. *Christian Science Monitor*, May 28, 1968. The Peshawar base, located only 150 miles from the Soviet border, enabled the United States to monitor Soviet military radio communications and the space exploration center in Central Asia. It was also used, until the aborted Francis Gary Power's mission in 1960, for U-2 overflights of the USSR.

announced that the USSR would sell small quantities of military
equipment to Pakistan. (The terms of the agreement were not public knowledge at the time of writing.)[11]

Two Crisis Situations
The Middle East and Czechoslovakia

An example of close Indo-Soviet diplomatic cooperation on a
major international issue occurred during the Middle Eastern War
of June 1967. Both nations sought a Security Council resolution
strongly condemning Israel's "aggression" and called for an immediate withdrawal of Israeli forces. During the first days of the
Security Council session, India's chief delegate at times used
language akin to the Soviet lexicon in denouncing the "ruling
circles of Tel Aviv."

Since the end of the conflict, India has continually urged the
withdrawal of Israeli forces from the "illegally occupied territories." Among the reasons for India's unequivocal support for
the Arab nations were (1) an obvious arithmetical consideration—
there are about a dozen Arab states plus a number of predominantly
Muslim nations sympathetic to the Arab cause; (2) the desire to
ensure continued Arab neutrality on the Indo-Pakistani dispute
over Kashmir; (3) the close diplomatic ties between Mrs. Gandhi
and President Nasser; (4) the opportunity to reflect the feelings
of the Indian Muslims on an international issue, thereby demon-
strating India's commitment to secularism. (The Muslims were
the only group within India, aside from the Communist parties,
to unequivocally applaud the Government of India's stand during
the June Security Council session.)

At the behest of the USSR, in November 1967, India sponsored
a draft resolution in the Security Council, the purpose of which
was to thwart any American role as the initiator or guarantor of
an Arab-Israeli compromise. Subsequently, along with the other

11. According to the *New York Times*, July 22, 1968, the Soviets might supply
Pakistan with personnel carriers, ammunition, and spare parts for the tanks
and aircraft which the Pakistani's received from China.

nations represented on the Security Council, India approved the selection of the special UN representative, Gunnar Jarring, to visit the Middle East for consultation with the parties immediately involved.

On August 21, 1968, after Soviet, Polish, Bulgarian, Hungarian, and East German armed forces had occupied Czechoslovakia, Madame Gandhi expressed her government's regrets before the Indian Parliament. Her statement recalled the tragic events which befell Czechoslovakia in 1938–39 and then read in part:

Our relations with the Soviet Union, Poland, Hungary, and Bulgaria are close and many sided. We value these friendships and wish to preserve and extend them. However, we cannot but give expression to our anguish at the events in Czechoslovakia. . . . I am sure I reflect the opinion of the House when I express the hope that the forces which have entered Czechoslovakia will be withdrawn at the earliest possible moment and the Czech people will be able to determine their future according to their own wishes and interests, and whatever mutual problems there may be between Czechoslovakia and its allies, will be settled peacefully. The right of nations to live peacefully and without outside interference should not be denied in the name of religion or ideology. . . . We have always stood for the right of every country to its own traditions, aptitudes and genius. India has always raised her voice whenever these principles have been violated.[12]

There are a number of contrasts and parallels in India's reactions to the Czechoslovakian and the Hungarian (1956) crises. In speaking out immediately against the reentry of Soviet troops into Prague, Mrs. Gandhi did not repeat her father's reluctance to commit himself while fighting was taking place in the streets of Budapest. It can, of course, be said that there was less danger of an escalation of the conflict in 1968 than in 1956. Nehru had hesitated partly because he judged that the Hungarian conflict might lead to a general East-West war and that nothing should be done to add

12. As reported in "The Czech Crisis," *India and Foreign Review*, 5 (September 1, 1968) : 5.

to the tension. In 1956 the crisis situation mounted quickly at a time when India was preoccupied with the Suez conflict, whereas in 1968 the situation built up gradually over a period of months and was a focal point of world attention. From India's standpoint it was uncertain whether the Western powers were involved in the Hungarian upheaval, while in 1968 the Communist party of Czechoslovakia itself was clearly in control of the situation and was leading the reform movement. The Hungarian insurgents had threatened to leave the Warsaw Pact, while the Czechs stressed their intention to remain within the Soviet-led alliance. India has always accepted Eastern Europe as a legitimate sphere of Soviet influence, but it could not accept Moscow's explanation for the Czechoslovak intervention.

India, however, did not support the Seven Nation Security Council resolution of August 22, which condemned the armed intervention of the USSR and its allies. (Pakistan also abstained on the resolution, which the Soviets ultimately vetoed.) The Indian delegate to the Security Council objected to the use of the word "condemns" in the resolution and therefore abstained in the voting. India requested that the delegations be permitted to vote on each paragraph of the resolution separately and expressed a willingness to support all of the paragraphs except the one containing the word "condemns." There was nothing to be gained from using provocative language, explained Mrs. Gandhi to the Indian Parliament on August 23. India's concern, she said, was for "the withdrawal of foreign troops, restoration of the legitimate government to power and restoration of the sovereignty of the people."[13] Mrs. Gandhi replied to her critics in the opposition parties by saying that "after all we have given expression to our feelings, . . . political realities remain and the government will have to deal with them."[14]

Given its overall situation, the government of India's reaction to the Czechoslovak crisis was about as strong as might have

13. Ibid.
14. *New York Times*, August 27, 1968.

been expected. Not to have spoken out would have placed India with the handful of Arab and African nations which—because of their military and/or economic dependence on the USSR— remained silent or supported the Soviet action. To have said less would have made Mrs. Gandhi's government more vulnerable to its domestic and foreign critics. But to have been any more outspoken in deploring the Soviet action would have incurred Moscow's extreme displeasure.

Spheres of Cooperation

Thus far Brezhnev and Kosygin have equalled the pledges of Soviet economic and technological aid to India made during the latter years of Khrushchev's rule. However, India's Fourth Five Year Plan has been delayed until 1969–74 and in the interim the timetables for many Soviet projects have been set back (see chapter 7). The largest single outlay scheduled for the Fourth FYP was approximately $220 million for the Bokaro steel plant and another $220 million for commercial credits. According to an agreement signed on December 10, 1966, assistance will be rendered to about 50 projects that are already in various phases of production. A 100,000 ton annual capacity aluminum smelting plant will be constructed in the Korba region of Madhya Pradesh, and the capacity of the Bhilai steel plants will be increased from 2.5 to 3.2 million tons per year. Other aid will assist coal and ore mining, geological and prospecting work, thermal power stations, and the training of personnel for deap-sea fishing. A number of technical schools will be set up at industrial centers for training skilled technicians and workers for the heavy engineering, metallurgical, electrical, heavy machine building and other industries.[15] The above projects are funded by long-term credits. As non-repayable grants the USSR sent 200,000 tons of wheat early in 1967 to help allay the foodgrain shortage in India and has provided about two million dollars worth

15. *New York Times*, December 11, 1966; and *Hindu Weekly Review*, December 19, 1966.

of equipment and agricultural machinery to assist in the setting up of five new state seed-growing farms.

Since 1953–54 the volume of Indo-Soviet trade has increased almost every year. Currently, the USSR is India's third leading trade partner. The value of trade during the 1960–65 period averaged slightly more than $100 million per year in each direction. An agreement signed in January 1966 projected that trade levels for 1966–70 would exceed the previous five years by approximately 250 percent. Among the most important products from the USSR are machinery and spare parts for maintaining and expanding the projects built with Soviet economic assistance. Under the agreement the USSR will supply almost all of India's imports of petroleum products. India's exports to the USSR continue to feature such products as spices, tea, wool, and skins; but increasingly the USSR is becoming a leading importer of Indian textiles and light electrical manufactures.[16] The Soviets later also contracted to receive a million tons of Indian steel and a large quantity of railway cars. (See chapter 7) India, though, has never been portrayed by the Soviets as a developmental model for other newly-independent nations to emulate. There has been concern in Soviet writings over the continuing domination of private capital within the Indian system. Two decades after Indian independence, "reactionary" elements of the bourgeoisie remain in control of India's economy. The Soviets undoubtedly were disappointed that the trend set by Nehru's adherence to a "Socialist pattern of society" did not develop further, but this has not altered the pattern of Indo-Soviet commercial transactions established in the late 1950s.

Since 1965 the USSR has been the largest single supplier of military equipment to India. Some influential Indian military and political figures have had misgivings about this increasing inde-

16. Additional Indian exports include vegetable oils, tobacco, jute products, knitwear, shoes, handicrafts, carpets, storage batteries, refrigerators, textile processing machinery, and electric fans. Manufactured products will account for 40 percent of Indian exports representing a four-fold increase over the 1961 level. See *Hindu Weekly Review*, January 17, 1966.

pendence upon the USSR, but the concern has been subordinated to the Indian government's conception of its defense needs. Because the United States and Great Britain have not resumed shipments of "lethal" military eqiupment to India, New Delhi's dependence on the Soviets has increased. The situation has its more positive side for India, as the abrogation of Anglo-American military aid has been felt even more strongly by Pakistan. Continuing American economic aid frees funds for military purchases. India is also rapidly increasing its own domestic manufactures of military equipment and ordnance.

Soviet weaponry sold on liberal terms to India since 1963–64 includes helicopters, ground to air missiles with launching and radar facilities, tanks, and SU-7 supersonic fighter-bombers, submarines, and surface naval craft, and surface-to-air missiles. After agreeing in 1962 to build the MIG-21 factories in India, Moscow apparently had some second thoughts. This may have been due in part to an increase in the estimated cost of the project, but probably it was more attributable to China's vehement reaction. Noting this, the Indian Defence Ministry periodically reminded the Soviets of their commitment. By 1965–66 the USSR was less concerned with China's reaction. In 1967 manufacturing of component parts was begun at the Nasik and Hyderabad plants, and production at the Koraput site was scheduled to begin in 1968. Some MIGs, assembled from Indian and Soviet-built components, were delivered to the Indian Air Force by the end of 1967. There has been concern expressed in New Delhi, however, that the MIGs may be obsolete by the time India's factories start manufacturing the fighters without Soviet components.

An Indo-Soviet Agreement calling for "the reciprocal exchanges of scientific information and for visits of specialists in the various aspects of the peaceful uses of atomic energy" was signed in October 1961. There has been very little implementation of this agreement thus far; India has not pressed the USSR on the matter, and the Soviets have not made any significant offers. Any future Soviet assistance is likely to come in fields that do not duplicate

India's present nuclear program. The USSR, for instance, might become interested in a project which would supply nuclear energy to mining technology. Through the years, the Soviets have supported India's contention that her nuclear reactors (almost all of which were acquired from Western nations) should not be subjected to International Atomic Energy Agency surveillance.

Since the first Chinese explosion of a nuclear device in October 1964, the Indian government has been under increasing pressure to develop a nuclear weapons capacity of its own. Prime Minister Shastri, as one means to avert this pressure, called upon the United States and the USSR to provide a "nuclear guarantee" for the protection of non-nuclear nations. While sympathizing with India's concern, the USSR indicated that it was not interested in providing a protective umbrella for the nuclear have-nots.

The Government of India has often reiterated its intent to use nuclear energy only for peaceful purposes. But as Sisir Gupta, writing in 1965–66 pointed out, a body of opinion has emerged which favors India's utilization of her existing capacity to manufacture nuclear weapons. While this opinion has not succeeded in changing the government's policy, it "created a national controversy, and focused attention on the various aspects of India's admittedly difficult choice."[17] There are a number of considerations which made the Indian development of atomic weapons

17. "The Indian Dilemma," in *A World of Nuclear Powers?* ed. Buchan, p. 55. Discussing Indian opinion on the issue, Mr. Gupta wrote: "It is not easy to indicate the relative strength of the two contending schools of thought; but it is clear that a large majority of what consitutes effective opinion today is opposed to a change of policy. A majority of the members of the Congress party in the Lok Sabha, the right-wing, pro-western Swatantra party, the pro-Soviet Communist party, a large number of Socialists, the leading national dailies, some senior Army officers and civil servants, most of the Indian economists and the body of public men known as the Gandhians are opposed to any Indian nuclear weapons program. Against this formidable combination of forces stands the important minority in the Congress party which wants a new policy, the militant nationalist Jana Sangh, which has a large number of scientists, some noted Indian experts on international affairs, a number of officers of the armed forces, some younger civil servants in the foreign and defense ministries, and a few leading columnists and commentators of the Indian press. Together they constitute a significant minority." (Ibid., 66–67.)

highly unlikely. These include the following: (1) The nation's traditional position has been that of a strong advocate of the cessation of testing and the ending of the nuclear threat to mankind. (2) The costs in terms of finances and skilled personnel involved in a nuclear weapons program would be more than India could bear. India could readily produce a crude atomic weapon on her own, but she would be unable to finance the development of a "credible nuclear deterrent" and delivery system without massive additional assistance from abroad. Such financial assistance would not be forthcoming from any quarter. (3) Pakistan would insist on a nuclear weapon if India acquired one. (4) The United States and the Soviet Union would disapprove of India's going against their mutually sponsored treaty on the nonproliferation of nuclear weapons.

Those who seek Great Power status for India see a token *force de frappe* as a means of enchancing India's credentials. In return for its support of the Soviet-American agreement on a draft nonproliferation treaty, the Government of India wants assurances that peaceful nuclear development in India would be positively encouraged and that an attack or threat of nuclear blackmail against India would be met by an appropriate international response. India also wants some indication that the present nuclear powers will stop production of new weapons and begin a program of gradual disarmament of existing nuclear stockpiles. The fact that India is not alone in its reservations about the nonproliferation treaty strengthens her bargaining power. The United States and the Soviet Union will undoubtedly attempt to meet at least some of India's demands, as well as those expressed by such countries as Japan, West Germany, Brazil, Italy, and Switzerland. Thus far the USSR, on its part, has attempted to persuade, but has not exerted strong pressures on New Delhi to ratify the non-proliferation agreement.

Brief mention may be made here of other examples of Indo-Soviet cooperation. The Cultural Agreement of May 1966 called for continued exchanges of individuals and delegations in such fields as education, sport, medicine, social welfare, art, and cinema. Under the agreement, there was an estimated 50 percent increase in the number of visiting Indian and Soviet scientific personnel. The USSR provided teachers of technological subjects, and Indians studied at Soviet and Eastern European universities, institutes, and industrial sites. India also receives meteorological data from Soviet sputniks.[18] It was also announced that the USSR would provide the payloads for French rockets during tests conducted in 1967 at the Thumba Range in Kerala. These examples of Soviet cooperation with India stand in marked contrast to the discontinued Soviet projects in China, the great decline in Sino-Soviet commerce, the cessation of cultural and educational exchanges, the volatile border situation, and the all-but-severed Moscow-Peking diplomatic relationship.

Soviet scholars have taken an increasing interest in the study of Indian languages and in the translations of Indian literary works into Russian and of Russian works into the vernacular Indian languages. In recent years the USSR has printed a substantial number of texts on scientific and technological subjects for Indian schools and colleges. In addition, the USSR publishes low-cost periodicals for distribution in India, the proceeds for which help to subsidize publications and activities of the Communist party of India. The Indian government permits all publications that are not deemed "tendentious and undesirable," and as the years pass fewer Soviet publications are so designated by Indian censors.

Areas of Friction

The USSR has accepted the steps taken by the Indian government to secure the nation's borders. When India asked for and received large-scale American and British military aid during the 1962 fighting with China, the USSR remained silent. Likewise the

18. Soviet citizens scheduled to visit India under the 1966 agreement included 23 scientists, 15 postgraduate students, 48 teachers of Russian and technological subjects. Those going to the USSR included 37 scientists for research and advanced studies and 55 students for postgraduate work. Others participated in lecture tours, athletic events, international conferences and festivals, and artistic performances (*Hindustan Times*, May 19, 1966).

Soviets did not criticize Prime Minister Shastri for permitting American warships to make courtesy calls in Indian ports, a practice which Nehru had adamantly forbidden. Pro-Soviet newspapers in India, such as *Patriot, Blitz,* and the Communist party of India's *New Age,* were not critical of Shastri's acquiescing to the operation of American submarines armed with Polaris missiles and nuclear warheads "in Asian waters."

On matters involving Indian domestic policy, however, the Soviets have been more critical. Pressure was brought to bear after the Indian government (in 1964) had agreed to let the United States provide a high-powered transmitter for All-India Radio under terms which would permit the Voice of America to use the transmitter three hours daily. The agreement was subsequently shelved after sharp Soviet and CPI protests. An American proposal in 1966 to provide small transmitters in India's districts for the dissemination of agricultural and birth control information met a similar fate, at least temporarily.[19]

Occasionally the USSR has chided India for its slowness in developing and implementing programs for land reform, reduction of socioeconomic disparities, and nationalization of industries. Concern has also been expressed about the influence of Western private investment and governmental aid on Indian economic and political life. Mrs. Gandhi's government, for example, was criticized in 1966 for allegedly compromising too much on the agreement under which American firms will build fertilizer plants in India. Yet on the whole the Soviets have not been critical of Indian acceptance of P.L. 480 grain shipments from the United States. (Indian Communists have been more overt than the Soviets in criticizing the "sorry dependence" on American surplus food.) In weighing its policy toward India, Moscow has to consider whether a successor government would be more or less sympathetic to the Soviet viewpoint than is the present Indian government.

The USSR nonetheless has been seriously concerned about the general shift of the balance of power within the Congress party to

19. *New York Times,* June 19, 1966.

the more conservative, or as the Soviets put it, more reactionary, elements. The process has been a rather natural one in that Nehru was not representative of the rural and business elements which through the years have given the Congress party much of its electoral and financial support. To these groups the image of the USSR raises the spectre of such evils as nationalized industries and banks, a leveling of society, wide-scale land reforms, and so forth. The Soviets have made very little attempt, for ideological and other reasons, to cultivate the rural and business elites; and such an attempt would be almost fruitless. (The USSR has on occasion invited some Indian businessmen for visits to the USSR and once offered Mr. Tata funds to expand one of his steel mills, but the Government of India turned down the offer while Tata was still thinking about it.) The Soviets are afraid that a further shift to the right within the Congress party will halt the growth of the Indian public sector and bring about some undesirable reorientation in Indian foreign policy.

Moscow also deplores the rapid growth of the rightist Swatantra and Bharatiya Jan Sangh parties. For several years after its inception the Swatantra party strongly advocated an alliance system with the United States and Pakistan directed against China. Since the (belatedly acknowledged) Sino-Soviet cleavage and the Indo-Pakistani fighting in 1965, Swatantra has modified the nature of its plea for alignment.[20] A distinction is made between Russia and China, although the USSR is still mistrusted.

The Jan Sangh has a better potential for continued electoral growth than does Swatantra. The party thus far is narrowly nationalistic and communalist, has pushed for the supremacy of Hindi,[21] and is suspicious of all Communists—Chinese, Soviet, or

20. For a detailed exposition of the Swatantra and Jan Sangh foreign policy views through 1965, see Erdman, "The Foreign Policy Views of the Indian Right."

21. As the party seeks to grow in electoral strength, it is modifying (at least officially) some of its extremist policies; note, for example, the relatively moderate position taken on the language question at the Jan Sangh Conference held in Calicut, Kerala, late in December 1967.

Indian. Although the major animus through 1968 has been against the Chinese and Indian Communists, the Soviet variety is not excluded from verbal attacks by the Jan Sangh. The Jan Sangh has not accepted the fact that Pakistan controls Azad Kashmir, and is not fully reconciled to the continuing existence of Pakistan itself. By contrast, the USSR wants to see a permament Indo-Pakistan settlement on the basis of the territorial status quo, a condition which the Indian government would be willing to accept. The Jan Sangh would prefer to draw closer to the West and away from the USSR; but its main goal is to build a militarily strong, self-sufficient India. Such an India, its leaders maintain, could coexist peacefully with the USSR and other world powers.

Thus, new irritants have developed in Indo-Soviet relations over the past few years. As one Indian journalist aptly put it, "a certain amount of disenchantment was unavoidable after the honeymoon."[22] The Soviets are alarmed at the "drift" within the Congress party and at the increased influence and electoral strength of the rightist Jan Sangh and Swatantra parties. This concern is expressed in various ways; for example, through broadcasts on Radio Peace and Progress, which since before the 1967 elections has been making critical remarks about certain conservative Congress party politicians. Mrs. Gandhi has been largely immune from this criticism even though some members of her cabinet have been attacked.

A noteworthy article appeared in the Soviet government newspaper, *Izvestia*, on November 29, 1967. In a matter of fact tone it reported that 20,000 slum dwellers from the Delhi area were herded into trucks and driven twenty miles outside the city where they and their meager possessions were dumped and left without shelter at the mercy of the weather.[23] The fact that the Soviet government

22. Girilal Jain, "Indo-Soviet Relations: Old Warmth Missing," *Times of India*, December 20, 1967.

23. The *Izvestia* article was essentially accurate, although incomplete. The Municipal Council took the action to discourage squatters from building their

newspaper chose to print the article is significant; it marked (as best as can be determined) the first time in many years that a critical report about such a sensitive subjective appeared in the Soviet daily press.

The problem of Soviet defectors in India is of concern to the USSR, particularly with the large number of Soviet citizens in India on various missions. The defection of Stalin's daughter, Mrs. Svetlana Alliluyeva, presented a particularly embarrassing situation. Briefly, Svetlana's story was this: She came to India in December 1966 to accompany the remains of her late husband to his family home. When she asked permission to remain permanently in India, a high government official allegedly told her that it would be impossible "because of the strongest opposition from the Soviet Government which would inevitably arise."[24] Deciding to go to the West, Svetlana walked up to a surprised marine guard at the United States embassy on March 6, 1967, and announced her intentions. As she had a valid Soviet passport, she was put on an outgoing plane to Switzerland and eventually went to the United States. Had the Soviets known of Mrs. Alliluyeva's intent, she would probably have been whisked back to the USSR. On several previous occasions the Soviets are known to have forcibly returned potential defectors from India. The Russians were angered by certain important Indian officials whom they suspected of having

---

huts on public land. Beggars who come to the capital are also rounded up and sometimes sent outside the city. This particular action was taken by the government to "clean up" New Delhi before the influx of the delegates to the UNCTAD Conference held in January–February 1968, the largest group of foreigners ever to come to the capital at any one time.

24. Mrs. Alliluyeva wrote a letter from Switzerland to Dr. Ram Manohar Lohia, an Indian Socialist leader, explaining her position. The denial of her request to remain in India was made by Dinesh Singh, commerce minister, and a member of Mrs. Gandhi's inner circle. Speaking for the prime minister, Mr. Singh spoke with Svetlana in January 1967, telling her that if she could settle the matter with the USSR first, then assistance from India would be available. Svetlana did not take the matter up with Soviet officials and apparently decided to go to the West only a few days before her scheduled return to Moscow. See *Statesman Weekly*, April 9, 1967, and *New York Times*, March 28, 1967.

known of Svetlana's intent. Svetlana herself has denied that she spoke with anyone prior to leaving.

Another notable defection occurred on December 21, 1967, when Aziz Ouloug-Zade, twenty-eight-year-old son of a famous Tadjik poet, sought asylum in the American embassy in New Delhi. The youth had studied Hindi at Delhi University from 1961 to 1963 and was currently in India heading a three-member Comsomol youth delegation. The American ambassador, Chester Bowles, handled the situation well by inviting the Soviet ambassador to speak with Ouloug-Zade, thus squelching the rumor that he was being held against his will. Then, after several weeks of "protective custody" by New Delhi authorities, Ouloug-Zade was permitted to fly to Britain.[25]

Soviet concern over these defections has been considerable. Since there exists a possibility that a Soviet version of the Peace Corps may be established in India, the thought of India's becoming known as a good place for defectors is especially unwelcome. Under pressure from the USSR, therefore, the Government of India announced in January 1968 that no foreign embassy would be permitted to grant political asylum to defectors from another nation.

The Soviets were also concerned about the dismissal of the Communist dominated United Front government in West Bengal in November 1967.[26] Although the government was formally removed by a ruling of the Speaker of the West Bengal House, the act was done with the permission of the central government. In

25. *Times of India* and other New Delhi newspapers, December 21, 1967–January 11, 1968.

26. One cannot begin to get into the complexities of Bengali Communist politics here. As of January 1968, there were three distinct parties and several other groups. In May 1967, sharecroppers and landless laborers in the Naxalbari district of West Bengal rose up when local landlords refused to implement government land reform laws. The Left Communists were caught in the middle between the police and peasants. The rebels were condemned by the West Bengal United Front Government as "adventurist" and expelled from the Left-Communist party.

attacking the constitutionality of the dismissal of the Ajoy Mukherjee government and its replacement by a Congress-led coalition, the USSR indirectly criticized New Delhi. The December 20, 1967, issue of *Pravda*, for instance, cited the continuing mass demonstrations in Calcutta as proof that the United Front enjoyed widespread support.[27] The Soviets urged that mid-term elections be held to resolve the matter. The National Council of the CPI (Soviet-oriented) which met in mid-December 1967 denounced the Congress party and the central government for their alleged role in undermining non-Congress coalitions. Despite its conflicts with the Left Communists, the Right CPI called for the unity of all "Left and democratic forces" to meet the danger of reactionary forces within India.[28]

On its part, New Delhi in 1967–68 was bothered by the appearance of critical comments about India in the Soviet media. The Congress "left" feels that the USSR should understand why the government is obliged to follow a centrist policy. One point of concern in India is the future direction of Soviet relations with Pakistan. Few high ranking Indian officials have expressed any objection to Soviet assistance to Pakistan short of military aid, and some have surmised that the USSR might even prove a "restraining influence on Pakistan." The Indian public, nonetheless, had grown accustomed during the Khrushchev years to the USSR's immediately siding with India on matters involving Pakistan. But in the Rann of Kutch dispute in mid-1965 the USSR only called for a halt to the senseless hostilities. The war with Pakistan a few months later brought anti-Pakistan sentiment to a fever pitch among many Indian nationalists. After the Tashkent Conference the rumor was circulated among such groups as the Jan Sangh and R.S.S. that Premier Kosygin had somehow deprived India of the fruits of victory won on the battlefield.

The Kashmir question, of course, continues to be a highly sensi-

27. As reported in the *Hindustan Times*, December 22, 1967.
28. See *Link*, December 17, 1967, p. 21.

tive one. The Defense of India Emergency Act promulgated in
1962 finally came to an end at the close of 1967, but in its place
was passed the Unlawful Activities (Prevention) Bill. The new bill
in effect made it unlawful for an Indian citizen to advocate any
detrimental change in India's present borders.[29] Such statutes
inhibit meaningful discussion on a volatile subject like Kashmir.
The new mood has been to talk less, but to show Pakistan and dissident Kashmiris firmly that the issue is resolved once and for all.
The parties with militant attitudes toward Pakistan are concerned
that the USSR may try to pressure India into some undesirable
settlement.

In the above paragraphs we have pointed to some areas of
emergent tension between the USSR and India. Neither country
wishes to be taken for granted by the other. To restore the sense
of perspective, however, it is necessary to emphasize that these
tensions as of September 1968 have scarcely interfered with the
many cooperative ventures of the two governments.

A Final Note

At this juncture the Soviet leaders do not appear to have a great
interest in the entry of "revolutionary-democratic" or "national-
democratic" regimes of Afro-Asia into the Marxist-Leninist fold.
The establishment of new Communist regimes no longer need
mean an extension of Soviet influence. In today's polycentric
world the USSR cannot exert control over some of its former
satellites in Eastern Europe, let alone the Communist nations in
Asia. Moscow welcomed Castro's Cuba as a fraternal socialist
nation, but Cuba's subsequent needs for military protection and

---

29. Under the bill, "unlawful activity" means any action or words which
support any claim to bring about the cession or the secession of a part of the
territory of India from the Union, or which incites any individual or group of
individuals to bring about such cession or secession (reported in the *Times of
India*, December 27, 1967). The vote in the Lok Sabha was 117 to 15 in favor
of the bill; all of the opposition parties except Swatantra and Jan Sangh walked
out before the vote was taken (*Indian Express*, December 21, 1967).

economic aid have dampened the initial Soviet enthusiasm. A fellow Communist state may launch strong ideological attacks on the USSR, as did China, when the Russians did not fulfill Peking's expectations. There are probably fewer risks and obligations involved in having friendly, cooperative relations with non-Communist nations of the third world whose international policies are in general accord with those of the USSR.

This accounts in part for Moscow's ambivalent attitude toward India's Communists. The Soviets do not want to unduly antagonize the party in power. If need be they would play down the interests of the CPI, as they have done on some previous occasions, rather than harm inter-governmental relations. What the Soviets would probably prefer is the emergence in India of a leftist faction within the Congress party similar to the Menon-Malaviya group of several years ago. Such a faction would keep the Congress party more in line with the Soviet notions of anti-imperialism and rekindle the goal of a "socialist pattern of society."

Although there exists the possibility of a revolutionary movement(s) developing in India,[30] the USSR does not encourage excessively disruptive activities by the CPI. With the Chinese problem foremost in their minds, the Kremlin leaders do not seek the coming to power of a militant Communist regime in India. Until Mao's victory in China, Stalin had dealt satisfactorily with Chiang's Kuomintang, occasionally against the interests of the

---

30. In a recent article entitled "The Indian Revolutionary Potential" (*Monthly Review* [New York] 20, no. 9 [February 1969]: 23–36), Kathleen Gough points to the increasing numbers of landless laborers and unemployed in many areas of rural India. Her analysis concluded: "The social force and numerical strength of [a movement based on these rural classes, on urban workers in hand-mills, semi-processing industries, services and transport, and on the millions of unemployed] would be so great that it could afford to let the rich and middle peasants, the petty bourgeoisie, and the small industrialists relate themselves to it at will, without being obliged to make weakening concessions to their interests. The rebel Left Communists, under Chinese influence, seem to be moving in that direction. . . . Their approach therefore seems the most hopeful, provided they can avoid too mechanical a dependence on Chinese experience, and get on with the work of organizing and liberating the Indian countryside."

Chinese Communists. Similarly, one could say that Moscow would hypothetically favor a left-leaning Congress leadership in India to an unpredictable revolutionary regime which might put heavy demands on the Soviet state. But in any event, the liklihood of a Communist regime seizing power in India is much less than the probable suppression of such an attempt by forces of the Right. The USSR, which lost a considerable investment in Indonesia after the aborted coup and subsequent removal of Sukarno, would deplore a repeat performance of the Indonesian experience in India.

Indian commentators in the 1950s were fond of saying that the roots of India's foreign policy were inherent in the country's history and culture. After India's clash with China, spiritualistic notions about India's policy were more often than not replaced by those of *realpolitik*. Sometimes quoted in the 1960s is the pithy remark of Lord Salisbury, a nineteenth-century British Foreign Secretary that England had no permanent friends or enemies, but only permanent interests.

However, even "permanent interests" are subject to change. At present it appears that India and the USSR have a long-term mutual interest in containing the spread of Chinese influence in Asia. Yet sixteen years ago, the USSR and, to a lesser extent, China spoke with hostility about India's leaders and sociopolitical system. Then China and the USSR sought cordial state relations with India. But by the end of the 1950s antagonisms had grown between China and both Moscow and New Delhi, bringing the latter two nations even closer together. From the perspective of the mid-1960s the Indo-Soviet detente vis-á-vis Peking appears to be a long-term arrangement. But there is nothing to prevent new, unforeseen factors from emerging at some future date, or the pendulum from swinging again. Hopefully, the future will someday bring about a realization in Peking, New Delhi, Moscow, Rawalpindi, and Washington that the permanent interests of each in Asia can be furthered best in conciliatory settlements of unresolved problems and not in the perpetuation of coalitions and intrigues.

Short of a radical change in Soviet or Indian leadership which would bring about a basic policy reorientation or of an unforeseen catastrophe like world war, it would appear that Indo-Soviet relations should continue on a fairly even keel. It is difficult at present, for example, to conceive of a situation in which Soviet and Indian interests in the Himalayan regions would strongly clash. In the latter decades of the nineteenth century there was much friction (although never war) between the expanding imperial domains of British India and Russia. A number of factors strongly work against a recurrence of the nineteenth century pattern: First, the immediate causes for much of the present trouble in the Himalayan area lie in rival claims to territory—India and Pakistan over Kashmir, China and India over Aksai Chin and Eastern Ladakh, Pakistan and Afghanistan over the Pathan areas. There is, however, no common boundary between the USSR and India, and both nations since 1947 have respected the political and territorial integrity of Afghanistan. Second, both the USSR and India (except for some Indian rightist elements that are not reconciled to the existence of Pakistan, and those who would like to retake Aksai Chin from the Chinese) are essentially interested in maintaining the status quo of their present boundaries. Finally, there is the rise of a strong but unsettled China from which emanates a challenge to the leadership and the societal arrangements of both India and the USSR.

Since 1953 the gradual decline of dogmatism in the Soviet doctrine and Moscow's willingness to coexist with the prevailing Indian socio-political system have paved the way for an era of "peaceful cooperation" between the two nations. The shared interests perceived by the leaders of both nations during the Nehru-Khrushchev era kept the inevitable discords toned down. The pattern of close cooperation has continued through 1968, even though the tone of the relationship has become more business-like and existing tensions are more apt to rise to the surface.

Appendix A

The Soviet Assistance Program to India
(Through March 1966)

The Government of U.S.S.R. has so far extended seven credits up to the 31st March 1966 for a total value of Rs. 4843.1 million[1] for the implementation of development projects included in India's five year plans. This does not include Rs. 53.2 million increased by the Soviet Government for Bokaro Steel Plant in August 1966. The Indo-Soviet economic collaboration which began with a credit of Rs. 647.4 million for the Bhilai Steel Plant in 1955 has been extended through the years to a variety of development projects in the public sector. Notable examples of such projects are the Bhilai Steel Plant, the Heavy Machine Building Plant at Ranchi, the Heavy Electrical Equipment Plant at Ranipur, Mining Machinery Plant in Durgapur, Oil Refineries at Barauni and Koyali Power plants at Neyveli, Korba, Bhakra and Singarauli, Oil Exploration at Cambay and other areas, Drugs Projects and the proposed steel plant at Bokaro.

Reprinted (with the permission of the Indian Finance Ministry) from the Government of India, Ministry of Finance, Department of Economic Affairs publication, *External Assistance, 1965–66* (New Delhi: Govt. of India Press, 1966), pp. 75–85.

1. Rupee equivalents in this section are all at the pre-devaluation rate of 1 Rupee = $.21 U.S.

285

2. The Soviet Credits carry interest at $2\frac{1}{2}\%$ per annum and are repayable over a period of 12 years, except in the case of the credit for Drugs Projects amounting to Rs. 95.2 million which is repayable in seven years. The repayments towards the principal begin one year after the completion of deliveries of equipment required for putting the respective projects into operation. Both the payments of interest and repayments of principal are made in rupees which are utilised by the Soviet authorities for the purchase of goods in India in accordance with the Indo-Soviet Trade Agreement.

3. The entire credit amounting to Rs. 647.4 million extended in February, 1955 for the Bhilai Steel Plant has already utilised. Contracts have also been placed on the Soviet Organisations for the expansion of the Bhilai Steel Plant. The ordering has also been completed for most of the projects financed out of the Soviet Credits. The Oil and Natural Gas Commission has embarked on a large programme for exploration, development and production of oil and gas with Soviet assistance and several contracts for equipment etc., have been placed on the Soviet Organisations.

4. Against the availability of Rs. 4896.3 million under the Soviet Credits, contracts of the value of Rs. 3160.4 million have already been placed on the Soviet Organisations and a sum of Rs. 2820.8 million has also been disbursed upto the 31st March, 1966. A statement indicating the particulars of the credits, the projects financed thereunder, the value of contracts placed on the Soviet suppliers and the amount drawn upto the 31st March 1966 is annexed to this chapter.

5. Up to March, 1966 a sum of Rs. 534.7 million has been repaid as principal under the Soviet credits. Out of this, a sum of Rs. 437.1 million is towards the repayment of Bhilai Credit of Rs. 647.4 million. The balance of Rs. 210.3 million under the Bhilai Credit is to be repaid in about 4 years.

6. A brief account of the projects financed out of the Soviet credits is given below.

(i) BHILAI STEEL PLANT (BHILAI M.P.)

The erection of the Steel Plant with a capacity of one million tonnes of steel ingots to be rolled into about 770,000 tonnes of rolled products, like rails, structurals crossing sleepers, merchant bars etc. along with mechanisation of mines at Rajhara for iron ore and Nandini for limestone was completed before the end of the Second Five Year Plan. The expansion of the steel plant to 2.5 million tonnes was started in September 1962. Excepting the wire rod mill the other units of the 2.5 million tonnes expansion stage are expected to be commissioned shortly. The wire rod mill is likely to be commissioned in the first quarter of 1967. The sixth blast furnace complex constitutes the first phase of the expansion of the Steel Plant beyond 2.5 million tonnes ingot capacity and envisages installation of seventh coke oven battery, sixth blast furnace, additional sintering plant and ancillaries. The partially expanded plant is now working at a capacity of 1.8 million tons of ingot steel.

(ii)   HEAVY MACHINERY BUILDING PLANT (RANCHI BIHAR)

The Heavy Machinery Building Plant is designed to produce 80,000 tonnes per annum of mechanical equipment out of which approximately 65,000 tonnes are meant for integrated iron and steel plants. The ability to increase installed steel plant capacity by means of machinery produced in the HMBP is of great significance. For other branches of Heavy engineering, such as oil drilling rigs, excavators and high pressure chemical plants, necessary equipment will also be manufactured in the HMBP. Excavators have been supplied to the National Coal Development Corporation and oil drilling rigs are to be supplied to the Oil and Natural Gas Commission. HMBP has also supplied a complete Pig Casting Plant for the Durgapur Steel Plant. HMBP will supply a part of machinery required for the Bokaro Steel Plant and for the sixth blast furnace of the Bhilai Steel Plant. By March 1966 about 65% of the total equipment to be imported from U.S.S.R. has been erected. Erection of machine tools and other processing equipment is expected to be completed in 1967. The value of the output at full capacity is expected to be about Rs. 500 million.

(iii)   COAL MINING MACHINERY PLANT (DURGAPUR)

The Coal Mining Machinery Plant is designed to produce 45,000 tons of coal mining machinery such as conveyors, coal cutters, loaders, haulages and winders, pumps, fans, locomotives, coal beneficiation equipment, etc. The Plant is to attain its full capacity by 1971–72 in stages. The Plant has produced 5178 tonnes of mining machinery and allied products during 1965–66.

(iv) DRUGS PROJECTS

The Drugs Projects are:
   (1) Antibiotics Projects, Rishikesh, (U.P.).
   (2) Synthetic Drugs Projects, Hyderabad.
   (3) Surgical Instruments Plant Madras.

These three projects will manufacture antibiotics, synthetic drugs and surgical instruments, some of which are being imported now. All the equipment imported and received has been erected/installed. The Antibiotics Project will have a capacity for manufacture 300 tons per annum distributed over a product-mix of 7 antibiotics drugs. The synthetic Drugs project will have a capacity for manufacture 826 tonnes per annum distributed over a product range of 15 synthetic drugs. In addition about 4560 tonnes of intermediates will also be produced at the Plant of which about 270 tonnes will be available for sale in the market and the balance will be used for producing drugs. The Surgical Instruments Plant will have a capacity of 2.5 million pieces of surgical instruments of 167 different types.

The Surgical Instruments Plant went into production in September, 1965 and the other two projects are in an advanced stage and are likely to be commissioned in the near future.

(v) POWER PROJECTS

(a) Neyveli Thermal Power Station (Neyveli, Madras)

A Thermal Power Station of 250 M.W. capacity consisting of 5 units of 50 M.W. each under the first stage of the project was completed in June, 1964. The expansion of the Power Station to 400 M.W. by installing two units with one of 50 M.W. and the other of 100 M.W. is under progress. The sixth unit of 50 M.W. was commissioned in August 1965. The seventh unit of 100 M.W. is likely to be commissioned in the near future. The Madras State Electricity Board is able to meet a great part of the demand for power for industrial and agricultural loads in the State with power supplied from Neyveli Thermal Power Station.

(*b*) *Singrauli Thermal Power Station* (*Singrauli, U.P.*)

The Project which is being set up in the South-East part of U.P. covers the installation of 5 units of 50 M.W. each. The generating plant along with boilers and associated equipment have mostly been delivered and the first unit is expected to be commissioned by December, 1966 and the remaining units at intervals of 4 month each.

(*c*) *Korba Thermal Power Station* (*Korba, M.P.*)

The expansion of the Korba Thermal Power Station provides for installation of 4 units of 50 M.W. each. The equipment imported for the project is presently under erection. The first unit has been erected and is likely to be commissioned shortly. The remaining three units are expected to be commissioned with an interval of 4 to 5 months thereafter.

(*d*) *Bhakra Right Bank Hydro-electric Power Station* (*Bhakra, Punjab*)

The hydro-electric power station provides for installation of 5 units of 120 M. W. each. The first unit was erected and commissioned in May, 1966 and the work of erection of the remaining units is in progress. It is expected that all the five units will be completed by September, 1967.

(*vi*) OIL PROJECTS

(*a*) *Exploration, development and production of oil and gas*

A large number of Soviet specialists in drilling, oil and gas production have been assisting the Oil and Natural Gas Commission in the exploration and development of oil and natural gas fields. The Indian technicians of the Commission have also been receiving training in the U.S.S.R. in oil technology. Contracts of the order of Rs. 373.6 million have concluded with the Soviet organisations for supply of drilling equipment, materials, accessories, geophysical and geological equipment etc. and bulk of the equipment costing about Rs. 320 million has already been received. So far oil and gas have been discovered at Ankleshwar, Kalol, Cambay, Nawagam, Sanand, Kosamba, Olpad and Kathara in Gujarat and Rudrasagar and Lakwa in Assam. Since the start of trial production in September, 1961, production by the end of March 1966 was 3.4 million tonnes of crude oil from the Ankleshwar oil fields.

(b) Barauni Oil Refinery (Barauni, Bihar)

The Barauni Oil Refinery was designed to process 2 million tonnes of crude oil per year and is being expanded to 3 million tonnes capacity per year. The first million tonne unit was commissioned in July 1964, the second million tonne unit is expected to be commissioned before the end of 1966 and the third million unit by the middle of 1967. During 1964–65, the total production of the Refinery was 1,73,378 tonnes and during 1965–66 the production was 6,13,000 tonnes.

(c) Gujarat Refinery (Koyali, Gujarat)

The Gugarat Refinery is also designed to process two million tonnes of crude oil per year and is also being expanded to 3 million tonnes per year. The first million tonne unit was commissioned in October, 1965, the second million tonne unit is expected to be commissioned in June/July, 1966 and the third million tonne unit is expected to be completed in early 1967. During October 1965 to March 1966, the production of the Refinery was 3,69,022 tonnes.

(vii) COAL PROJECTS

(a) Korba Coal Mining Projects (Korba, M.P.)

It is proposed to establish two underground mines, viz., Banki and Surakachhar, one open-cast mine at Manikpur and a Central Electrical and Mechanical Workshop in Korba. The annual output of Banki and Surakachhar mine will be 0.6 million and 1.1 million tonnes of non-coking coal respectively, and that of the Manikpur mine will be 1 million tonnes of non-coking coal. The Korba Workshop will cater mainly for the repairing and overhauling needs of equipment of various projects of the National Coal Development Corporation in the Korba region. The workshop will also manufacture spare parts. All these projects are under final stages of construction.

(b) Kathara Coal Washery (Kathara, Bihar)

The Washery will beneficiate 3 million tonnes of coking coal per annum out of which about 1.5 million tonnes of clean coal will be for use of steel plant and about 1.2 million tonnes of middlings will be used as a fuel in a Thermal Power Station. The Project is in an advanced stage and is expected to be completed by April, 1967.

(*viii*) Precision Instruments Plants

It is proposed to set up two Instruments Plants—one at Kota (Rajasthan) for manufacture of electronic and electro-magnetic instruments and the other at Palghat, (Kerala) for manufacture of mechanical, hydraulic and pneumatic instrument and ancillary equipment for Industrial process control. The contract for supply of equipment and machinery for Kota Plant has already been placed on the Soviet organisation and part of the machinery has also been received. The Kota Plant is expected to start commercial production by the end of 1966. A detailed project report prepared by the Soviet Organisation for the Palghat Plant is under consideration. This plant is likely to go into production by the middle of 1968. The total value of annual production of the two Plants when they attain full production will be approximately Rs. 200 million.

(*ix*) Heavy Electricals Plant (Ranipur, U.P.)

The Plant is designed to produce annually 1500 MW. of Steam Turbines and Turbo-alternators and 1200 MW of Hydro Turbines and Generators. The Plant will also manufacture large Electric Motors required for steel, mining and other industries totalling to 515000 KW annually.

Production of Turbo-sets of 300 MW and even higher capacities are contemplated when needed. Steam Turbine manufacture will start in 1967 with 100 MW and the first set is scheduled for delivery in December, 1968. 200 MW sets will be taken up a little later and units of this size will be available from the first quarter of 1971. The scope of manufacture at this Plant will include Condensers, Heaters and Coolers.

Hydro Turbines with runner diameters up to 6600 mm, perhaps the largest that may have to be catered for will be produced at this plant. The manufacture of Hydro Turbines and Generators will closely follow the steam Turbines and delivery of large Hydro sets is programmed from the middle of 1969.

The rated output of 1500 MW of Thermal Station equipment and

1200 MW of Hydro equipment from Hardwar is expected to be reached in 1973–74.

The civil construction works in progress will be completed early in 1967. All major equipments have been ordered and their installation will be phased to suit the production programme. Partial production of Electric Motors of medium sizes has started in early 1966. The main activities during 1966 and 1967 will be progressive manufacture of motors up to 700 MW, Jigs, Fixtures, etc.

(x) OPTHALMIC GLASS PROJECT (DURGAPUR, WEST BENGAL)

The project envisages the production of 300 tonnes of Opthalmic Glass including processing of 10.3 million lenses per annum. The bulk of the machinery has been received. The construction of buildings and erection of equipment are expected to be completed by the middle of 1967 when pilot production will commence.

(xi) PUMPS AND COMPRESSORS PROJECT (NAINI, U.P.)

The Plant will manufacture heavy pumps and compressors required for the fertiliser industry, chemical plants, petroleum and petrochemical plants and steel plants. A techno-economic study has been prepared for establishment of manufacture of compressors and pumps with a capacity of 16,700 tonnes per annum and a captive grey iron foundary of a capacity of 25,000 tonnes per annum. A contract for the preparation of detailed Project report has been signed and the report is expected to be received in September, 1966.

(xii) BOKARO STEEL PLANT (BOKARO, BIHAR)

An agreement was signed with the U.S.S.R. Government for assistance in the construction of a steel works at Bokaro with a capacity of 1.5 to 2 million tonnes with provision for expansion to 4 million tonnes. The Soviet Government have agreed to extend a credit of 200 million roubles (Rs. 1058.2 million) for the purpose of meeting the foreign exchange cost of the steel plant. The credit will carry an interest of 2.5 per cent per annum and is repayable in twelve years. The detailed project report has been prepared and the contract for the supply of machinery and equipment is expected to be signed in the month of May, 1966. The Soviet organisations will supply during the period 1966 to 1969 such equipment as are not available in India. The steel plant is expected to be commissioned early in 1967.

GRANTS TO THE CENTRAL GOVERNMENT

The Central Mechanised Farm at Suratgarh set up in August, 1956 with the agricultural machinery valued at Rs. 7.9 million received as a free gift from the U.S.S.R. made steady progress in 1965. During the year 1965–66 it was possible to bring under crops an area of about 9,600 acres only due to lack of rains and acute shortage of irrigation facilities.

A free gift of equipment worth 3 million roubles (Rs. 3.6 million) was also received by the Indian Institute of Technology, Bombay under the Indo-Soviet agreement signed in December, 1958.

SUPPLY OF SMALL POX VACCINE

The Government of U.S.S.R. have offered to supply a total quantity of 650 million doses of Small Pox Freeze dried vaccine. Out of this we have so far received 590 million doses valued at Rs. 38.08 million. The balance of 84 million doses is being received in monthly instalments of 11 million doses each.

The vaccine being both potent and thermostable is likely to give greater protection to the people of India.

SPECIAL FOOD ASSISTANCE

The Government of U.S.S.R. have offered emergency food aid in the form of milk powder, vegetable oil, biscuits, milk powder and baby food etc.

The table below will show the assistance authorised and utilised during the plan periods:

	Loan		(Rupees million) Grants	
	Authori-sation	Utilisa-tion	Authori-sation	Utilisa-tion
Up to end of First Five Year Plan	647.4			
During Second Five Year Plan	3,190.7	748.5	11.5	11.5
During Third Five Year Plan				
1961–62		245.7		
1962–63		324.3		
1963–64		472.9	20.0	20.0
1964–65	1,005.0	649.7	9.8	9.8
1965–66		379.7	8.3	8.3
	4,843.1	2,820.8	49.6	49.6

ANNEXURE

Table showing particulars of Soviet Credits and the Projects financed under them

(Rs. Million)

Name of Loan	Date of Agreement	Amount of loan	Project	Contracts placed	Amount drawn 31–3–1966
1. Bhilai credit	2–2–55	647.4	Bhilai steel Plant	647.4	647.4
2. Credit for Industrial Projects	9–11–57	595.3	1. Heavy machine building plant.	159.4	152.6
			2. Coal Mining machinery plant.	99.1	93.5
			3. Opthalmic glass project.	11.8	10.5
			4. Korba coal mining project.	51.9	49.0
			5. Neyveli lignite power project.	139.1	138.2
				461.3	443.8
3. Credit for drugs project	29–5–59	95.2	Drugs project	95.2	94.6
4. Barauni credit	28–9–59	119.1	Barauni Oil Refinery.	119.1	113.1
5. First credit for Third Five Year Plan	12–9–59	1,785.8	1. Expansion of Bhilai Steel Plant.	576.1	544.2
			2. Expansion of Neyveli Thermal Plant.	84.1	73.8
			3. Singarauli power station (OBRA).	145.7	133.7
			4. Expansion of HMBP.	65.2	57.2
			5. Kotah Precision Instruments Projects.	17.2	9.2
			6. Expansion of coal Mining Machinery Plant.	22.4	11.3
			7. Expansion of Korba Thermal Power Station.	114.3	108.1

ANNEXURE—*contd.*

Name of Loan	Date of Agreement	Amount of loan	Project	Contracts placed	Amount drawn 31-3-1966
			8. Barauni Oil Refinery.	39.5	39.5
			9. Heavy Electricals plant.	149.5	42.4
			10. Carrying out prospecting & production of oil & gas.	330.0	313.1
				1,544.0	1,332.5
6. Second Credit for Third Plan Projects	21-2-61	595.3	1. Bhakra Right Hydro Elc. Power Station.	58.7	60.1
			2. Koyali Oil Refinery.	80.1	80.1
			3. Coal Washery at Kathara.	28.8	21.9
			4. Refractories plant	1.6	1.1
			5. Exploration development & production of oil in cambay, Ankaleswar & in other areas.	43.6	10.2
			6. Production of pumps and compressors preparation of technio economic report.	0.2	0.2
				213.0	173.6
			Additional projects agreed for financing under the savings from the Soviet Credits. 1. 5th Unit for Bhakra Right Bank Power Station.	9.9	—

ANNEXURE—*concld.*

Name of Loan	Date of Agreement	Amount of loan	Project	Contracts placed	Amount drawn 31-3-1966
			2. Kerala Precision Instruments Plant.	2.3	0.7
			3. Expansion of Refineries:—		
			(i) Barauni	8.1	9.8
			(ii) Koyali	8.9	
			4. Compressors & Pumps Project.	2.6	1.2
			5. Steel Foundary for Railways.	1.5	—
			6. Sixth Blast Furnace at Bhilai.	44.5	3.6
			7. Neyveli Thermal Power Station Expansion (400 MW to 600 MW).	2.6	0.5
			Total	80.4	15.8
7. Bakaro Credit	25-1-65	1,058.2	Bakaro Steel Plant	—	—

Appendix B

There are some minor discrepancies in the available trade figures on Indo-Soviet Trade. For the sake of consistency I have decided to use data from the United Nations publications, *Direction of International Trade, Yearbook of International Trade Statistics,* and the *Statistical Yearbook.*

Indo-Soviet Trade
(In Millions of U.S. Dollars)

	Indian Imports (C.I.F.) from USSR			Indian Exports (F.O.B.)		
Year	Total Imports	Imports[1] from Russia	% of Imports[2] from USSR	Total Exports	Exports to USSR	% Exports to USSR
1938	$ 566.5	$ .7	.1%	$ 616.7	$ 1.3	.2%
1948	1616	9.8	.5%	1251	16.2	1.3%
1951	1792	1.6	.09%	1645.8	13.6	.8%
1953	1200.7	.9	.07%	1116.2	.7	.06%
1955	1413.4	6.4	.4%	1276.5	5.2	.4%
1956	1708.7	31.3	1.8%	1251.1	26.2	2.1%
1957	2154.2	47.6	2.3%	1350	36.7	2.7%
1958	1814.8	45.6	2.5%	1215.8	49	4.2%
1959	1986	35.	1.8%	1304.	63.7	4.9%
1960[3]	2327.	33.3	1.4%	1331.	60.4	4.5%
1961	2277.	84.	3.7%	1386.	67.3	4.9%
1962	2361.	123.	5.3%	1403.	79.8	5.7%
1963	2477.	143.8	5.8%	1626.	109.1	6.7%
1964	2876.	165.4	5.8%	1705.	163.6	9.6%
1965	2912.	173.7	6. %	1688.	194.	11.5%

Sources: United Nations, *Statistical Yearbook,* 1960–67 [For total annual imports and exports]; *Direction of International Trade,* 1953–60 [Indo-Soviet bilateral imports and exports]; *Yearbook of International Trade Statistics,* 1961–67.

1. Dollar totals converted by author at rate of 1 Indian rupee = .21 U.S.

2. Calculated by author on basis of $\dfrac{\text{imports from USSR}}{\text{total imports}}$.

3. Indian statistics until 1959 based on calendar year; from 1960 onward, beginning April 1 of year stated.

Selected Bibliography

The publications listed below include some works which contributed to the author's general understanding of the subject, as well as those which, representing a broad spectrum of views, deal directly or peripherally with the many aspects of the Indo-Soviet relationship. Specific citations of most of the newspapers, periodicals, government of India and UN publications, etc., are not listed, as they appear contextually in the individual footnotes.

The Indian sources vary widely in their significance for this study. Official government publications such as the *Foreign Affairs Record* provided useful verbatim accounts of Indo-Soviet agreements and joint communiqués, official statements of policy, etc. The proceedings of the Indian Houses of Parliament, the *Lok Sabha Debates* (lower house) and to a lesser degree the *Rajya Sabha Official Record* (upper house) were of considerable value. During the general debates and in the question hours a number of aspects of the government's attitude toward the USSR were discussed. While the debates themselves had little effect on the formulation of policy, they did serve the purpose of calling upon the government to explain its course in foreign affairs. Within the Parliament almost every shade of Indian opinion has at least token representation. Addresses by the late Prime Minister Jawaharlal Nehru and other Indian leaders are best evaluated in the context in which they were delivered rather than in the official compendia of speeches.

The daily newspapers contained a good deal of relevant information that was not available elsewhere. It was worthwhile scanning daily issues of *The Hindu* from the early 1950s through 1967. *The Hindu* provided good coverage of matters pertaining to foreign affairs in general and Indo-Soviet relations in particular. Also, its editorial position at any given moment more often than not was similar to the government's policy towards the USSR, and therefore provided a well-articulated rationale for this policy. Particularly during critical periods it was fruitful to crosscheck and compare the accounts of events in such leading dailies as The *Times of India*, The *Hindustan Times*, The *Statesman*, and the *Hindu*. In doing so I was better able to place the important developments in Indo-Soviet relations in the context of other considerations—both domestic and external—of the two nations.

Among the more prominent nonpartisan journals which contained a number of relevant articles were *The Economic Weekly* (now the *Economic and Political Weekly*), *The Radical Humanist*, and *The Eastern Economist*. Reflections of Congress party thinking appear in the *A.I.C.C. Economic Review* and the *Congress Bulletin*. In the mid-1950s the *India Quarterly* published several anonymous articles written by high government officials which discussed the Soviet Union. Of more recent origin are *Seminar*, which has devoted a number of issues to foreign affairs, *International Studies*, the Indian School of International Studies' quarterly, and *Mainstream*, a journal of Marxist intellectual thought.

The *New Age* weekly (formerly *Crossroads*), official organ of the Communist party of India, reflects a Soviet orientation toward international affairs. *Link* magazine, the orientation of which has been described as a "link" between the left-wing of the Congress party and the right-wing of the CPI, has had close contacts with Communist parties of Eastern Europe and has generally provided good coverage of intra-bloc relations. Information on the exchange of delegations between India and the USSR, projects involving mutual cooperation, and literary news was often contained in the monthly issues of *ISCUS*, journal of the Indo-Soviet Cultural Society.

To supplement the available published materials, numerous interviews and discussions were held with Indian diplomats, government officials, journalists, and scholars. Over a five year period similar discussions also were conducted with Soviet, East European, Pakistani, American, and British scholars, journalists and diplomats. The interviews helped in corroborating evidence obtained from published sources, and in giving me a sense of the outlook and opinions of those who have been involved in the policy-making process. In researching an admittedly sensitive subject, I have neither sought nor received classified information from any Indian nor non-Indian source.

I. *Indian Sources*

A. *Government Publications*

Government of India. *Foreign Policy of India: Text of Documents, 1947–59.* New Delhi: Government of India Press, 1959.

———. Lok Sabha Secretariat. *Debates.* New Delhi: Government of India Press, 1954–1965.

———. Ministry of External Affairs. *Foreign Affairs Record* (monthly). 1955–.

———. Ministry of External Affairs. *Notes, Memoranda, Letters and Agreements Signed between the Governments of India and China, 1954–59.* New Delhi: Government of India Press, 1959.

———. Ministry of Information and Broadcasting. *Jawaharlal Nehru's Speeches, 1946–49; 1949–53;* and *1953–57.* New Delhi: Government of India Press, 1953, 1954, 1958.

———. *Notes, Memoranda, and Letters Exchanged between the Governments of India and China: White Paper II* (1959) ; and *White Paper III* (1960). New Delhi: Government of India Press, 1959, 1960.

———. Parliament Secretariat. *Parliamentary Debates,* 1950–54.

———. Planning Commission. *Second Five Year Plan.* New Delhi: Government of India Press, 1956.

———. Planning Commission. *Third Five Year Plan.* New Delhi: Government of India Press, 1961.

———. Rajya Sabha Secretariat. *Debates.* 1954–1965.

B. *Newspapers*

Amrita Bazar Patrika, The (Calcutta).
Hindu, The (Madras) 1947–67.
Hindu Weekly Review, The (Madras).

Hindusthan Standard, The (New Delhi).
Indian Express, The (Bombay, New Delhi).
New Age (New Delhi).
Patriot (New Delhi).
Statesman, The (Calcutta, New Delhi).
Times of India, The (Bombay, New Delhi).
Tribune, The (Ambala).

C. *Periodicals*

A.I.C.C. Economic Review (New Delhi).
Congress Bulletin (New Delhi).
Eastern Economist, The (New Delhi).
Economic Weekly (Bombay).
Economic and Political Weekly (Bombay).
India Quarterly (New Delhi).
International Studies (New Delhi).
ISCUS (New Delhi).
Link (New Delhi).
Mainstream (New Delhi).
Radical Humanist (Calcutta).
Seminar (New Delhi).
Socialist Congressman (New Delhi).
Thought (New Delhi).

II. *Other Sources*

A. *Public Documents*

United Nations. *Direction of International Trade.*
————. *General Assembly, Official Records.*
————. *Security Council, Official Records.*
————. *Statistical Yearbook.*
————. *Statistics in World Trade in Steel.*
United States Congress, Joint Economic Committee. *Hearings together with Compilations of Studies [on] Dimensions of Soviet Economic Power.* 87th Congress, 2nd Session, December, 1962. Washington: Government Printing Office, 1962.
————. *New Directions in the Soviet Economy.* 89th Congress, 2nd Session. Washington: Government Printing Office, 1966.

B. *Books and Reports*

Balabushevich, V. V. *Some Problems of History of India*. Moscow, 1963. Paper delivered to 26th International Congress of Orientalists in New Delhi, January, 1964.

Balabushevich, V. V., and Diakov, A. M., eds. *Noveishaia Istoriia Indii* [Modern history of India]. Moscow: Eastern Languages Publishing House, 1959.

Bayley, David H. *Public Liberties in the New States*. Chicago: Rand McNally, 1964.

Berkes, Ross N., and Bedi, M. S. *The Diplomacy of India*. New York: Harper, for the Council on Foreign Relations, 1960.

Berliner, Joseph S. *Soviet Economic Aid: The New Aid and Trade Policy in Underdeveloped Countries*. New York: Praeger, for the Council on Foreign Relations, 1958.

Black, Joseph E., and Thompson, Kenneth W., eds. *Foreign Policies in a World of Change*. New York: Harper, 1963. Chapters by A. Appadorai, "The Foreign Policy of India," and V. M. Khvostov, "The Foreign Policy of the Union of Soviet Socialist Republics."

Bolshaia Sovetskaia Entsiklopediia [Large Soviet encyclopedia.] 2d ed. Moscow: State Scientific Publishing House, 1950–58.

Bottomore, T. B. *Elites and Society*. New York: Basic Books, 1964.

Brecher, Michael. *India's Foreign Policy: An Interpretation*. Secretariat Paper no. 1, Proceedings of the Institute of Pacific Relations, 1957. New York: Institute of Pacific Relations, 1957.

———. *Nehru: A Political Biography*. London: Oxford University Press, 1959.

———. *The New States of Asia: A Political Analysis*. London: Oxford University Press, 1963.

Brown, W. Norman. *The United States and India and Pakistan*. 2d ed. Cambridge: Harvard University Press, 1963.

Buchan, Alastair, ed. *A World of Nuclear Powers?* Englewood Cliffs, N. J.: Prentice Hall, 1966.

Chakravarti, P. C. *India's China Policy*. Bloomington, Ind.: Indiana University Press, 1962.

Crankshaw, Edward. *The New Cold War: Moscow v. Peking*. Baltimore: Penguin (paperback), 1963.

Crocker, Walter. *Nehru: A Contemporary's Estimate*. Oxford: Oxford University Press, 1966.

Diakov, A. M. *New Stage in India's Liberation Struggle*. Bombay: People's Publishing House, 1950.

Dutt, Vidya Prakash. *China and the World*. New York: Praeger, 1964.

Eden, Sir Anthony. *Full Circle: The Memoirs of Anthony Eden*. Boston: Houghton-Mifflin, 1960.

Fisher, Margaret W.; Rose, Leo E.; and Huttenback, Robert. *Himalayan Battleground: Sino-Indian Rivalry in Ladakh*. New York: Praeger, 1963.

Friedmann, Wolfgang G.; Kalmanoff, George; and Meagher, Robert. *International Financial Aid*. New York: Columbia University Press, 1966.

Gafurov, B. G., ed. *Politika S. Sh. A. v Stranakh Yuzhnoi Azii* [Policy of the United States in the countries of South Asia] Moscow: Eastern Languages Publishing House, 1961.

Gelman, Harry. "The Communist Party of India: Sino-Soviet Battleground." *Communist Strategies in Asia. A Comparative Analysis of Governments and Parties*. New York: Praeger, 1962.

George, T. J. S. *Krishna Menon: A Biography*. London: Jonathan Cape, 1964.

Gupta, Sisir. *Kashmir: A Study in India-Pakistan Relations*. Bombay: Asia Publishing House, 1966.

Halle, Louis J. *The Cold War as History*. New York: Harper and Row, 1967.

Harrison, Selig S. *India: The Most Dangerous Decades*. Princeton: Princeton University Press, 1960.

Karaka, D. F. *Nehru: The Lotus Eater from Kashmir*. London: Derek Verschoyle, 1953.

Karanjia, R. K. *The Mind of Mr. Nehru*. London: Allen & Unwin, 1960.

Karunakaran, K. P. *India in World Affairs, 1950–1953*. Calcutta: Oxford University Press, 1958.

Kautsky, John H. *Moscow and the Communist Party of India: A Study in the Postwar Evolution of International Communist Strategy*. New York: Wiley and Sons, 1956.

Kavic, Lorne J. *India's Quest for Security: Defence Policies, 1947–65*. Berkeley: University of California Press, 1967.

Khrushchev, Nikita S. *The Present International Situation and Soviet*

Foreign Policy. Report to the Supreme Soviet of the USSR on December 12, 1962. Reprinted in *Political Affairs*, 42 (January 1963) : 27–61.

Kidron, Michael. *Foreign Investments in India*. Oxford: Oxford University Press, 1965.

Kundra, J. C. *Indian Foreign Policy, 1947–54: A Study of Relations with Western Bloc*. Bombay: Vora, 1955.

Lall, Arthur. *How Communist China Negotiates*. New York: Columbia University Press, 1968.

Lamb, Alastair. *The China-India Border*. London: Oxford University Press, 1964.

Lewis, John P. *Quiet Crisis in India: Economic Development and American Policy*. Washington, D. C.: Brookings Institution, 1962.

Malenbaum, Wilfred. *Prospects for Indian Development*. London: Allen & Unwin, 1962.

Martin, Laurence W. *Neutralism and Nonalignment: The New States in World Affairs*. New York: Praeger, 1962.

Marx, Karl. "The British Rule in India." In *Selected Works II* (New York, n.d.)

Masani, M. R. *The Communist Party of India: A Short History*. New York: Macmillan, 1954.

Mehnert, Klaus. *Peking and Moscow*. Translated by L. Vennewitz. New York: Putman, 1963.

Menon, K. P. S. *The Flying Troika*. London: Oxford University Press, 1963.

Myrdal, Gunnar, *Asian Drama*. Vol. 1. New York: Pantheon, 1968.

Namboodiripad, E. M. S. *Problems of National Integration*. Calcutta: Nation Book Agency, 1966.

Nehru, Jawaharlal. *Soviet Russia: Some Random Sketches and Impressions*. Bombay: Chetana, 1929.

――――. *The Discovery of India*. New York: John Day, 1946.

――――. *Toward Freedom: The Autobiography of Jawaharlal Nehru*. New York: John Day, 1942.

Norman, Dorothy. *Nehru: The First Sixty Years*. 2 vols. New York, 1964.

Overstreet, Gene D., and Windmiller, Marshall. *Communism in India*. Berkeley: University of California Press, 1959.

Palmer, Norman D. *South Asia and United States Policy*. Boston: Houghton Mifflin, 1966.

Panikkar, K. M. *In Two Chinas, Memoirs of a Diplomat*. London: Allen & Unwin, 1955.

————. *Problems of Indian Defence*. New York: Asia Publishing House, 1960.

Park, Richard L., and Tinker, Irene, eds. *Leadership and Political Institutions in India*. Princeton: Princeton University Press, 1959.

Patterson, George N. *Peking versus Delhi*. London: Faber and Faber, 1964.

Pavlov, V. *India: Economic Freedom versus Imperialism*. New Delhi: People's Publishing House, 1963. (Translated from original Russian edition.)

Rajan, M. S. *India in World Affairs, 1954–56*. Bombay: Asia Publishing House, 1963.

Rajkumar, N. V., ed. *The Background of India's Foreign Policy*. New Delhi: All-India Congress Committee, 1952.

Rimalov, V. *Economic Cooperation between the U.S.S.R. and Underdeveloped Countries*. Moscow: Foreign Languages Publishing House, n. d. (c. 1962).

Rosen, George. *Democracy and Economic Change in India*. Berkeley: University of California Press, 1966.

Rubinstein, Alvin Z. *The Soviets in International Organization*. Princeton: Princeton University Press, 1964.

Rudolph, Lloyd I., and Rudolph, Susanne H. *The Modernity of Tradition: Political Development in India*. Chicago: University of Chicago Press, 1967.

Sager, Peter. *Moscow's Hand in India*. Bombay: Lalvani Publishing House, 1967.

Samra, Chattar Singh. *India and Anglo-Soviet Relations, 1917–47*. New York: Asia Publishing House, 1959.

Sar Desai, D. R., *India's Foreign Policy in Cambodia, Laos and Vietnam, 1947–64*. Berkeley: University of California, 1968.

Sardesai, S. G. *India and the Russian Revolution*. New Delhi: New Age Printing Press, 1967.

Sawyer, Carole A. *Communist Trade with Developing Countries, 1955–65*. New York: Praeger, 1966.

Sheean, Vincent. *Nehru: The Years of Power.* New York: Random House, 1960.

Shils, Edward. *The Intellectual Between Tradition and Modernity: The Indian Situation.* The Hague: Mouton, 1961.

Smith, Donald. *India as a Secular State.* Princeton: Princeton University Press, 1963.

———. *Nehru and Democracy.* Calcutta, 1957.

Survey of International Affairs. Vols. for 1952, 1953, 1954, 1955–56, 1956–58. Royal Institute of International Affairs. London: Oxford University Press, 1953, 1956, 1957, 1960, 1962.

Thornton, T. P., ed. *The Third World in Soviet Perspective.* Princeton: Princeton University Press, 1964.

Tidmarsh, Kyril. "The Soviet Reassessment of Mahatma Gandhi." In *St. Antony's Papers on South Asian Affairs.* Edited by R. Iyer. No. 8. London: Oxford University Press, 1960.

Tinker, Hugh. *India and Pakistan: A Political Analysis.* New York: Praeger, 1962.

Triska, Jan F., and Finley, David. *Soviet Foreign Policy.* New York: Macmillan, 1968.

UNCTAD. *Problems arising in Trade Relations between Countries Having Different Economic and Social Systems: Case Study Prepared by the UNCTAD Secretariat on Trade and Economic Relations between India and the Socialist Countries of Eastern Europe.* Geneva, July 1967.

Varma, S. N. "Trends in Indian Foreign Policy, 1954–57." In *Aspects of India's Foreign Relations.* Prepared for Thirteenth Conference of the Institute of Pacific Relations at Iahore, February 1958. New Delhi: I.C.W.A., 1958.

Visit of N. A. Bulganin and N. S. Khrushchev to India. Moscow: Foreign Languages Publishing House, 1956.

Weiner, Myron. *The Politics of Scarcity.* Chicago: University of Chicago Press, 1962.

Zagoria, Donald. *The Sino-Soviet Conflict.* Princeton: Princeton University Press, 1962.

Zeleznev, I. A., *Voina i ideologicheskaya borba* [War and ideological struggle]. Moscow, 1964.

C. *Articles*

Adic, W. A. C. "China, Russia and the Third World." *China Quarterly*, no. 11 (July–September, 1962), pp. 200–213.

Bragina, T. A. "The Third Five Year Plan and the Indian Economy." *Narody Azii i Afriki*, no. 3 (1963), pp. 33–48.

Brecher, Michael. "International Relations and Asian Studies: The Subordinate State System of Southern Asia." *World Politics* 15 (January 1963) : 213–35.

Chaudhri, M. A. "Pakistan's Relations with the Soviet Union." *Asian Survey* 6 (September 1966) : 492–500.

Erdman, Howard L. "The Foreign Policy Views of the Indian Right." *Pacific Affairs*, 39 (Spring, Summer 1966) : 5–18.

Fisher, Margaret W. "India's Jawaharlal Nehru." *Asian Survey* 7 (June 1967) : 363–73.

Gelman, Harry. "Russia, China and the Underdeveloped Areas." *The Annals of the American Academy of Political and Social Sciences* 349 (September, 1963) : 130–42.

Ghosh, Ajoy. "A Visit of Great Historical Significance." *New Age* (December 25, 1955), p. 1.

Gopal, S. "India, China and the Soviet Union." In *The Australian Journal of Politics and History* 12 (August 1966) : 241–57.

Graham, Ian. "The Soviet MIG Deal and its International Repercussions." *Asian Survey* 4 (May 1964) : 823–32.

Gupta, Sisir. "India and the Soviet Union." *Current History* 44 (March 1963) : 141–46.

Ilchman, Warren. "Political Development and Foreign Policy: The Case of India." *Journal of Commonwealth Political Studies* 4 (November 1966).

Imam, Zafar. "Soviet Aid to India: Time for Reappraisal?" *Mainstream* 6 (April 20, 1968) : 12–14.

"India and the U.S.S.R." *Eastern Economist*, no. 52 (December 30, 1955), pp. 984–91.

"India and the World." *Seminar* no. 56 (April 1964).

International Studies (special issue on "Chinese Aggression") 5, nos. 1 and 2 (July–October 1963).

ISCUS, 9 (March, 1962) (special tenth anniversary issue of Indo-Soviet Cultural Society Journal).

Kautsky, John H. "Russia, China and Nationalist Movements." *Survey*, no. 43 (1962), pp. 119 ff.

Kotovsky, G.; Pavlov, V.; and Redko, I. "Some Indian Economic and Political Problems. *New Times*, no. 1 (January, 1964), pp. 18–22.

Kremnyev, M. "The Non-Aligned Countries and World Politics." World Marxist Review 6 (April 1963) : 29–36.

Letters exchanged between C. Rajagopalachari and N. S. Khrushchev. *International Affairs* (Moscow), no. 2 (February, 1959).

Levi, Werner. "Pakistan, the Soviet Union and China." *Pacific Affairs* 35 (Fall 1962) : 211–22.

Malaviya, K. D. "Indo-Soviet Trade Pact." *A.I.C.C. Economic Review* 5 (December 15, 1953) : 10–11.

Mehta, Asok. "India's Foreign Policy: The Soviet View." *India Quarterly* 7 (April–June, 1951).

Namboodiripad, E. M. S. "Agrarian Problem and National Liberation Movement." *World Marxist Review* 4 (January 1961) : 69–72.

Nayar N. P. "Growth of Non-alignment in World Affairs." *India Quarterly* 18 (January–March 1962) : 28 ff.

Nehru, Jawaharlal. "The Basic Approach." *A.I.C.C. Economic Review* 10 (May 15, 1958) : 3–6.

Nesterov, M., and Sergeey, V. A. "Economic Cooperation between India and the Soviet Union." *Foreign Affairs Reports India* 8 (December 1959) : 142–52.

"Our Neighbors." *Seminar* no. 37 (September 1962).

"P" (N. R. Pillai). "Middle Ground between America and Russia: An Indian View." *Foreign Affairs* 32 (January 1954) : 259–69.

Palmer, Norman D. "India's Position in Asia." *Journal of International Affairs* 17 (1963) : 126–41.

Power, Paul F. "India's Foreign Policy: The Age of Nehru." *The Review of Politics* 26 (April 1964) : 257–86.

Pye, Lucian. "The Non-Western Political Process." *The Journal of Politics* 20 (1958) : 468–86.

Rangaswami, K. "India's Reaction to Khrushchev's October 30 Speech to Supreme Soviet." *Hindu*, November 4, 1959, p. 1.

R. K. "Deterioration of Relations between India and China." *Review of International Affairs* (Belgrade) 10 (September 16, 1959) : 10.

Rosario, J. A. "India's Trade with the Socialist Bloc." *Economic and Political Weekly* 2 (October 28, 1967) : 1948–1951.

Roy, M. N. "Communism in Asia." *Radical Humanist*, October 30, 1954. (Last installment of Roy's incomplete *Memoirs*.)

———. "Disagreement with Lenin over Colonial Countries." *Radical Humanist*, January 24, 1954, 42.

Sen, Mohit. "Soviet Aid to India: Implications for Indian Revolution." *Mainstream* 6 (April 20, 1968) : 15–16.

Singer, J. David. "Inter-Nation Influence: A Formal Model." *American Political Science Review* 57 (June 1963:) : 420–30.

Skorov, G. "L'Aide Economique et Technique de l'U.R.S.S. aux Pays Sous-Developpes." *Tiere Monde*, October–December, 1960, pp. 491–510.

Stein, Arthur. "India and the USSR: The Post-Nehru Period." *Asian Survey* 7 (March 1967) : 165–75.

Vaidyanath, R. "Izuchenie SSSR v Indii i Ego Perspektivy" [The study of the USSR in India and its prospects]. *Istoriia* SSSR, no. 2 (Moscow, 1965), pp. 170–80.

———. "Some Recent Trends in Soviet Policies Towards India and Pakistan." *International Studies*, January 1966, pp. 429–47.

"X." "Destalinization." *India Quarterly* 13 (July–September 1957) : 237–41.

Yudin, P. "Can We Accept Pandit Nehru's Approach?" *World Marxist Review* 1 (December 1958) : 42–54.

Zhukov, E. "Gandhi's Role in History." *New Times*, no. 6 (February 2, 1956), p. 15.

D. *Unpublished Material*

Boland, Gertrude C. "India and the United Nations: India's Role in the General Assembly, 1946–57." Ph. D. dissertation, Claremont College, 1961.

Budharj, Vijay Sen. "The Soviet Image of India." Ph. D. dissertation, American University, 1958.

Noonon, Norma C. "Soviet-Indian Relations, 1953–63." Ph. D. dissertation, Indiana University, 1965.

Satyapalan, C. N. "India's China Policy: The First Decade." Ph. D. dissertation, University of Pennsylvania, 1964.

E. *Newspapers, Periodicals, and Miscellaneous*

Asian Recorder
Asian Survey
Australian Journal of History and Politics
Christian Science Monitor
Current Digest of the Soviet Press
Current History
Current Soviet Documents
Economist (London)
Foreign Affairs
India and Foreign Review
India News (Washington, D. C.)
Indian Institute of Public Opinion, *Monthly Public Opinion Surveys*
    (New Delhi)
Indian Press Digests (Berkeley)
International Affairs (Moscow)
Journal of Asian Studies
Journal of Conflict Resolution
Journal of International Affairs
Keesing Contemporary Archives
Mizan (London)
Morning News (Dacca)
New China News Agency, Daily Press Releases
New Times (Moscow)
New York Times
Pakistan Observer
Peking Review
Pravda
Review of International Affairs (Belgrade)
Times (London)
USIA, *Developments in International Broadcasting by Communist
    Countries*
World Marxist Review

Index